AFTERLIFE

ISBN: 1499604629
ISBN 13: 9781499604627
Library of Congress Control Number: 2014909932
CreateSpace Independent Publishing Platform
North Charleston, South Carolina

AFTERLIFE

A PSYCHIATRIST EXPLORING LIFE BEYOND DEATH

DR MARCEL WESTERLUND

translated into English by Sebastian Westerlund

Contents

CONTENTS

The Author's Introduction

Hypnosis is possibly as old as mankind itself. Despite its impressive age, hypnosis has over time, both been regarded as a key to higher understanding and wisdom and yet also often questioned and sometimes regarded as pseudo-scientific nonsense, and dangerous. How is it possible that such an old science is neglected in favor of conscious control of the mind through modern psycho-therapeutic techniques like CBT (Cognitive Behaviour Therapy)? Despite its reputation, is it possible to use hypnosis as an advanced technique to cure victims of severe emotional, physical, sexual and violent abuse? Is it even possible that clients tell the truth when they relate to previous lives, reincarnation and a vast and highly complex spiritual world?

This book will give evidence of this from numerous cases in England and Sweden. It is also an inner journey not only for the client but also for the doctor. A breath- and painstaking journey that opens up a new whole parallel invisible world to our own limited physical existence. Before you enter this journey you might need some background information.

The book is divided into three major sections. The first major part takes you to all the clients and their journeys. Sometimes it might become confusing when past, present and future tense are mixed. This is exactly how hypnosis works. Time is of no essence and suddenly you discover that everything is present in the moment of now. I have deliberately given you these live interviews, collected from over more than 10 years of work. This will help you to understand how challenging, wonderful and mind blowing this work can be. Suddenly we are unable to control by thinking. Instead we are offered to explore the mind by visual imagery and timeless travel. It becomes increasingly clear that time does not exist and that everything exists within the moment of now.

The second part of the book is a simple attempt to start trying to map the spiritual world. If the human genome can be mapped, why not the spiritual world?

The third and last part of the book deals with possibilities to prove and explain that we actually never die, and that physics is the most likely candidate to explain and prove life beyond death. You can read any part and yet benefit from what you read. But how old is hypnosis?

Hypnosis as an art of healing goes at least back to the first dynasty of the ancient Egyptian civilization. Evidence of this can be found in the papyrus Westcar, containing stories about marvels performed by priests and magicians at the court of Pharaoh Khufu (2589-2566 BC).

Perhaps hypnosis bad reputation was created by the Viennese doctor, Franz Anton Mesmer, who during the late 18th century, amused the Austrian court with his skills, called animal magnetism. The ancient Egyptians would perhaps regard him as a true conjurer.

During 1840's James Braid, a surgeon from Manchester in England, by mistake gave hypnosis its current name. In 1852 James Esdaile, a Scottish surgeon in India, published a pamphlet called "*The introduction of mesmerism as an anaesthetic and curative agent into the hospitals of India*". During his time in India Dr Esdaile perfomed more than 300 painless surgeries. Unfortunately Mortons discovery of ether 1846, put an end to Dr Esdailes work.

Ambroise-Auguste Liebault (1823-1904) and Berheim (1840-1919), two French doctors, founded the so called Nancy school in France in the late 19th century, which proved to be very significant in the acceptance of hypnotherapy. Sigmund Freud, the father of psychoanalysis, visited Nancy in 1889, and on this visit he became convinced of the *'powerful mental processes which nevertheless remain hidden from the consciousness of men'*. Freud never really got to grips with hypnosis, abandoning it after he discovered 'positive transference', and developed psycho-analysis.

William James (1842-1910) was a famous psychologist at Harward University, USA. James was interested in Hypnosis because it seemed to involve alterations in conscious awareness. He authored a chapter on Hypnosis in his famous Principles of Psychology (1890). Later P. C.

Young, a psychologist, did the first systematic experimental work on hypnosis in his doctoral dissertation completed at Harvard in 1923.

The modern study of hypnotism is usually considered to have begun with Clark Leonard Hull at the University of Wisconsin in the 1920s and continued at Yale into the 1930s. As an experimental psychologist, his work *Hypnosis and Suggestibility* (1933) was a rigorous study of the phenomenon, using statistical and experimental analysis. Van Pelt wrote the *"Hypnotism and the power within"* and also *"Hypnotism and its therapeutic value in medicine"*, 1949.

Studies continued after the Second World War. Ernest Hilgard and Andrei Witzenhoffer created the Stanford scales in 1961, a standardised scale for susceptibility to hypnosis, and properly examined susceptibility across age-groups and sex. Hilgard went on to study sensory deception (1965) and induced anesthesia and analgesia (1975).

Hilgard further developed Janet's earlier work on dissociation (the fragmented self) into his theory of neodissociation, posing three stages of consciousness within hypnosis:

- The distorted reality
- The hidden observer
- The observing consciousness.

This model, when brought together with the then contemporary Pain Gate Theory of Melzack and Wall, gave an elegant paradigm which remains just as fresh today, to explain the way in which hypnotic interventions can be so effective.

John Hartland was a British psychiatrist, member of the British Society of Dental and Medical Hypnosis (BSDMH), and editor of the Journal of Medical Hypnosis. His comprehensive textbook on clinical hypnotherapy, Medical & Dental Hypnosis was published in 1966. Hartland described straightforward techniques for ego, employing direct suggestions of a general nature, aimed at increasing the patient's self confidence. The book, now in its fourth edition, became a 'bible' for the medical or dental student of hypnosis.

The study of psycho-neuro-immunology (PNI), the conduits through which our emotions and thoughts may affect our health came into prominence in the 1980s, and a major influence in this study remain Dr Ernest Rossi. In his early years Rossi worked with and co-wrote many papers with Milton Erickson. He is also editor of Erickson's collected papers. In 1986 he published a major book, 'The Psychobiology of Mind-Body Healing'. His painstaking research into psychobiology and state dependent learning has resulted in a large number of publications in which he describes the mind-body pathways, and applies hypnotic techniques in utilising these pathways to bring about healing.

Modern hypnosis has survived the controversies, mistrust and open hostility to reach its present position amongst the healing arts. Hypnotherapy has survived because enough determined people have fought on, and because enough people have benefited from it. We struggle and desperately try to comprehend our own existence, caught as we are between the alienation of existential separation and the promise of spiritual unity.

This book is dedicated to all those brave clients and souls I have encountered over my years as physician, psychiatrist and healer. Without their willingness to share their many lives, suffering and joy, all this would be hidden except for the All Seeing Eye.

From hundreds of interviews and from my reading I intend to show that there is life after death and that it can be accessed by clients to help them better understand their present lives, their possible future needs, and a whole host of techniques that will bring them into a fuller understanding of themselves, their souls, and their purposes in life.

Dedication

I am eternally grateful to my loving and spiritual family, and particularly my oldest son who decided to translate this from Swedish to English. It is my sincere hope that this book will bring you all love, hope and strength. By the end we are all spiritual beings trying to gather some physical experience!

I have been given the great gift to publish this work, and without support and help both from the physical and spiritual world, this would never have been achieved.

What is known cannot be unknown.

Hamilton, Bermuda

25 March 2015

The Priest from Karnak

*T*he sun was burning hot, and it was only in the shade of Ramses II's enormous columns that brief respite could be found. The columns surrounding me in circular rows, described magnificent battles and epic adventures, with hieroglyphs cut into the substantial sandstone. Along the ceiling cobalt blue and gold shone against okra red and mustard yellows. The painted scenes described Ra, Osiris, Hathor, Thoth and a pantheon of other gods. A regal, dark and silently watching Anubis stared blankly as Maat raised her wings for protection. No building in the world could compare with Karnak. The most beautiful building my eyes have ever seen. My whole life I had dedicated to its construction, until finally I had been initiated into the larger mysteries and the road lay open for me to become the High Priest. But now I lay attentive and brooding with my face down on the smooth stone tiles before the feet of the High Priest of Karnak. He gazed with saddened eyes down upon my bald head and bare torso as he slowly began to speak.

'Why? Why this misfortune Ptah-Amun-Ra? You who more than anyone embodied the since long forgotten knowledge of the power of the light. You who have been Karnak's and the initiates' long anticipated hope. Why?'

'Master, I have not touched the Queen. I only used my ability to embody the light,' I said.

'One who has touched her can never be pardoned. The Pharaoh demands I make the decision. You must die. But as you are Karnak's most skilled priest, you have been given the mercy to choose which way your life ends,' said the High Priest.

In waves of despair, sorrow and meaningless words of my innocence I finally managed to make my last difficult decision. To be buried alive was my greatest fear. To have my throat cut I imagined as a messy and painful death. 'I choose the spears,' I said as I slowly stood up and was led away by the guards.

***

Everything began the day Martin asked if I had ever tried a regression. Of course I had read all about this. I was familiar with professor Brian Weiss, Sylvia Brown, Edgar Cayce, Madame Blavatsky, Anton Mesmer, Jung, Freud and the rest of the long line of psychics, priests, doctors, scientists, "self-proclaimed" healers and various charlatans. Nevertheless I had never tried it myself. As a doctor I had never felt the urge to search for early traumas, through regression, for myself. The reason for this was that reincarnation is to me as natural as night and day to me, and nobody would have to spend time and energy in order to convince me. I really did not require any proof. The possibility to convince just a single individual about a truth that no one would believe felt like wasted energy, as I had since long passed the point where it felt important to convince others about my beliefs. Everyone should find his or her own truth.

'Okay, I'll come along,' I said. 'It might be interesting as an experience for my patients.'

I could never forget the day we travelled to Berndt in Bettna. I once again had intense pain from gallstones, and six months later I had intensive surgery in Falun. In addition to the piercing gallstone pains I had a bad toothache in my left mandible. I was tired, irritated, and in heavy pain, unaware that the pain was the beginning of something new. In spite of the pain I sank ever deeper. Berndt's calm and friendly voice made me relax and finally completely disappear in archaic memories of myself. When Berndt asked what I was doing I was on my knees in front of the High Priest with difficult spiritual pains. As a doctor it had always been my goal to help the suffering, but finally even I had lost respect for the power of the light and my own role. I was a tool, nothing more, but love had made me naive and helped me lose my judgment, a fault which I have repeated several times even in my current life. Slowly I started to realise the shocking truth that past lives traumas, mistakes and teachings return, sometimes as flashing short-lived images or the intuition of something archaic and deeply grounded. Something we recognize but lack words to describe. Something that for a sudden moment releases materialistic behaviour, encouragement and challenges. Something the religious sometimes describe as a revelation or an idea of salvation.

My time as a revered and knowledgeable healer was out. My death would finally also transfer a degree of wrath into my future lives. The wrath over being unjustly punished for a crime not committed. Was this what has been described as cellular memories? Was this what time upon time made its mark on my current life? To always uphold the importance of truth, to feel recurrent wrath over the world's never-ending capability for unfairness, to like Sisyphus labour to accomplish the impossible.

**

The Temple of Karnak was as always bustling with activity. As the other priests stood and conferred, I amused myself by focusing energy. I took a number of dead flies and sent them up in the air above the small group of chattering colleagues with playful energy. The flies fell without a sound down on their bald heads. With a wide smile I saw them one after another brush off the falling flies. One of them suddenly burst out: 'Not again! It's Ptah-Amun-Ra who's entertaining himself. Will he never grow up? We must inform the High Priest!'

A few days later I got reprimanded by the High Priest and instructed to focus more on my work and not use the pure energy for selfish nonsense. 'When will you grow up and understand,' he finally said with a friendly smile. His admonishment educated and also always protected me.

**

I felt instinctively that although he was forced to make the decision regarding my execution he was still my closest friend and confidant. A small perhaps insignificant detail that was to return even in this life. Where others believed I had failed I returned like a Phoenix, often protected by the person my colleagues would think of last. Not infrequently an individual high up in the hierarchy. Was this also a coincidence, a Jungian synchronicity?

**

3

A few days later there was a large commotion surrounding the holy lake. For some inexplicable reason a young boy had fallen into the water. While the priests who did not know how to swim ran around looking for something to save the boy with he was gradually sinking to his death. By drawing upon all my power, I focused the pure light on the boy. Slowly, I saw how he was invisibly pulled up during the time it took for the other priests to finally find a long stick with which to reach out to him. Gradually the boy was pulled back in to the edge, and I went away quietly and pleased. There was no reason to talk about what had just happened. Perhaps the High Priest might be the only one to believe that what had occurred was true.

Time no longer existed in this state of consciousness. The events suddenly shifted away from the holy lake. A large contingent was approaching the Temple of Karnak from the south. It was apparent that it was someone of importance. Male and female servants were followed by guards and soldiers. All of a sudden someone shouted out: 'It's the Queen of Thebes approaching! By Ra's inscrutable mercy, what is she doing here?'

The images shifted abruptly and in the next moment I was standing with the High Priest in front of the Queen of Thebes. Her beauty was radiant. Her raven black hair shone against her copper yellow skin. Her painted eyes observed me kindly yet intensely.

'The Queen has come here to seek grace from Ra, the priests and Thoth. She seeks healing. Her body will not give her and her ruler an heir. She has heard that there exists someone who masters the ancient forgotten knowledge to heal with light,' said her councillor.

The High Priest looked around himself anxiously. Now there was no way out. Karnak had always been protected by the Pharaoh and the temple was never wanting for anything. Now was the time to repay old debts. 'Not I, but my most excelled student shall help the Queen.'

The next moment I had on my own initiative been left alone with the Queen in a small dark closed off room in the temple. While the Queen sat with crossed legs in front of me I spoke calmly and respectfully to her. 'Her Highness has no illness. It is the mother to the child who needs energy.' The same moment I saw myself form an intensely blue ball between my hands. I threw it softly up and down through the air as the intensity of the blue ball's colour and energy slowly increased. I then took the ball of energy and put it above the Queens heart.

'Should you not put it over my stomach?'

'No, I am giving you Ka,' I said as the blue ball disappeared into her chest.

It was maybe a year later that the Queen returned to Karnak. She was radiantly happy and in addition to her royal cortege she was accompanied by a beautiful little boy. The future of the upper and lower kingdom was secured.

A short while later she returned. This time she drove a war chariot with two striking white horses. She was definitely a very unusual woman. Strong, intense and possessing a will of steel. In my deeply regressed condition I felt instinctively that a Queen did not normally drive a chariot like this. There were soldiers that guarded her progression but none dared to intervene and slow her down. 'You shall come with me to Luxor. There is something I wish to give you,' she said smiling as she eagerly urged the stunning animals.

The ride through the Alley of Sphinxes down towards the palace in Luxor made me buzz with relish. The horse's hooves thundered against the stones and the breeze gave a pleasant cool in the burning sun. The journey in the Queen's golden chariot was the most wonderful experience in my whole life as a priest in Karnak. How can I have forgotten all of this, I thought to myself as I went forward through the Queen's carriage.

Having arrived in Luxor we walked slowly through the summer palace's garden. We spoke softly and I suddenly felt an intense love for her. In my regressed state it was as if I knew that my love was reciprocated, but such love was naturally unthinkable.

'I wish to give you a gift for what you did.'

'No, I have not done anything. It was not me. It was the light.'

'Perhaps,' she said decisively as she reached for something golden. 'This is a scarab of pure gold, an immaculate piece of craftsmanship. It is forever yours,' said the Queen as she clasped it around my neck.

In the next moment I understood why I was to die. I heard murmurs, whispering silent voices conspiring and I saw dark glances thrown from behind high pillars. Everyone retreated. I was shunned, as if I was walking down a road alone surrounded by people who refused to look at or acknowledge me. Nobody wanted to risk getting involved in something beyond their control. Instinctively I felt that this was a revolting, low but human characteristic. Something we all can see in our everyday lives. 'Oh, they think I have touched the Queen physically *because she received a child after the visit in Karnak. What scheming jackals. I signed my own death the same moment I was left alone with her,' I thought to myself as I lay on the couch, and started to feel increasing pains under my right ribs and in my jaw. Were these pains similar to those I felt when I was executed by the spears at the temple of Karnak?*

The next instant I saw the Queen bitterly and mournfully speak a curse over my tomb. Her wrath was enormous, and she spoke that all who dared touch the tomb of my remains would die. She consciously ensured that a sufficient number saw and heard her curse. It was a way of exploiting peoples' superstition for a final protection. I saw her put the golden scarab in the grave. Outside I saw people take detours and spit towards the tomb out of fear to fall victim to misfortune. The Queen had sealed this tomb for eternity.

***

I remember that the first thing I asked about as I slowly returned to Berndt and Martin was the time. To me it felt like maybe half an hour had passed. We had started around five o'clock. I was shocked to learn that the time was now half past seven. It took several weeks before I was able to mentally and spiritually recover from what had occurred. Something had happened that would forever change my work as a doctor. There was no way back. The journey back to my secret, which had been well hidden for millennia, had begun, and I soon regained the knowledge of the light and its healing power.

SWEDEN

2000-2002

You Shall Cure Me Without Drugs

The lady was formally dressed. She was thin and sat still and observant in my office. Her face had sharp features and her eyes watched me with experience. 'I have met six different doctors. They have prescribed me antidepressants to cure me. I certainly do not want any more drugs. It just made me feel weird. Some have had a conversation with me, and subsequently given me sick leave. I want you to cure me without medicine.' I got a strong feeling that I was standing at a crossroads. The time had come where a patient had put me against the wall to choose my path. Elisabeth continued. 'I want help, but I cannot get it with medicine.'

As she spoke I thought of professor Weiss in the USA and all the other therapists who had stepped into the unknown. They had stridden into a jungle filled with dangers without any protection. Every single step could lead to a merciless battle from doctors, scientists and religious fundamentalists hunting for another victim to burn on the pyre of renegades. A pyre made of intellectual protectionism, capitalistic ruthlessness and various sectarian and religious dogmas.

'A single ticket into a jungle of problems, but perhaps there is a hidden treasure deep inside... I have made up my mind Elisabeth, you will become my first patient. This is only possible because you want to do this and you have given your consent. I cannot promise any results, nothing at all. But I will give it my very best in order to help you. Then, if I fail, at least we tried. And you can stop it whenever you want.' I then detailed how we were going to work. We would strictly follow professor Weiss' model, mainly in order to provide a frame of reference to guide both me and Elisabeth. We also agreed to work together openly and in full confidence of each other. I was decisive about keeping a detailed record. 'No one will be able to complain about my documentation even if they dislike my methods.'

When Elisabeth left the clinic I felt a massive inner happiness. I knew in my heart I had chosen the correct path. In contrast to many times when I had only acted intellectually and traditionally I had this time followed my strong intuition, which had always been my guiding star at times where knowledge had not sufficed. That force which Einstein himself described as a scientific necessity.

The House in Portugal

Elisabeth was getting more and more relaxed. Her breath was almost unnoticeable. Methodically, almost chanting, I gradually took her down towards hypnotic relaxation. 'Your breathing is calm and still. Nothing bothers you. Every sound just reinforces the feeling of complete relaxation. You are safe and calm. Your muscles are completely relaxed. You see yourself bathe in the light of your favourite colour. The light relaxes all your muscles.'

The music of Björn Melander gently lulled her to peace. The melody of "Eternal Waves" proved itself to be a hit. Later on, it would be proven, that by using a background of sea waves each patient I treated was able to experience an inner peace I never thought possible to achieve.

'You are walking on a beach along the sea. The waves slowly roll towards the beach. The blue sky meets your eyes. The sea salt in the air fills your nostrils and the breeze caresses your skin. You can feel the sand under your feet. Far away you see a door along a large wall. A strong light shines through the gaps along the sides of the door. The light is unstoppable. It penetrates every hole, every crevice. You cannot resist getting pulled towards the light. All the capability to heal exists within you. All the power to understand. All the solutions to your problems exist deep within yourself. I am your guide. I will not abandon you. You do not need to be afraid. Nothing can hurt you. When I have counted from ten to one you will then be inside the light. You will then be in another life, in another age.'

I slowly counted down by increasing her muscle relaxation between each number. With surprise I witnessed how her body became lifeless. Suddenly her eyelids exploded with movement, precisely as the REM-phase that precede dreams and the deep sleep state. Elisabeth appeared to be seeing something. I became curious. 'What are you doing?'

'I am standing by a body of water and looking out,' Elisabeth answered.

'A body of water? What is on your feet? What kind of clothes are you wearing?'

'I have nothing on my feet. I am wearing a blue dress.'

'Are you standing by a sea?' I asked.

'Yes.'

'Walk towards where you live. Look around you. What do you see?'

'I see a large stone house. Further away there is a large number of people working. I do not understand their words. Yes, I live in the large stone house.'

'When I have counted from three to one you can understand what they are saying. 3, 2, 1, now you can understand. Walk into the house. Is there any furniture?' Sometimes the answers came slowly. I steeled myself not to push her, not to force the answers, not to direct the questions, not to make her as confused as she had been when she arrived at the clinic. It was as if she has landed on a different planet in a different era. My questions must have seemed strange to her.

'Yes, there is furniture,' Elisabeth answered.

'Walk into the room where there are people. What are they doing?'

'There are several men in red coats sitting around a table. Mm, they have books open in front of them. I am 15-16 years old. I am learning something. It is important. They look seriously at me, she continued, almost annoyed at my presence.

'Look all the men in the eyes. Do you recognize anyone?' A long moment of silence followed my question.

'Yes, it is my brother. Not as you would think of it, it is my uncle. It is he who is my maternal uncle in this life.'

'Are you learning mathematics?' I asked.

'It is something in that direction, but not quite right...'

'Go up to one of them. Look in his book. Open the first page. What year do you see?'

A moment of silence followed. 'It says 17.... 176... 1763.'

'We are now moving forward five years in your life. What are you doing?' I asked.

'I am looking out through a window. I wish to travel far away, but I cannot leave. I have everything but cannot leave this place. It is difficult.'

'We move further along your life. Now you are working. What do you do?'

'I am sitting at a desk signing documents. I have control over people,' Elisabeth answered.

'What are you? A judge? Governor? Queen?' I didn't get an answer. Elisabeth said she didn't know. 'We now move towards your death. Are you at home? Are you alone?'

'I am not at my home, and I am not alone. I am old.'

Elisabeth returned slowly by reverse order through every muscle with calm deep breaths. She sat up and rubbed her eyes. She shook her head. She told me that her uncle is a professor of macroeconomics. 'He has been like a brother to my family. But he can be overbearing and demanding. He always wants so much from us.'

The Pathfinder

Elisabeth had spent a lot of time contemplating during the two weeks that had passed. Unobtrusively she had decided not to tell either her brother or husband. It was as if the world had changed. As if its depth and quality had transformed to new unexpected and concealed dimensions. Her nerves and apprehension during the first few sessions had changed into expectations, happiness and surprise. Her eyes were lit up with wonder. Unremarkably I could perceive how our doctor-patient relationship strengthened and deepened without intruding on her integrity or weakening my professional role. Elisabeth made me take myself much more seriously. I realised that I mastered something I had had with me my whole life. Not a single one of thousands of hours spent studying had been dedicated to this. How could this be?

'I know precisely where I was last time. I know what land it was. It was Portugal. A few years ago I went with my husband to Lisbon. My uncle, the professor, who can be rather encumbering was with us. By chance we passed a large stone house I recognized instinctively. After our last session I remembered it. The book I was reading was in Portuguese, which was why the language was so difficult. How did you manage to make me see this? What is happening? I am a slightly scared yet curious. Do you think it might be dangerous?'

Sitting in the relaxation room she looked at me deeply, almost searching. Candles were lit and the atmosphere in the room was perfectly fitting. The female orderlies at the clinic had stubbornly worked with relaxation therapy using ear acupuncture. With great respect I recognized how they just as the barefoot doctors of China accomplished small miracles with simple tools.

I spoke open-heartedly about mankind's search for spirituality with Elisabeth. I told her she had her own strong ability, but that she might have suppressed it during all the years of work, and that it was time for her to listen to herself and no one else. I comforted her by reminding her of humanity's strange ability to only learn as much as we can handle. I believed this was just as true for Elisabeth. In her professional work Elisabeth had always been dutiful and conscientious. She always tried her best and was dependable, accurate and possessed great integrity. She was pleasant and attentive to strangers but profoundly committed to her friends and family. I offered her a closure without proviso but she wanted to carry on, so we mutually agreed to continue the inner journey.

Elisabeth lay calm and comfortable. Her regressed state was getting easier to evoke. I only had to gently and carefully guide her. The water splashed pleasantly in the background music. I watched how her eyes started to move as in a REM-phase under her eyelids. She quickly reached the relaxed state this time.

'You are walking along a path towards the door with light. You are extremely curious Elisabeth. You cannot resist walking towards it. When I have counted down from ten to one you will be in the light. You will then have decided yourself which life we shall visit. Then you will be there,' I told her.

'We are sitting in a circle... There is a fire in the middle,' Elisabeth answered.

'What shoes are you wearing? Do you have clothes? How does your skin look? Describe the faces of those around the fire.'

Sometimes I bit my own tongue. I was too forceful, too hasty. I forgot my old professor's words of wisdom in Malmö – to focus on the simple things first and then the more difficult to follow. Professor Bergentz once told me during an oral examination: 'You are able to do so much of those things others cannot, but you also have to learn how to do the simple things. You must learn patience' he said as he mildly watched me through his black glasses. He probably also possessed strong intuition because his remarks were dead-on accurate.

'I am only wearing something tiny, nearly nothing. My skin is brown, dark. They have curly hair,' Elisabeth said.

'Are their noses wide?' I asked leadingly.

'Yes they are wide. There are only boys and men around the fire... The women are further away, in the background... It is dry...' she answered after a long period.

'Elisabeth, you can now see a spinning globe above the fire. On it you see all the countries slowly spin by. What country do you recognize on the globe?'

'Ooh, it is Australia, but I have never been there.... The tribe is so safe. Everyone helps each other.'

'Look into the eyes of everyone around the fire. Do you recognize anyone?'

'Yes, it is as if we are all related,' Elisabeth answered.

'Am I there?'

'Yes, you are also sitting there.'

'Am I a medicine man... a dream walker?'

'Oh, I see, yes you are.'

'What am I telling you? What am I teaching you about the spirit world?'

Elisabeth remains silent. I see her eyes move under the eyelids but I do not get an answer. She leaves the question unanswered. I should not have asked about myself I thought. Even though I know that I have lived in Australia as aboriginal I should not transfer that onto the patient. My critics will smell blood since they can then obviously claim I have created everything in my mind and projected it onto Elisabeth. I will give her a test as I know she has never been to Australia in this life. I will ask her how the aboriginals wash themselves. Yes, that will work. It is a difficult question. How many people could answer that?

'Elisabeth, you now walk with the tribe. What do you do, what is your task?'

'I am walking ahead of everyone else', she said.

'Are you leading them?'

'Yes, I know my way around'

15

'Do you have any children, a wife?' I asked.

Elisabeth was silent for a long time before she answered. 'No, she died.'

'She died?' I asked.

'Yes.'

'Was it an illness or an accident?'

'Some kind of animal attacked her,' Elisabeth answered.

'You are now back before she died. You love her. Look her in the eyes. Who do you recognize?' I instructed her, changing the scene.

'Oh my, it is my mother,' Elisabeth said.

'Tell me Elisabeth how you wash yourself. How do the aboriginal do it?'

Elisabeth is again silent for a long moment. I do not believe she will be able to answer the question. 'Yes it is sand,' she said, suddenly to my surprise. 'We wash ourselves with sand.' She answered it correctly. I was stunned to say the least, and slightly worried about her incredibly strong ability, her absolute consciousness.

'We now move forward to your own death Elisabeth,' I said changing the scene. Are you afraid?'

'No not at all.'

'What does the shaman say about death?'

'He says we all meet. That we will meet again.'

'You are now in the afterlife Elisabeth. You meet your mother. You are happy. What does she tell you?'

'She tells me that she is doing well.'

Suddenly I get an egoistic impulse and ask Elisabeth if she can ask her mother if what I am doing as a doctor is important.

'She does not know,' Elisabeth answered.

'Ask her to relay the question to a master' I say almost abruptly and unexpectedly even to myself. The answer is delayed. Elisabeth remains quiet for a long time. She lives another life inside her eyelids. Both present but also far away in a state outside space and time.

'She says it is important. You should continue. She is happy that you are helping me.'

I ask Elisabeth if I have told her about Australia. I then tell her that I have always suspected and also been told by a medium that I have acted as a 'dream walker' in a tribe. She tells me that she did not know this. I tell her that during my and my partners visit to Australia in 1987 we learned in the desert that the aboriginal wash themselves with sand. A piece of information few people know about.

I slowly wake Elisabeth who rises faster than before. She sits up and tells me she can see everything clearly.

'Did you know I saw you in about 3-4 years?' she says. 'We are going to meet at a party. I walk up to you and shake your hand and thank you for your help,' she tells me.

The Cave of Death

Elisabeth unwinds faster now. She only requires a few instructions before she slips over into the regressed state of deep relaxation. At the same time I have experienced a personal change in myself. It is as if her change is not independent of me. I have discovered a still increasing intuitive understanding between me as a doctor and her as my client. The gap between us decreases each session. Maybe soon our roles will be reversed and she will be teaching me, I thought.

Elisabeth is laid down fully relaxed. I have given her an instruction to stay where she experiences healing and understanding most clearly.

'I am holding my dad's hand. I am wearing a blue dress, gloss black leather shoes and a white ribbon in my hair. I am happy. My dad is bringing me to work. We are going down by elevator. There are a lot of machines around,' Elisabeth said.

'Are you in a mine?' Elisabeth had told me during our first session that her father had worked within the mining industry.

'Yes, it is a mine. He is working there... It is so dark... I am really scared...' Elisabeth's grimaces and I rapidly realise she is experiencing something difficult and unpleasant.

'Do not be afraid, Elisabeth. There is nothing here that can hurt you. I am with you constantly. Move towards that time and place where this fear started. Do not be afraid. I am with you. What are you doing?'

'We move towards a mountain. There are lots of people. They lead me into a cave.'

'Are they forcing you?' I asked.

'Yes, they are. They shut me into the cave. They are blocking the entrance with stones until only the slightest streams of light are able

18

to pass through some crevices. I cannot escape. I am so afraid. It is horrifying.'

'What have you done to deserve such a fate? Listen and look back in time. What crime do people speak of that you have committed?' I asked.

Elisabeth falls silent for a while. 'I think I have been unfaithful.'

'Is your husband part of deciding your punishment?'

'Yes he is,' Elisabeth said.

'You are now dead Elisabeth. Free. Do not be afraid, I am with you. You can once again see the spinning glowing globe in the air before you. What country do you recognize?'

Again she falls into a lengthy silence. 'Italy, yes it is Italy,' she said.

I bring Elisabeth back. When she wakes up she is exhausted. She tells me that she feels completely worn out after each session. It seems she uses an enormous amount of energy during each session. A normal therapy session in the form of, for instance, cognitive psychotherapy, appears like pure rest in comparison to Elisabeth's description of the amount of energy she felt she was losing.

We are often prone to discussion, Elisabeth and I, both before and after each session. There is a growing trust and intimacy in our doctor-client relationship. For me, this experience allows me only to be her guide and I felt joy at observing Elisabeth's growing change. I realised that the courage to step beyond the common treatment of symptoms in order to reach the deepest core and identify the cause of the anxiety was a hard journey, the kind of journey that can be likened to conquering an impossible quest that no ordinary human challenges. That is the way the world is for me. When taking that into consideration, it is a huge privilege for me to journey with each of my clients through the aeons of their past selves. Of course, within the context of modern science the notion of being able to do this is insane and completely impossible to prove. Yet, it seems, my best ally is modern science, it is physics. It is from that branch that I receive reinforcements. My clients are not the only ones in need of courage.

However, deep in my mind I never doubt. Giordano Bruno may not be physically alive, but as a father of ideas he will always live on, threatening and indomitably rebellious against the pseudo-democratic establishment's global monopoly on truth. The natural sciences explain everything yet at the same time they do not. The paradigm shift lies right around the corner. As soon as the change occurs everyone who previously fanatically fought against the new ideas will say "But that is what I have always said!" Elisabeth is changing, whether I want her to or not.

Often, my thoughts stray to as how those close to Elisabeth are reacting. Are they happy that she is recovering? Or disappointed that she might now choose a completely different path for her life? I try to ask my questions openly and without bias. She has improved, but there is still a long way to go until complete recovery.

An Account from the Afterlife

Before the session Elisabeth tells me she has been having nightmares about the episode in the cave. She tells me she has suffered panic-anxiety and says that for the first time in a long time, life has felt very challenging. I tell her that she is free to quit whenever she would like. Nothing is demanded of her. At the same time I confess to her that it would be unprofessional of me to not try and reach the source of her anxiety. I admit that it is a difficult dilemma. The current increase in anxiety might make stopping the treatment seem like the best option.

Elisabeth still seems pleased. She affirms that even with the anxiety she feels happier. She says that she has greatly changed. Her close relatives have noticed her recovery but also perceived that she has lost her previous need for control and detailed planning. 'Now I do not have the compulsion to clean – sometimes I just end up daydreaming and pondering instead.'

After she has reached the relaxed state I consciously guide her to the afterlife. I make the new discovery that she cannot answer any questions unless she has been given instructions to regress or meet some dead individual in the afterlife.

'I am just floating in the light,' Elisabeth said.

'Speak to your mother and father. Ask them to pass on the question regarding the source of your anxiety to a master, someone who knows. Ask why!'

'My mother says I have to accept that it was that way.'

'Go back to your life in Italy. You can now see your husband and the people who were living after your death. Describe what is happening!' I encouraged her.

Several minutes pass as time slowly drags forward. 'I was innocent. My husband's conscience devoured him. He told someone that he had lied. He was hanged afterwards,' Elisabeth said.

'Look into your husband's eyes. Do you recognize them from your current life?'

Several minutes of silence follows. Elisabeth's eyes move under the eyelids. 'No.'

'Do you have any children?' I asked.

'Yes, I have a son.'

'Look into his eyes. Do you recognize them?'

'Yes, it is my son from this life.'

Her face shines up during the regression. I take her back to the afterlife. I explain that she has now gotten the explanation for the cause of her anxiety. She was unjustly convicted and suffered deeply. Now she can understand the source of her anxiety even if it is returning in a new shape. When she is in the afterlife I ask if there is anyone close to her.

'Yes, several soar around me' she says decidedly.

'Do they want contact with you or me?'

'With you.' She seemed to be far away, sometimes almost confused, as if she was standing in a crowd of people where everyone tried to get her attention. Suddenly she spoke: 'He keeps drifting around me and urges me to say 'I am Bo, your brother."

What Elisabeth did not know was that my biological father was named Bo and had passed away 1965. At that point I had already spent several years in an orphanage and ended up in a permanent foster home in Småland. It is strange how all the threads are weaved together into one large human web. My own apprehension makes me lose control. I stop acting professionally and ask about my father-in-law who is close to death. 'How can I help him? He does not like me but I still want to help him,' I ask.

'You only need to go to him and hold his hand.'

My father-in-law's death was very painful. That Saturday morning when he lay dying, I and my three sons travelled to him ahead of everyone else. Fate must have really wanted me to give him strength at death's threshold as, when we arrived, screams of despair could be heard throughout the ward. It turned out to be my father-in-law who had suddenly lost all his strength and was now gripped by fear and angst as he was slipping towards his death. He was moaning deeply and with each breath came an intense tormented shriek. My eldest son became like steel and took his grandfather's hand. My middle son swelled up with sadness and cried softly. My youngest reacted with anxiety and later complained of stomach pains. Yet my sons all remained in the room without fear and watched as their grandfather died. Their fear of death somehow appeared lesser than that of the adult world.

I took my father-in-law's hands and calmly spoke to him. I told him that he could leave this life without fear. I said that I had no fury or bitterness remaining towards him, and that he could let go. That there is a light and another world awaiting him. That he could leave his heavy and painful body behind. That his daughters would reach him – we would all be there. His breathing slowly got lighter and his anguished cries more scarce. Almost unnoticeable tranquillity crept over his face. When his daughters arrived his breaths had started to gradually reduce in frequency. As his normal breathing came to a stop he finally gave out his heavy last breath. Everything became silent

The Death of a Chinese Noblewoman

Elisabeth was once again far away in another life. The visualising globe was as effective as always. A simple instruction makes it instantly materialize in front of Elisabeth's inner eyes. She does not hesitate a single time during all our sessions.

Elisabeth says she lives in China. 'I am living with my husband and three children.'

'Are you part of the imperial family or just well off?' I ask.

'No, we are not part of the imperial family but close. We have a high position.'

Elisabeth then describes her clothes. 'I have such beautiful clothes. They are shining of green and dark orange. I do not work but stay at home and take care of my children. I have a good life,' Elisabeth said.

Suddenly she describes her abrupt death. 'Someone pushed me down the stairs. I cannot see who it is clearly. Someone came up from behind. My children are very distressed and gathered around me. My husband is standing at the top of the stairs and is looking straight ahead with eyes that do not care.'

After the session Elisabeth tells me that she thinks it was a woman who murdered her. She could not determine what relation there was between her husband and the woman. For the first time Elisabeth tells me that throughout her current life she has suffered an intense fear of heights and that she has always feared getting stuck in an elevator.

The Painter in the Desert

It is a day in July 2002. Elisabeth is once again lying deeply relaxed in the room. Several candles are burning on a small table along the windowsill. The blinds are shut as usual. The room is quiet and the atmosphere soft and pleasant.

'What is under your feet?' I ask.

'Sand. I think it is a desert.'

'Do you see anyone else?'

'Yes,' Elisabeth said.

'How many do you see?'

'There are twelve of them.'

'What are you doing?' I ask.

'I am walking with the others. I have a stone in my hand.'

'Are you using it for anything?' I ask.

A long silence follows, as if Elisabeth is standing on the seashore and I am standing and shouting from the opposite shore far away. 'Hmm... I am painting.'

I decide to use the globe again in order to enable me to localise myself in the non limitless time-space dimension Elisabeth is journeying through. 'You can now see a slowly spinning globe before your inner eyes. The continents are green, the sea is blue. In what country are you living?'

'Australia,' she answers without hesitation.

The next moment I ask her to visualise a clock before her inner eyes. A clock in which time is running backwards towards her past life. 'You can now see a big board with clearly defined glowing numbers. There are six digits on the board. The four last ones show our current year 2002. You now see how the digits are reversing. When you can see and feel that it is the correct year the digital numbers will come to a stop. What do you see?'

She never hesitates even though I feel doubtful of my method. I am only making an attempt as an impulse. The advantage is that there is no one who tells me "Stop!" or "This is forbidden". Only fear and respect for the scientific method imposes a limit. Elisabeth answers: 'I see 608.'

'Do you think it is before or after Christ?'

'608 AD' she says without a doubt.

'Time passes. You and the tribe have reached your goal. What are you doing?'

'We have reached water,' Elisabeth said.

'Water... Are there any animals there?'

'Yes but they disperse as we arrive,' she said without hesitation.

'You now move to the most important moment in this life. What are you doing?'

'I am alone, the others are standing a bit further away.'

'What are you doing?' I ask.

'I am giving birth to my child.'

'In the sand?' I exclaim astounded.

'Yes, but I under the shade of a tree.'

'You now clearly see your child. Look into the child's eyes. Is it someone you recognize?' A long moment of silence follows. 'Hmm, it is not possible, is it?'

'No.'

'The light now takes you forward in time. You are holding your child and can clearly see its eyes. Who do you see?'

Silence. Elisabeth seems to be experiencing so much that I have to remind her of my existence. Time is becoming more of a hindrance. It becomes scarce and it is obviously impossible to compare all Elisabeth's experiences during her short "time" towards that outer time I am representing myself. It is as if a stranger laws of physics, different from our own, rule that dimension Elisabeth is visiting. I suddenly realise that I have read something about hyperspace and the absence of human "time' from multidimensional spaces. I remind myself of the physics professor Kaku's book "Hyperspace – a scientific odyssey into the 10th dimension".

'I see my brother from this life, yes that's who it is,' Elisabeth says suddenly and rouse me from my inner thoughts.

'The light and time move you forward. Your child is older now. What are you doing?'

'We are walking with the tribe,' she said.

'Is your son with you?'

'Yes,' she answered.

'What role does he later fulfil in the tribe?'

'He becomes a waterfinder,' she quickly replies.

'I see,' I answer surprised.

'You are now with your tribe at a place where you use your stone. What do you do?'

'I believe I am drawing lines with the stone. I have a stick I am using to paint.'

'Do you have a paint that you are using? Red, black, white?' I ask leadingly.

'It is a dark colour.'

'We now move to your own death. Are you old?'

'Yes, I am old.'

'Are you alone?' I ask.

'No. I am lying on the beach. The others are standing around me.'

'Are they touching you?'

'No.'

'You are dead now. Free. How was this life?'

'It was a good life.'

In later conversations and letters Elisabeth has told me that out of all her lives, the life in Australia was the best one. She returned several times to when we according to her perception sat together in the night at the campfire.

'Life was so easy because we had so much love to give each other. No one had to feel left out. Yes, I do long back to that life.' Elisabeth wrote in one letter.

From Peru to Egypt

Elisabeth wished to meet me one last time, perhaps to gain some perspective. Perhaps for one last journey through time and space before she left the clinic to walk out into the tough reality. Björn Melander's "Eternal waves" was playing on low volume in the background as usual. The candles cast a pleasant light in the room that was increasingly dominated by the autumnal darkness outside the care centre.

'What are you doing?' I ask.

'The ground I am standing on is dry.'

'What kind of shoes do you have? What kind of clothes are you wearing?'

'I have leather clothes and leather shoes,' Elisabeth answered.

'How old are you?'

'I am 17-18 years old. I have long dark hair braided in a plait. I am beautiful. My father is the tribe chieftain. I get to follow a medicine man into the rainforest and learn about medicinal plants. I am proud,' she spontaneously tells me.

Her life was extinguished as abruptly as it had begun. She told me that everyone in the tribe had fallen ill. 'I die in a fever before I ever get to apply my knowledge.'

'Is it the black death, the plague?' I ask inanely.

'No.'

With the visualization of the globe and the clock I learn the time and place.

'It is Peru... year 1200.'

There was time left of our 45 minute session. Often it would become a full hour. I never had time for a break, only quickly dictate the session and then move on to the next patient. The women working at the clinic

28

wondered how I could cope. The reason was simple–I got to take part in an astonishing experience. I would never ever wish it undone no matter what everyone else would say when this was released.

By curiosity and the spur of the moment I took Elisabeth to Egypt. I cannot explain why. Perhaps it was the thoughts of Peru, Inca tribes, pyramids and my earlier visit to Egypt that by instinctive curiosity made me take here there.

'Time is short, soon all our appointments will be over. Soon I move to London. Will she get well in time?' I thought to myself as I instructed her.

With the visualisation of the power of the light I move her to Egypt. I become surprised when I discover that she is not occupying a body. She floats around as a silent observer. No one seems bothered about her invisible presence. I start to worry that I have made a huge mistake.

'She really does not have a life in Egypt,' I think anxiously.

'I am floating above the pyramids. There are so many people building them,' Elisabeth says spontaneously.

'Are there only humans? Do they have ropes and long paths up the pyramid where they drag the stones?' I ask.

'No, there are three Masters dressed in white. They are standing on floating platforms above the pyramids,' she says without any hesitation.

'What do the Masters do afterwards?'

'They return home in a silver coloured ship. They seem pleased over their accomplishment,' she answered.

She later described the Masters using a beam of light to move the stones. 'It felt completely natural. I could feel that the secret of the creation of Earth was buried within the pyramids. I saw two sphinxes, one with a large human head. The other one I could not see clearly.'

Without success I tried to make her visualise what year before zero it was.

***

Elisabeth stayed long after the session as she was the last patient that Friday afternoon. We had a long discussion about her experiences. She told me that she felt completely recovered, but going back to her old job was now unthinkable. Her life had completely changed. It was as if she had been reborn.

Had she wished for this? Was it an acceptable side effect of the treatment? As I watched her smile and leave, I considered these questions and the effect her radical change of personality might have on her family. Was it ethically acceptable to make use of a treatment which could lead to such radical changes?

The Three Masters

It had been one and a half months since the last session when we met to conclude Elisabeth's treatment. She no longer acted with rigid movements and with eyes full of anxiety. Her face glowed with self-confidence and joy. She had changed. In a short reply to the referring GP I had written that the patient had recovered from panic anxiety, elevator phobia and claustrophobia. I felt silly, and feared being misinterpreted. What would they think? Recovery without medication?

During the last relaxation it was unusually difficult to reach a certain point. Elisabeth had wished to go backwards. First she couldn't see anything, and she complained that it was half-light, half dark. I put her into deeper relaxation, and she suddenly exclaimed: 'I am on a silver disc. There are three masters here. They speak to me. They are almost transparent. I think I can almost see through them. They tell me that I shall learn to tell good and bad people apart. They say that even in the evil there is something good,' she said. She spoke without being questioned. I sat still in my chair.

'Can I learn this?'

'You are already able to, they say.' Elisabeth went silent for longer than ever before. Her eyes moved actively under the eyelids in REM-phase. Occasionally she twisted her head lightly, and once or twice she started to breathe rapidly. Then she said:

'I have known all along, why has no one said anything?'

It seemed as if she was experiencing and hearing a lot of stuff I was not allowed to take part in. After several minutes of impatient waiting I could not remain quiet any longer. 'What is happening? What are you doing?'

'They are telling me that I am their observer. I was to meet you so that you would take the step. I would find you. That is what they are saying.'

'You mean that there was a plan all along,' I said.

'Yes, it was decided. Oh, it is so difficult. They say that my dog will die soon… and that soon a friend will pass away…oh…'

'I understand that it is difficult. Perhaps they are telling you so that you will use the time right. To appreciate everything in a completely different way,' I said. To get her away from the troubling subjects I needed to distract her, so I asked her: 'How many lives have you lived Elisabeth?'

'93.'

'So this is your 94th life?'

'No, my 93rd. I will live two more lives. You will also live two more lives,' she said.

For the first time the session was out of my control. It was as if someone else had just suddenly come and taken control over Elisabeth. I didn't think that she was schizophrenic. It seemed as if Elisabeth turned to me after an instruction from someone else, or her own inner experience. The only way to handle what was happening was to not judge anything. Instead I had to observe, and listen. At the end of the session Elisabeth suddenly said: 'They say that you should take care of your eldest son.'

When Elisabeth returned to a normal conscious state she told how three men had been seated in front of here, two at the front, and one in the middle behind them. The experience had made a strong lasting impression on her. She had a feeling that they wanted us to mainly help those people with evil intentions who commit serious crimes.

'The thought transfer was hard to receive… have you tried the method on murderers… but that is how they must have thought,' she said questioningly.

I thought to myself that she was right, but who would dare and who would think that it is a priority?

We spoke about what she had experienced for half an hour. She was firmly convinced that her dog and friend would pass away-nothing could shake her conviction. She was sad, tense yet calm. I marvelled at how this woman with her panic anxiety and phobias had been able to become so strong and carefree.

I pondered her journey as I travelled home towards six in the evening. The sky was grey and ready to rain. The autumn leaves swirled down the birches along the avenue down to the town. The dark and heavy autumn evening seemed light and colourful after the session, a return journey to three masters on a silver disc. What was one to think?

***

A few months later I watched the movie "Minority Report" together with my oldest son. An indescribable emotion of pleasure and discomfort went through my body. When I saw the three precognisant people bathe in photon light it was not just an emotion from seeing an imaginative film with no connection to reality. No, there was something more serious in the background which I had seen and which would never leave me untouched. Elisabeth who had seen the future had also seen mine. The future I must meet with love and without fear. Elisabeth had surely some similarities with Agatha in the film.

I considered the struggle ahead of me and the possibility of human free choice. Do we truly possess it, or are all our choices made before we are born? I felt tired. I understood why Elisabeth became exhausted by visiting the future. To view light as compressed photon images of future events, to feel the pain, to know. Any government would pay anything to control such a weapon, yet there seemed to be some kind of dimensional barrier hidden somewhere in the whole, something which ensures you never receive more knowledge than you can handle. I wondered if that was why several of my patients had reported that they could see the light, yet the door leading there remained closed.

The Farmer from Born

The man who had received an emergency appointment sat deeply depressed in front of me. His breath was shallow and irregular. His eyes were deprived of joy and he constantly fiddled his hands, almost as if he tried to wash them of something invisible and inescapable.

Leif had just turned 45 and should have been at the height of his life, yet his eyes were filled with tears. Gawkily and quietly he tried to tell me about himself using few words. Everything in his life had turned into chaos. It was his wife who had arranged his appointment.

Leif had walked into a serious existential crisis. He was the father of two healthy children, and he had always put his family first. One day everything changed, not instantly as a bolt of lightning, but as a seducing gradual irresistible change. Leif had met a new woman at the same time as the relationship with his wife had become more and more strained.

Leif did everything he could to protect his family. But slowly the truth dripped out as the water from the gutters on a spring day, until finally he drowned in a massive spring flood of emotions and reactions from those close to him. Ultimately, he could not bear it.

It was a small town and soon everyone knew what Leif could not bear to tell his family. When his wife at last confronted him, his ability to handle the relationship burst and everything became emotional disarray. In the end the crisis turned into a deep depression. Leif sat as if, during the worst storm of his life, he had turned to stone.

A few months treatment on antidepressants had improved Leif unremarkably. He was quiet and reclusive. Yet our relationship became stronger as I met his wife and obtained the confidence of both parties. One day I asked Leif if he was interested in getting to know himself deeper. Perhaps he might be able to understand how he, who had never known anyone other than his wife, had ended up in conflict over two different women.

Was there a deeper explanation? We decided, together, to use relaxation exercises to help the process. The starting point was to be an experience that Leif had had as an 11 year old. He'd seen a close friend almost killed in a motorcycle accident and felt immense mortal dread. This was where we would start to find Leif's deeper knowledge of himself.

**

The first session went unexpectedly well. Leif was very emotional after having found himself at his beloved grandparents' farmhouse. On a calendar on the kitchen wall he saw the year 1966. He walked around in his mind and experienced a subjectively intense reality. For the first time, Leif had started to change more noticeably in himself. Spontaneously he walked into my office when I was dictating and remarked 'I really believe in this!'

During the second session he found himself at his school desk in year 1. Without hesitation he described his friends' names and where they were sitting. Under the deep hypnosis he was simply sitting in the classroom. 'Yes, Räven is sitting there, and Erling is over there,' Leif said.

During the third session Leif started to speak spontaneously. He told me about his blue trousers, a dark coat and brown shoes. He was on his way to collect a dog from a friend. In Leif's current life he had just had to put his golden retriever to sleep. The pain had been made easier, I believe, as I had recommended that he do it together with his wife and children. That way they could, by way of the sorrow over their dog, on a deeper level start to process their grief from other issues within the family. According to Leif it worked much better than he had expected.

During the session Leif told me of how he lived in a cottage on a hill above a lake. He worked with some form of wood and leather. By my instruction he walked about his cabin and described it in detail. He looked upon the calendar on the kitchen wall and saw the year 1887. Leif spoke of his beloved dog and told me that the grief after its death made him pass himself soon thereafter. Upon the question of the meaning of this specific life he answered: 'That I should find peace.'

He then spontaneously said that he did not wish to be born to his parents in 1957. 'Mum knew this. It is dark but calm in here.' When he later sat up he told me that he had never throughout his life experienced such an inner calm as during the experience in his own mother's womb. Later something about the story turned out to be inaccurate. It could be the year, the location or both. What was revealed later showed that parts of this story still had a connection to the farmer in Born. But the farmer in Born did not die 1887. He died in 1899.

And even though he died, he has been resurrected. The movie "The Sixth Sense" suddenly appeared meaningful in an age of searching for spirituality. The farmer in Born came to show both Leif and me that it appears we live more than once.

'I am standing by a hay drying rack. The Dane is here with his horse.'

'Do you not own a horse?' I ask.

'No,' Leif answered.

'What kind of wagon does the Dane have?'

'It is a wagon with iron wheels'

'Go to your home now. Describe what your home looks like.'

'There is a barn to the right. The house lies to the left and in the middle is the earth cellar,' Leif answered.

'You are now inside your cottage. What does it look like?'

'There is one room. The kitchen is yellow. The bed I sleep in is on the first floor,' he answered serenely.

'Do you have any books, a calendar, anything you can see?'

'No books, but I have a calendar on the kitchen wall.'

'What year does it say? Look closely, take your time!' I encouraged him.

'It says 1887,' he replied without hesitation.

'Are you married?'

'No, I have never had a woman. And no relatives.'

'What do you work as?' I ask.

'I work in the forest. I sell milk and egg. I have seven cows and a couple of chickens,' he told me without having to be asked.

For each minute the farmer in Born became more and more alive. I had so many questions. Who was he? Why was he so alive to Leif? What was his name? Would it maybe be possible to trace him?

Just imagine if only a single patient could be traced! To maybe really find the person and their grave. To maybe receive a letter from an authority confirming the impossible. Initially I repelled the thought, but it successively became stronger. There was no return. I decided to try and reach a conclusion with the farmer in Born. Leif was an excellent subject. Calm and safe. Before we had started the sessions he had told me that he did not believe in life after death. Neither had he read any special literature. He was a grounded and reliable person. No one could accuse him of being wishy-washy or escapist. For my purposes, it was probably better that he was a non-believer. It was not necessary to believe. The process would still work just as well. It really did not matter whether Leif was Muslim, Christian or Buddhist, white or black. The result is really the only thing that mattered in the end.

'I am happiest when I am working at the farm.'

'You are breathing in and out. All your muscles are completely relaxed. The sounds around you just reinforce the feeling of relaxation. Nothing threatens you. I am constantly by your side Leif. You are within the light. When I have counted from three to one you will be back to that time you were a child... Three – you are floating in the light completely relaxed. You breathe in and out... Two – you are taken backwards. Nothing is dangerous. Everything exists. Nothing hurts you. You can observe yourself freely from the outside... One – you are there. You are once again a child in the middle of the 19th century. It is the time before you became a farmer. What are you doing?' I instructed.

'It is an orphanage. There are many children without parents here. They are poor but do not starve. There is a curvy little lady who runs the home. She likes me.'

I suddenly got an idea. 'Ask her what the orphanage is called!'

He seemed to disappear. The eyes moved under the eyelids. He mumbled something. 'She says.... Bo... Born she says.'

'Born certainly sounds strange,' I thought. 'Is there really such a place?

***

Later he was back at his farm. You could see that Leif in his regressed condition really took pleasure in his experiences. It was as if he was the main character in a wonderful movie he never wished to stop watching.

'Do you live secluded?'

'Yes. The Dane with the horse lives nearest. He helps me sometimes,' Leif answered.

'Are there any close towns?' A long pause.

'Mm, Örebro. I once travelled there for a market,' he said spontaneously.

'How did you get there? What did you do?'

'It took a day to get there by horse and carriage. It is a party. People are drinking liquor,' he continued openheartedly.

'Oh, don't you make your own?'

'No, I buy mine.'

During a later session Leif spoke more in depth that his trips to Örebro were intensive. 'I make such a trip to Örebro once a year. It covers all needs. You buy alcohol and meet women' he told.

We moved forward to the farmer's death. 'I am lying on the wooden bench in the kitchen. I am unable to keep food down.'

'Do you go to the doctor?' I ask.

'No, my neighbour brings me medicine... it is a strong liquor.'

'What year can you see on the calendar in the kitchen?'

'1899,' he replies instantly. It seemed as if the farmer himself never realized he was actually dying. 'I was sick for about a week... and then I died.' Leif seemed very pleased and serene. He seemed to be experiencing something special.

'Why are you so happy?' I asked curiously.

'Well, I am sitting outside my house looking out at the fields. The work for the summer and autumn is done,' he answered.

'What did you learn from the life in Born?'

'To be satisfied with a good life... to be satisfied with peace and quiet.'

I let him rest in the light of his own inner experience. It seemed obvious that Leif longed back to his life as a farmer. In his internal world which I could not question there was a strength I could not help but envy. 'What can you learn from the life in Born in regards to your decisions in your current life?

'To not say no to good things... To not be afraid of peace,' he continued.

Such wonderful perspicacity. Why does he not possess it as distinctly in his everyday life? And why can't one keep all the knowledge that exists in the active biological brain. There must exist a deeper answer as to why one has to reach their own enlightenment of the self. I pondered as to why he had ended up here with me.

***

The next session we worked once again with the farmer in Born. I had decided to once and for all try and establish an identity. Leif calmly lay down as he always did. We started to chat about his current situation. He had not yet made a decision about his life and that was making his wife feel very bad. I stressed to him that the decisions he was to make had to be his own and I could not pressure or persuade him in any direction. He understood.

Leif never had any trouble reaching the deep regressive state where he literally left the room psychically and spiritually. Once when he stood up he was completely dizzy and had to support himself on the walls. He seemed completely drained. It was truly a strange process.

And yet they still wanted to go through all of this. No mumbling from a psychoanalytic therapist trying to find an unresolved internal conflict. All the established schools and theories paled in comparison to what patients achieved with themselves in the deeply relaxed state.

My God, what will the pharmaceutical industry say if people do not need drugs against their mental issues? If there are alternative but demanding processes, which yet can heal relatively quickly, what does that mean? Are we mature enough to enter ourselves in order to survive?

***

On several occasions during the sessions where the farmer in Born manifested himself it also happened that Leif visited other lives. One of these was particularly interesting and painful. Leif had returned to a short life where he lived with his maternal aunt and uncle. For ease of reading I have collected the extracts of interest from these sessions.

'I am with a fair woman... it is my current wife... I follow her into a large house as she shows me around,' Leif said.

'Is there a calendar anywhere on the wall?'

'Yes, there is a hand sewn one on the kitchen wall. It reads 1949.'

The scene changes and he finds himself at the side of a road, observing an old motorbike lying in the ditch. A number of people appear to stand further away. 'They do not want me here.' Leif describes a wounded man lying on the road. 'It is Åke.'

I then instruct Leif to return to his childhood in this life.

'My parents are going away... a large boat... it sank.'

'Try to see if your grandmother and uncle are reading about this in a newspaper,' I urge him.

'Yes, I can see the text about the accident. I can see them reading about it in the paper... but I cannot see any names.'

During a later session he could see his grandmother reading about the accident. And later on he found himself at the docks looking up at the ship.

'I am standing very close. I cannot quite see the name on the boat as there is a house in the way. Excel...sius...Exelcius... I am uncertain. The ship collided with something at sea. There was some sort of drawing in the newspaper of the place of the accident. 498 people died.'

'Do you miss your parents?'

'Yes, but I did not know them well... they were young,' Leif said.

I now took Leif to the moment of his death.

'I am working in the forest... A tree falls on me.' He does not seem to realise he is going to die. There is no fear in his recollection. After the death I instruct him to see his grandmother and uncle reading his obituary in the local newspaper. 'Yes, I can see the years... Born 1928... Died 1952. It is hard to read because the paper is folded.'

Later he could also read the tombstone of the young man.

'I can see a long letter... L... Li... Linus, yes Linus.'

I think to myself that Leif surely must have something wrong. That it would now prove that some details are constructs of his or my mind. When he wakes up we discuss this.

'Leif, something is not right. You are born 1956 and this man died 1952 in the forest. Your parents in the last life were already dead, and that means your own parents must have been reincarnated very quickly in order to have you... it does not add up,' I said.

'My current parents are born 1934 and 1937,' Leif answered.

'In the last life you were born 1928... That means your current parents must have died sometime between 1928 and 1934. That in turn means that they were reborn before you died in your last life,' I answered. I immediately realised that there was room for this possibility.

***

Leif was once again in Born, his body completely relaxed and his breathing calm.

'You walk around your house. Is there a deed for it anywhere? Something with your name on it?' I ask.

'Yes, yes... I received the farm as a gift from the woman from the poorhouse. A third person witnesses as she hands over the deed to me... Yes, I am signing it,' he said.

'What name is on the documents? What name are you writing?' I ask, now more curious than ever.

41

'Erik... Erik Andersen... Andersson... Andersen... it is a bit difficult to see and read it,' he says. I felt completely amazed at the prospect of having discovered a real, tangible name.

During one of the final sessions we decide to end the visits to Erik Andersson in Born. We knew his name, year of death and the place where he lived. That information was enough in order to search the archives. I asked Leif to contact the national archive in Uppsala. They could help him with the impossible task to find Erik if he really had ever existed. Leif promised to make an attempt and call them. He was himself curious.

'I am so glad. The fields are cut and the hay is collected,' Leif said.

'Oh? What do you have on your feet? What clothes are you wearing today?' I ask.

'A pair of wooden clogs, grey trousers... and a white shirt. It is Sunday today.' He continued like before to describe his home. He seemed incredibly attached to his farm. With great affection he once again described the farm to me.

'Leif, you have now moved forward to Erik's funeral. You can see the coffin, the people who are at the service. It is nothing dangerous. You are observing everything from the outside in order to understand.'

'Yes... There are quite a lot of people in the church... I never did anyone harm... Mm, I can hear the priest speaking,' he said rapidly.

Leif later said that he had seen his own gravestone with the name Erik Andersson written on it.

***

The 25th October 2002 Leif came to my clinic with a letter from the archivist G Ehnström from the research service at the national archive in Uppsala. The letter was dated 15th October with the registration number 421/02-5923 contained the following:

With reference to the telephone conversations on 2002-09-23 and 10-14 the national archive reports the following:

In the Nora parish register of deaths for year 1899 there was found only one Erik Andersson in Born, born 1822. It was Per Erik Andersson who died 16 Mars from cardioplegia and was buried on 23ʳᵈ Mars. Under the age 76 years, 4 months and 1 day, reads 22 Nov 15, which appears to be his date of birth, 15 Nov 1822. In the column for annotations reads: Nr 23 – Nora north kg kv 2 nr 139.

With kind regards,

Gunilla Ehnström

I was completely overwhelmed and speechless. A feeling of effervescence was mixed with the knowledge that the outside world was maybe not yet ready for the reintroduction of the knowledge of reincarnation. The impossible was true. Erik had been found in Born. At the same time the apprehension that the proof would never be enough where prejudice prevailed gnawed at me. There was a discrepancy between the 15 November from the parish records and the 16 November on the gravestone, but it seemed like a simple mistake.

'They will say that you made everything up before you went for help. Someone will try to find a point where you have visited Born, to show you have constructed everything.'

Leif seemed offended. He stood silent and contemplating for a while with the letter in his hand. 'But I have never been there. I did not even know of Born. I did not know the place existed. Surely they must believe me,' Leif said with indignation.

'Belief is reserved for the church. But sure, it is better than nothing.'

During the last session we jointly decided to make an attempt to visit the future-if it was possible. Leif gave his approval, and I emphasised that we would not try to uncover anything that could affect his current life negatively.

'I am standing by a beach. There is a woman on a sailing boat out on the lake,' Leif said. Later during the session he told me that the woman was his wife and he had built the boat himself.

43

'You have now come to your home. Describe what it looks like!'

'It is square. I work in the ground floor with designing sailboats. I have some form of larger computer and a smaller one for when I am travelling. Hmm, I enjoy my work very much... things are going well. We have one TV. The picture is projected onto the wall by a thin beam of light from a smaller lens. Yes, I can see it clearly.'

'Describe how you live. What do the cars look like?' I asked him.

'There are not a lot of cars. There is some type of train, they travel soundlessly on rails between the houses. We do not have a car.'

'What country do you live in and what year?' I asked, using the instruction of the globe and digital chronometer.

'It is Sweden, but I do not know the name of the town. It is 2111.'

Thinking about Elisabeth's sessions I decided to take Leif forward to 2113.

'Has something special happened?'

'No.'

We went forward another few years. He and his wife then had a son and a daughter. When I asked him to look into the children's eyes Leif said: 'It is Daniel and Stina... it is my current children!'

Just like all the other sessions Leif returned to the present without drama. He looked up and shook his head when he was told the time. Like most patients he felt as though 10-15 minutes had passed. The last session had lasted about an hour.

***

The autumn colours were intensely defined. In a last brilliant act the October sun sparkled against crimson red maple leaves. The birch leaves mixed mustardy yellows and oranges with small fading strips of pale green. Along the mountain lakes south of Grängesberg the clear blue water glistened fresh and inviting. Only a few cars met us along the winding roads down towards Nora and Born. Elisabeth drove her new Toyota softly and pleasantly. Leif was in the backseat, pleased and at peace. It felt almost unreal.

It was strange sitting with Leif in the backseat of Elisabeth's car. He had accepted her request of being allowed to come along. I questioned if I had acted ethically, but felt secure in my decision as I had never broken patient confidentiality. Leif had been allowed to make his decision before Elisabeth was made able to contact him. I hoped that they would both gain something from their meeting. And then we were there. Out under the clear blue October sky with its blinding cascade of colour lay a few houses and farms gathered around a couple of creeping roads that met at a crossroads. Born, our goal. We had decided to unite and make a foolish attempt to find Erik's grave. Before we went to the graveyard in Nora we drove a few times back and forth in order to allow Leif to process his impressions.

'No, it is further into the forest. That is my definite feeling. There was a road down to a village, I am certain of it. I lived rather remotely,' he said as laconic as ever.

After an hour of aimless driving we went to the graveyard. The ground was covered by a thin veil of the first snowfall. The day was cold and clear. We went back and forth between the old tombstones.

'Our beloved son, born 1824. Died 1873. The shoemaker Nils Andersson, born 1834, died 1888,' I read.

Not until Elisabeth suggested that we should follow the strict divisions and find division 2 number 139 did we realise we were on the right track. The stones were getting older, as we moved down the 19th and 18th centuries.

Abruptly I found myself in front of a plain, low granite stone. I could not make anything out clearly as the engraving had since long been worn by wind and weather. But there was a text. I used my feet to rub off the snow on the stone to make it more readable. Slowly P E Andersson became readable, and as I continued the rest of the text appeared. *16/11 1822 † 16/3 1899 Born it read. I looked down astounded. I called Elisabeth and Leif who quickly came over. We were all extremely happy, almost excited.

'What we see now is something completely unique, but we should not forget that no matter what evidence we could present from an individual's previous life there will always be someone to claim it is a lie, fabrication or God knows what. Nothing can change a true conviction,' I said.

We photographed the gravestone with each of us, and lastly even with Leif and myself squatting next to this strange memorial. Leif later handed me a floppy disc with the digital photographs.

'How does it feel to exist both above and below earth?' Elisabeth asked smiling.

'I have to admit I am slightly bewildered,' he said seemingly as collected as usual. Cynically I considered the advantage of having Leif as the subject of this particular story, as he had absolutely no belief whatsoever in these sorts of things before we had begun our sessions. It made me seem less likely as an impostor.

We had reached our goal. We had made one of the strangest discoveries possible by a human. We had rediscovered Erik's but also Leif's grave, and that was not all. All the details he had given were correct. And he had absolutely nothing in common with this place in his current life. He had never put his foot in this place, nor visited Nora north graveyard. One of my most thrilling years as a psychiatrist was going towards its end. Our labours had borne fruit. Nothing would ever be able to take away this joy from us. No one.

I felt intensely grateful towards Professor Weiss' achievements, and the path he had trod. Likewise Professor Ian Stevenson's work with "Twenty cases suggestive about reincarnation" had been a great inspiration. Everything has a meaning, but brave people are required in order to reveal the obvious truths for humanity. The physical body slows everything down in order to make pain, suffering and longing our teachers in life. The physical form gives us important experiences so we can advance spiritually and reach higher dimensions. How grateful I am for my clients who made me choose this path, and that I managed to resist the pressure from the world's illusions and fleeting rewards. As many times before my mind was a flurry of thoughts. Too many had misunderstood me in life. They thought I was always in a rush, but the answer was deeper and more difficult. Deep in my heart the conviction was crystal clear. I was very old. I had lived so many times and made infinite errors. Now for once I really wanted to act right, and not work according to the wishes of others but according to my true inner conviction. To find a dead person in a new life. The spiritual world's energies had always been unfathomably powerful inside me.

When I was young I had abused the power with which I influenced people and obtained what I wanted. Now I had put egoism aside and chosen to follow the path that finally had proved correct. I did not need to doubt myself. Many had been incensed by my words of truth, and some turned their indignity towards dark thoughts of hurting and stopping this too openhearted and controversial doctor. Thoughts and images flashed quickly through my mind. No, I shall never again be afraid, everything will be alright. The truth will slowly reveal itself just as gravestones under the melting snow, I thought to myself as I sat in silence in Elisabeth's car during our journey home towards Dalarna.

Leif was satisfied. He remained on antidepressants, but he had slowly improved, perhaps due to both the medicine and the therapy in combination. From the latter he had for the first time obtained a deeper knowledge of himself, and he seemed content with that knowledge. He never went around and told others about this. As always he moved slowly and carefully. He remained laconic and deeply attached to nature. Eventually he moved into his own apartment and after I met him one last time together with his wife he signed his divorce. He did so with pain and ambivalence, as he did not wish to sever the bonds with those that were closest to him. Just like Erik Andersson, Leif never consciously did any person harm. He was fundamentally a warm and affectionate person. When I left Sweden he was going to start working again. He had done what most people dream of but few dare. He had set out on an inner journey to discover himself.

I Chose to Become a Woman

Karin was referred to the clinic after a suicide attempt with pills and alcohol. The reason was that after a fight during a party her wife had left her for three days.

Like many other children in modern Sweden Karin grew up with parents and several half siblings on each parent's side. Most of the time she had to take care of herself, and she felt a constant lack of emotional involvement and closeness from her parents. Her father kept his previous children secret to Karin until she was 15 years old. Naturally Karin rebelled against the adult world's lies and false reality. She ran away and dreamt of a new family. She never found it.

Karin was strong and obtained a HGV driving license. In her 20s she had a son, but a few years later she started to feel uneasy. Only through private psychotherapy did she come to terms with her homosexuality. She started to feel relief and freedom. When Karin came to me she had been married for one year with her new partner. Even though both of her parents were alcoholics she had never abused drugs and she was physically fit. During the last two years before we met she had suffered feelings of loneliness and seclusion and she recurrently felt emotionally crippled and incapable of logical reasoning. Karin's emotional life went up and down like an elevator.

'Sometimes I feel like a 3 year old who is smoking... and soon thereafter like I am an adult again,' she said to illustrate her feelings to me.

I never diagnosed Karin as having a personality disorder. With the years I became less and less inclined to put that label on the people I saw. Too many regressed in their emotional life under the influence of depressions, sorrows and losses. Personality disorder is a diagnosis that should only be used after prolonged contact and careful evaluation by professional assessors. Karin received the diagnosis crisis reaction with anxiety and a symptom diagnosis of relationship conflict with partner. Just around the corner of psychiatric history lay the textbooks that said that homosexuality was a valid diagnosis. Luckily times have changed.

We decided that while Karin waited for the relaxation therapy she would continue with conversational therapy with our understanding and worldly counsellor. The relationship conflict with her partner resulted in Karin being treated for a few days in the psychiatric ward under the diagnosis crisis reaction. She was put onto sleeping pills and antidepressants, in common tongue happy pills. Karin started to sleep better and she found her appetite. At the start of September we started the relaxation exercises, and at that point she had herself quit her medication without any side effects.

The first session was as always focused on the relaxation itself. Everything went well. Karin was back to being a four year old and described graphically how she wore black trousers with suspenders.

'I am standing by the kitchen sink with mum. She is giving me medicine,' Karin said.

'Why?'

Karin was like all the other patients caught by an invisible but imaginable interdimensional phenomenon, the time paradox. Several lengthy minutes passed in waiting silence before the answers came. The psychologists and my colleagues would just dismiss such a theory as nonsense. They would note that the patients have been trapped in their own past sea of unconscious knowledge. "Freud and Jung knew that, are you not educated?" they would ask. But how would they explain past lives of which we find evidence, I wondered as I waited for Karin's answer. What made Karin special was that she often spontaneously started to talk about what was happening to her. Sometimes it was as if she was a living correspondent from another age.

'Mm... Mum wants me to take it because I am hyperactive. It feels so weird when I am speaking,' she ended abruptly.

When she returned to herself she described vividly how strange it was to experience herself as a child while speaking through the body of an adult woman. That phenomenon is well known and has been described previously in literature by, amongst others, my great inspiration professor Brian Weiss from the USA.

'What are you wearing on your feet?' I asked.

'Black boots,' Karin answered after a long silence.

'What kind of clothes are you wearing? Feel them,' I urged her.

'Mm, I am wearing a white shirt and, I believe, suede trousers. I am only travelling through. It is a market square... There are so many people here... The air is buzzing with conversation. There is a fountain in the middle,' she said before I had even had time to ask anything again.

'I see. How did you get there?'

'I came with the boat I work on,' Karin said. Once again I used the illusory globe in order to help her localise herself. 'I actually think it is Italy,' she said.

'What is everyone doing there? What is it that is happening?' I asked.

After a very long moment the answer came. 'Someone is to be hanged.'

'Do you know who? Ask someone in the crowd who is to be hanged' I ask on pure impulse.

'Mm, yes, it is a thief.'

Karin continued to describe her life. There was a great gravity and deeply buried sorrow in her story. I still did not understand why. 'What are you doing?'

'I am saying farewell to my wife and children. The children are so sad,' Karin said.

'Look into your wife's eyes. Take your time. Is it someone you recognize?'

'Yes, wow, it is Maria, my current wife.'

'Are you scared?' I asked.

'No.'

'What is happening on the boat?'

'We are out at sea. I lose my grip when I am reaching for something. I fall into the sea and drown.' Karin was now in the afterlife yet remarkably open to questions.

'Why were you a man then and woman in this life?'

'I chose to be born as a woman in this life because I was a man before. I need to learn to like my own feminine side in order to feel better as a man. I live together with Maria for the sake of love. You ask such difficult questions' she finished.

Karin gave me a different perspective on the concept of homosexuality. Apparently there did not have to be anything biologically "wrong". It was as if an individual chooses a child and gender even before conception with the purpose to evolve their spiritual life and to follow their group of soul friends on the continued cosmic line of development, which in turn would explain homosexuality based on a dominant female soul in a male body and vice versa. It would make everything so much easier – our body types would be completely arbitrary as in the end the only thing of importance is love.

'I am holding the reins. I am on my way to an old woman with bread.' Karin unexpectedly lifted her hand and touched her chin. Surprised I asked her what she was doing.

'Some bread is stuck on my chin.'

'What clothes are you wearing?' I asked.

'Hmm, it is some sort of birch bark shaped as a cloak,' Karin answered.

'Are you a man or woman, girl or boy?'

'I am a young boy.' A moment later she waved her hand again, this time in the air.

'What are you doing?'

'There are flies around the horse,' she answered.

Karin proceeded to describe how she once again was back in her village. She described small houses with clay roofs, as well as her parents, but she did not recognize either of them from her current life. Karin started to speak spontaneously. 'We make knives and arrowheads... We sell them to distinguished gentlemen.'

I used the technique of creating the illusory globe at the spot where Karin was standing. She could not tell me where she was until she had moved forward to a point where the village was visited by the weapon merchants. 'There are high gentlemen in the village. They are buying knives and spears. I can see where I am now,' she stated suddenly. 'It is England,' she said.

I now asked Karin to move to the most important moment in her life. 'What are you doing?' I asked.

'Oh... Yes... I'm holding a woman in my arms.' Karin spoke with genuine warmth, and she seemed blissful when she described the warm feeling of holding the woman in her arms. Once again she demonstrated her candour and spoke spontaneously. 'We have to be sneaky. She is dressed in some sort of cloak... not a dress... she is from a high family.'

'What family does she come from?' I asked.

'They have lots of land. We can never marry nor have children.'

Karin seemed unwilling to leave her moment of love, but I decided to move her to her moment of death. I listened to Karin's description, worried about what I had done. 'What is happening? Can you see how your life ends?'

'I am to be hanged,' she replied surprisingly decisively.

'What have you done to deserve such a punishment?'

'I have stolen food.'

'Are you scared?'

'No, it will be nice to leave everything behind,' she answered peacefully.

In the afterlife Karin could look back upon her life in England and I asked her what she had learned from that life.

'I was to learn to never give up.'

'But you never did.'

'Yes, it was exactly what I did. I gave up on love. I did not fight,' she answered so resolutely that I was astonished over her capability of insight. I continued curiously to ask her what happened after the death by hanging. 'It is cold and snowy. I see people far away waving at me' Karin answered. I then instructed her to move closer, and she then told me that the people gave her bread.

The episode was another confirmation of the difficulty in distinguishing the physically living and that which could be interpreted as the afterlife or the immortal existence. The question remains whether or not it was a fragment of an event from Karin's life in England, her own interpretations or wishes, or her experience of the moment just before death, a moment possibly filled with confusion, surprise and anxiety.

After several conversations Karin agreed to try the possibility of moving forward. It was now spring 2002. Without her knowledge I chose the 22nd Century in order to create a checkpoint in regards to Elisabeth. Would there be any similarities, or where there elements of fantasies and self made constructions?

'What are you wearing?' I ask.

'I am completely naked. It is so bright... there are people around me.'

It was unclear if it this was her birth, and Karin gave no clues. I moved her further along in life. 'I am in a home. It is very bright. There is a large TV-like screen. It is laid into a wall.'

'How do you contact friends and acquaintances?'

'I use the TV.'

'Do you have computers?'

'Yes... a small device in the form of some sort of remote control that I connect to and control something similar to a computer. I can go back in history on the computer. The environment is dreadfully cold. There are a few furnishings but no paintings on the walls,' she answered.

'Good. Look in your history encyclopaedia if you can see something about year 2113. Is there anything?' I asked tensely curious.

'It seems as if most animals went extinct. I do not know why.' She never gave any more details and gave the impression that they were very difficult questions to answer.

'Are you married and do you have any children?' I ask.

'Yes, I am married and have one son,' she replied.

'Do you love your husband?'

After a deep silence the answer came. 'It has something to do with social status.'

I transported Karin further along in this future life, and she described how she was eating a meal. Suddenly her breathing became strained. She twisted on her chair and her face became worried. 'It does not feel good. I have pains in my chest and it feels heavy.'

I brought her back and made one last excursion to the summer of 2003. 'What are you doing?' I ask.

'I am on vacation in Greece together with Maria. It feels great!'

When she woke up she told me there were no plans whatsoever to travel there. Karin expressed her joy that the regressions had made a definite effect on her relationships with other people. She felt she had made a positive development and moved forward. She was experiencing real, positive, inner change.

Do you believe traumas exist in this life?

Emma was referral by her local GP who did not quite know what to do with her. She was single and shared the care of her two children with their father. Emma had no higher education but was unemployed. Combined with being a single mum this meant a bad and fragile economic situation.

Until she was ten years old she had grown up together with her parents and a sibling. Her parents then divorced and eventually found new partners. For Emma her parental relationships had always been unstable. Her father had somewhat transgressed sexual boundaries and his presence always awoke a feeling of insecurity. During her upbringing Emma had always experienced that her relationship with her mother was defined by emotional coldness and a lack of support and appreciation. Emma felt constantly unsafe and insecure. She had never experienced a relationship where she could relax and be herself. Instead her mind was plagued with thoughts of not being good enough, of being sexually deviant, and of not fitting in.

Most patients with some form of anxiety, depression, panic attacks and compulsions were treated with drugs. The doctors did of course want to help the patients- there was but one problem. There was never enough time for deeper discussion, analysis or treatment. I have myself just as my colleagues many times used the prescription pad to stop the uncertainty and questions regarding the symptoms.

'You will find things work out. Take these tablets in a slowly increasing dosage. You may feel slightly ill, sweat, and get headaches and decreased sexual drive, but this will pass with time. Take the medicine each day

55

and try to avoid alcohol. If you can just cope during the first few days everything will get better.'

That was how we often spoke. There was nothing scientifically wrong in our method. The problem was that too many patients cancelled the treatment, never collected the medicine, or stopped taking it after the side effects had started during the first few days.

Emma was also aware of this. She did not accept any drugs but wanted me to help her anyway. Perhaps slightly arrogantly I started providing relaxation exercises. No matter the outcome, one thing was perfectly clear. Emma did really need to learn to relax. She often sat tense, nervous and uncertain in the waiting room. Even though she was young she found it difficult to discover a deeper purpose of life. She felt lost in a world that never really understood her.

The first session was uncomplicated. I only let her regress to when she was 5-6 years old. She described a warm and deep love to her father, but also a lack of any love from her mother towards her father.

When she started school she felt left out and she had no friends. When she was ten her father told her about the divorce, something that evidently made her suffer greatly. Like so many other children of divorce she lost the close contact with her father, and was left with a mother that she could never understand or get close to.

During the second session Emma is calm and pleasantly relaxed. Her tense movements are gone. She speaks peacefully without anxiety. In the deep relaxation Emma for the first time find pictures of something she has neither believed nor been interested in.

'What are you wearing Emma?'

'Leather... My feet are bare. There is a camp. I see an older woman... my mother. There are tents... other people... horses.'

As with the other patients I use the visualising globe and clock of time. I feel quite uncertain and don't believe Emma is able to handle some questions and statements. To my surprise she proves herself independent and certain.

'It is Peru... Yes, I am completely certain. Yes, I can clearly see the year... 1893. I am watching out over grey mountains.'

'Do you have children?' I ask.

'No, I don't believe I ever got any. I loved my father deeply, but my feelings towards my mother were cold.'

'You are now at your moment of death. What is happening?'

'I fell ill quite young. I can see myself lying in a small bed with mother by my side.'

'Were you scared after you had died?'

'No, I did not feel any great joy in the afterlife... but neither any fear nor terror,' Emma said. When she opened her eyes she was stunned to find that an hour had passed. 'But has it not been ten to fifteen minutes? I only laid down a moment ago!' Emma told me she felt uncertain regarding her experiences. She instinctively that some of what she saw was influenced by events from her current life.

During the following session Emma was irritated and tired. She had no energy to work on a deeper level, so I did not force her. The next session she once again visited her tribal life in Peru. She saw herself collecting sticks in the forest, and also told me that she had been full of social phobia since she was 3-4 years old. I suspected that Emma carried many secrets.

Emma's experiences are characterized by things getting mixed up. She becomes confused and sees several lives mixed together. Sometimes it is naturally difficult to distinguish truth from fantasy, yet one important observation remains. The process itself definitely seems curative even for Emma. At the start of September Emma has relaxed deeply during her session. Suddenly she laughs and speaks.

'I have clogs on my feet, apron and a skirt. It is nice weather...'

'Go to your home and your husband. Describe what you see,' I encouraged her.

'I live in a small house... maybe it is dark red in colour. I am married but we have no children. Yes, I see my husband before me.'

'Look into his eyes! Is it someone you recognize?' I ask.

'How strange... I recognize Jacob,' Emma said.

When I ask her to visualise the globe she sees Germany. She says that the year is 1859, after which I take her forward. It is possibly then that

I discover that in a flash of light Emma can be in another life, another epoch. I have no real control as to where she goes.

'What are you doing?'

'I see an airplane,' Emma answers.

I become confused because I'm not expecting an airplane. I am much too guided by myself and Emma's experience in the German countryside.

'Oh, I am bidding him farewell. He is going... some mission I think... Belgium I believe. He is wearing some special aviation gear.'

'Is the plane armed?' I ask.

'I cannot see it. Oh, we love each other so deeply. I am worried over his departure.'

I carefully take Emma forward, just a little bit of time. I give her careful instructions in order not to lose her. 'What are you doing?'

'Two armed men have come to tell me that my husband will never return,' she says mournfully.

'We now go forward to your death in this life Emma. Describe what you are experiencing!'

She constantly keeps calm and relaxed. 'I am a grey-haired woman who dies... sleeping in the bed.'

'What year is it?'

'1890.'

'What did you learn from the life in Germany?'

'To love and that one must learn not to be afraid,' she replies without hesitation.

When Emma arose after the session she was completely stiff. As usual she did not understand where the time had gone. She said that she could not explain why she saw the aircraft. She had seen that it was a so called biplane and that the man in the plane was the same man she had seen outside the farm in Germany in the middle of the 19th century.

There was certainly something that was not correct in her story. Probably one of the error sources where her dates. There was still no reason for me to start questioning this. These were details that hardly would contribute to her recovery. No, something was missing, but I never did find out what it was. Apparently Emma's experiences were fragmented.

A modern person with the same experiences would risk being classified as disassociated, subconsciously split and fragmented as a result of some type of difficult and early trauma. But in Emma's case we never found any such trauma. She was herself very conscious of this yet still insisted that there was a trauma. I did not understand what she meant. Not until she became Anna-Greta.

'What are you doing Emma?' I asked. She was already deeply relaxed and seemed occupied with something.

'I am walking along a dirty road. I have slippers on my feet and a long dress in brown and beige.' She replied without diffidence.

'Go to your house. Describe how it looks!'

'It is a large yellow house. Inside the kitchen stands a small round woman. It is my grandmother.'

'You now see the time-board before your eyes. Slowly the digits roll back from 2002 to that year you see now. Take your time. What do you see?'

'1920' she replied assuredly.

Thereafter I asked her to go forward to that life's most important event. Suddenly Emma became intensely scared, almost terrified. I became forced to repeatedly ask her to observe what happened from the outside. I reassured her that she no longer would feel any physical pain or anxiety. She would just observe and describe what she saw.

'I see a long row of horses with men?'

'Do they wear military uniforms?' I ask.

'They are grey in some way. No, I cannot really see? It happens... something very nasty. They... are holding me... one of these men rapes me,' she says almost agonizingly.

'Does no one interfere and defend you?'

'No, they leave me bloody and torn by the roadside. I never return home. Now I walk around begging in a city,' Emma says.

I move her forward to her death. 'What are you doing?'

'I am lying in a hospital bed. There are nurses around me.'

'Maybe the nurses and doctors mention your name? Do you hear anything?'

'Yes, they are saying Anna-Greta... I died without anyone at my side,' Emma said.

What hit me when Emma had woken up was that she actually expressed joy over her disturbing experience.

'I always knew there was something, but I didn't know what' she said spontaneously.

She told me in confidence that she had met a man with whom she had stayed the night. The man had been allowed to stroke her skin. For the first time Emma had been able to relax in the company of a man. The man she had stayed with was the man from the earlier life in Germany. The man she had bid farewell.

'How strange. Is there a purpose that she should meet him, is it random? Is it her fantasy and wishes or mine? No matter. She is feeling better,' I thought when Emma left the clinic.

During one of the last sessions Emma relived how she as a young girl stood watch over a green valley. She definitely contended that it was year 1010. She recognized her father and mother from her current life. At the end of the session she saw her house burning with her whole family inside. 'I stand at the side of the fire with my sprawling doll. I feel such despair, such anxiety' Emma told me.

I cannot claim that Emma made a full recovery, but she changed. She found her own deeper explanation for her anxiety, which was enough for her to be able to handle life without medication- and who could truly deny her that?

The Woman who could not Stop Grieving

The gloomy but kind and modest woman sat in my waiting room one day at the start of July 2002. As always I had given myself time to read her journal. The pages filled me with melancholy and pain.

I asked myself how much a single person should ever have to suffer as I entered the waiting room and took her hand. 'Welcome, I hope you have not waited too long' I said as our eyes met.

Within her eyes there was a sadness I had not encountered in a long time. Her handshake was firm and kind, but her body moved in slow melancholy. Anna carried deep sorrow. In her youth she had lost a childhood friend who got hit by a train. During her puberty she was sexually harassed by an older acquaintance and thereafter suffered a lifelong feeling of insecurity. She lost her daughter at the end of the eighties, during which time Anna had contact with our clinic.

During the last few months Anna had once again contacted the clinic. The warm and understanding staff had done everything possible to support her, yet she was still stuck in her infinite grief over her daughter. Counselling and ear-acupuncture had not had any effect. An investigation by her corporate health insurance with large resources had with understandable reasons not found anything deviant. In the end she was put onto relatively effective antidepressants. In October she was also given a tryptophan amino acid supplement which can sometimes increase the proportion of neurotransmitters and act as an adjunct antidepressant.

At the end of the eighties Anna and her husband lost their daughter Klara in a horrifying manner. Her husband was sawing down a tree at their house when the tree suddenly fell right on Klara. The girl died from her head hitting a stone right in front of her parents. The grief shattered them. Anna and her husband could not stand seeing their dead daughter in her coffin, but Anna sent Klara her clothes, her favourite teddy and a watch for the long journey.

'I was never given time to grieve. We both worked full time, and new things were constantly happening. Many friends betrayed us in our mourning, and I was thrown into another tragedy. As staff in a hospital I had to help relatives mourn their sons after an enormous ship accident.'

Anna and her husband simply tried to work themselves away from their grief. And during her work at the hospital she was confronted day after day by sufferers of cancer. In October 1994 Anna was on that boat which first arrived to the site of Estonia's accident where 852 people lost their lives. She was amongst those who helped the wounded that were taken aboard. Finally she had no strength left – she was completely mentally and physically exhausted. Who could blame her?

At the same time her husband was suffering from one illness after another. It was as if he tormented himself with diseases due to his guilt over his daughter's tragic death. At the time when Anna contacted me she also discovered that her husband had become an alcoholic. It seemed to never end.

Time was short during the autumn of 2002. I instantly realised that we would never be able to take Anna on in a more planned and constructive treatment of 10-15 sessions. I decided together with Anna's excellent family-therapist to do a couple of relaxation exercises focused on one single thing. Without the therapist's support and deep understanding my short entry would never have been possible. The plan was to give Anna contact with her daughter through the light. The sessions took place at the end of October.

'Dear Anna, you are now going to meet your daughter within yourself. I cannot promise you anything. You are breathing very calmly. You are completely relaxed. Soon you will be with your daughter,' I recited methodically.

Anna was breathing still and calm. For the first time she was lying relaxed at my clinic. Her facial expression was serene. For a few hours during the sessions she left my clinic in two of the strangest excursions I have experienced. Anna's inner journey would give her the greatest experience in a very long time.

'You are walking along a beach. You are alone. The sea peacefully rolls over the beach where you are walking. The sky is blue. The wind strokes your hair and you can smell the salt. Far away you suddenly see a door surrounded by a strange light,' I said.

Anna calmly went into the light with ease. It was as if her subconscious just had been waiting for a small nudge in the right direction.

'When I have counted to three you will be with your daughter Klara.'

Her eyes were moving beneath the eyelids, and she smiled a radiant smile and my eyes filled with tears. I had to summon all my strength to continue the process.

'What are you doing now Anna?' I asked.

'I am with Klara. She is standing right in front of me in a pink dress. Oh, how beautiful she is.' Anna seemed to chat with her daughter. Something happened. 'She says that I am reading it wrong. She always did. She knew very well what was written in the books.'

A few days passed and soon again Anna was back with Klara. Everything was easier now. They seemed to have a dialogue. I had difficulty reaching Anna in her delightful higher state of consciousness. 'Klara says that dad could not have known that the tree would twist. She says I have to let go of the grief and move on. She is really comfortable. She… says she will return during my lifetime… And that when it happens I will know. She says… that I should tell dad to take care of Ullis,' Anna said.

When Anna woke up she described clearly how she had spoken to her daughter, and that she had become very strongly conscious that her daughter was in another place of non-physical existence. She told me for the first time that the tree her husband cut down really did twist itself and fell over Klara. There was a strong inner conviction and joy with Anna over her experience, and I understood that no one could take this from her. Through her experience in her own consciousness

63

she had freed herself. Regardless of the experience's genuineness there was nothing in the world that could shake Anna's conviction. She had met her daughter and finally, through Klara, given herself permission to move on with life. Anna expressed delight at the prospect of meeting Klara again before her own life would end.

When she left the clinic that dark autumn day she left with clear eyes and decisive steps. Her change was in truth really strange, and she left me with Klara's supporting words: 'Mother, you must stop mourning me. Move on now. It's all good and I will return.'

Meeting Loved Ones beyond Life

Sari was a Finnish woman who came for an assessment one day at the suggestion of our counsellor, a profound and wise woman. Sari came to Dalarna County as a 6 year old. When she was 8 her brother died from a brain tumour. The night he died he was at home with his parents and two sisters. Sari remembered that she attended the funeral but that she was disappointed at missing school.

In close connection to her brother's death her parents got divorced. Her father had big problems with alcohol. A short time after, when Sari was 9 years old, her father also died. Sari grew up together with her sister whilst their mother worked hard to provide for the children with a meagre cleaner's salary. During her youth Sari often got to hear that she "would end up a charity case", due to her background. She never did. Despite all her misfortune she got herself a job and eventually three children. Her husband never understood her emotionally and finally he left her and the three young children.

During the conversation with Sari her deep and unprocessed misery was strongly prominent. She had been tormented by back pain and took painkillers. She had been prescribed antidepressants but with no effect on a deeper level. Her depression was the result of a much deeper and unresolved grief due to the loss of her brother and father.

Psychodynamically it was not difficult to understand her outbreaks of rage, despondency and unexplainable emptiness. Even after medication and good support from our counsellor she had not improved in five months following initial contact. After the pleas of the counsellor I made a vain attempt to try to help Sari during a few sessions before my departure to England.

At the start of July 2002 I helped Sari reach unexpectedly good relaxation. During two sessions she returned to her parents and witnessed her mother telling her that her brother had a brain tumour. After his death she was with a neighbour. As the tears ran down her cheek she painted a strongly descriptive picture of her grief.

'I can feel his fear... I am so sad that I could not help him... But I can feel that he remains,' Sari said.

Everything became intensely real. After the session she left the clinic relieved. Once again I was surprised by the inner strength that each patient seemed to possess. It seemed as if everyone had the potential to heal under the correct guidance.

***

Sari was breathing lightly, almost unnoticeable in the subtly lit room. Outside the pulled blinds the summer day was bright and hot.

'What are you doing?' I asked her.

'I am standing in front of a tent,' she swiftly replied.

I was surprised because I had not expected anything else other than her grief over her brother and father. 'What do you have on your feet? What clothes are you wearing?'

'I am barefoot...' As always time got drawn out. My tendency towards short patience was tested once again. Several minutes passed before Sari replied. 'I have a brownish dress with a belt... They are not usual clothes... they are made of skin.'

'Are you alone?' I asked.

'Yes, I don't see any people but a tent,' Sari responded.

'Enter the tent,' I encouraged her.

She experienced something in the tent but did not describe anything. She exited the tent and continued: 'I see a pine forest. There is no water, but a bit away there is another tent. It is empty.'

I decided to take her back a short amount of time so that she might find the other inhabitants of the place.

'Ah…. Someone is coming out from the edge of the forest. Two men, dressed in skin. One of them has half-long black hair,' Sari said.

'Look into their eyes! Take your time. Is it someone you recognize?' I encouraged her. Immediately Sari's eyes swelled up with tears.

'Oh, it is my brother… and my current father.' The men were suddenly gone and Sari continued. 'They are gone… they are looking for something… possibly other people… I will be married at a later point in that life.'

That gave me the opportunity to take her forward to when she herself had a family in that life. 'Tell me about your family,' I urged her.

'I am married and have a son. We are outside… It seems like large plain grassland.'

'Look your husband in his eyes,' I instructed her. 'Is it someone you recognize?'

'Mm… I do not recognize my son but I do know my husband. But I haven't met him yet in this life… Oh, he tells me that he is waiting for me… That I will meet him again in this life.' She seemed so genuinely happy and joyful when she said this, almost as if she based on her subconscious experience really believed that this would come true. I really didn't wish to take this feeling away from her. Afterwards I perceived that this specific event radically changed her. She seemed to have faith in the future again.

I took Sari to the moment of death in the life on the prairie. She lay on the ground in a tent. 'I am old and grey. I have died in my sleep. I feel calm and safe,' Sari said.

When she left the clinic her eyes were filled with tears, yet she had a smile that I had never seen before. It was almost as if she had undergone a religious revelation, something that long puzzled me. It still amazed me how radically a person could change from their inner experience during deep relaxation and regression. At the same time I wondered if it constitutes a problem that she describes events that I have no control over. In the end, do I really have any right to question her experience when it freed her from pain and suffering, particularly when it had been the sole purpose from the beginning?

***

A few days into September Sari came back to the clinic. She told me that she had stopped taking her medication but still felt energised and happy, even though she had just had a fight with her daughter. Sari described how her inner experiences had changed her and that she had found a completely new bliss and anticipation for the future. She wanted to be taken off medication, and why should I try to convince her differently. But it irritated me that I did not understand how these inner experiences changed my patients so dramatically. It seems as if the healing process by the method of past lives instigated a healing force widely superior to anything I could offer in terms of medication. It made for great news for the patients, but scarcely for the pharmaceutical industry.

'Well, I've only helped a few patients. The great masses will continue on as usual. The pills will help many to withstand everyday life, but I doubt that they can resolve the deeply hidden conflicts and losses that over eons of time seem to have left indelible scars on their souls. It will take a long time before we start using light quanta to cure mental suffering. Good thing no one can hear my thoughts, they would think I'm more ill than those who see me,' I thought to myself.

'I'm sitting in a kitchen… I am wearing a long dress. A table is in front of me… No, I don't have any books… cannot see a calendar,' Sari said slowly.

'Are you rich or poor?' I asked.

'Neither.'

'Exit the house. Look around. What do you see?'

'It is… a town street… with dark red brick houses on both sides. I distinctly feel that it is an English town. Strange, something about Australia.' Once again she took her time.

'What are you doing?' I asked.

'Oh, I am on my way to the docks. There are a lot of people and boats here?' Sari said.

'Try asking someone you see about the name of the town,' I encouraged her.

'I can't really hear. Someone says Miss Anne to me.'

I took Sari further in time. Instinctively I thought about the harbour. Reasonably there ought to exist some connection between England, a port and Australia. I asked her to describe the most important event from the life in England.

'A ship is leaving the harbour,' Sari told me.

'Is it someone you know?' I responded.

'Yes, it is my father and mother who are going away.'

Sari later told that the mother returned back to England after many years. Her father was not with her and she assumed he was dead. Sari calmly described her death at her home in England without fear. 'I died on a chair in my kitchen,' she said as calm as always.

'What did you learn from this life?'

'To not be rushed.'

Sari was a very calm and insightful woman. She never used big words, and like most Finnish people she was terse yet straightforward and unequivocal. She imparted a very strong feeling of strength mixed with a dash of Finnish melancholy and solitude.

During one of the last sessions in the middle of September 2002 she suddenly went very far back in her past lives.

'What shoes are you wearing? What clothes? What are you doing?' I asked.

'I have nothing on my feet... I am young... male... it is some type of animal skins I am wearing. Everything is black, I cannot see anything. It is dark,' she said.

'Do not worry! I am with you all along. You do not need to worry. Take your time. Look around carefully. What kind of place are you in?'

'A cave.'

Time passed. There was always this extreme time consumption, which would drive healthcare and hospital planners insane due to its apparent lack of efficiency. Still this was a clear indication that neither I nor the patients were equipped with the mental ability to interpret room-time and space-time. It was becoming gradually clear to me that all the patients experienced a great deal more than they were telling.

Several of them told me that they simply experienced so much that they did not notice there was a link back to "reality". They were completely preoccupied with the experience.

'What do you see?' I asked Sari again after a she had kept silent for an extended moment while her eyes moved intently under the eyelids.

'An extremely beautiful landscape outside the cave entrance.'

'Do you know where you are?'

'Sweden,' she replies without hesitation.

'What are you doing?'

'I'm at a large, open area... there are many other people there. I think... yes, it's some sort of market. People are trading things with each other.'

'What are you trading?' I asked.

'I own nothing to trade with,' Sari replied.

'What are you wearing at the market?'

'I have animal skins. And a knife.'

'Describe the knife. Is it hard, black, sharp?'

'It is so difficult... not metal... not wood... it is a dark grey material,' she replied. Things did not get more exciting than that. Her life seemed extremely tough, and she seemed to live alone as male. Sari said that he later died in the cave from old age. She never experienced any fear when he died.

The last session was unusual. Sari gave her consent to let a colleague sit in. She was doing her speciality training and had expressed a wish to work with me for several months. She became the first colleague who got to experience what most of us never dared to dabble with, and perhaps even less believe.

Sari lay relaxed and went completely into the inner state of comfort and light. In contrast to other patients she never had any problems with the deep relaxation, but perhaps my colleague's presence distracted her as it took her a long time before she experienced anything. For my own part I was deeply worried that it would be a failure and my colleague would leave with suspicions of me as a charlatan, as a delusional and egocentric nutcase.

'What are you doing Sari?'

Her reply lingered, but almost startlingly came a cheerful response. 'Ah, I'm on a picnic… he has brown eyes… he is dressed in black trousers and a black blazer… we have two children.' Everything came spontaneously and I was surprised by her cheerfulness. It was as if it was a different Sari. 'It's the 1830's… yes, America. We live in a yellow house. I am at home with the twins. I am 25 years old… Oh, I love him so much. He is so handsome, so beautiful.'

Here I made a mistake. Prone of doubting Sari, perhaps also due to my colleague's presence, I asked her if it was her twins from her current life. Her current twins are both girls. 'No, it is a boy and a girl. It is the same children in my current life,' she answered with affirmation.

'How do you travel to other towns, other relatives and friends?'

'By horse and carriage, of course,' she answered almost annoyed. Her experiences were so natural that her way of replying made me question if perhaps my own reality wasn't real.

'Sari, now go to the most difficult moment of this life. Describe what is happening,' I encouraged her.

Sari's face wrinkled up and her eyes rapidly filled with tears. Just as happy as she had been at her family's picnic, she was now filled with sorrow over something awful that she was seeing. 'It is my husband. He is at the hospital. I do not know what disease it is… It is so horrible. I could not do anything. He died.' Sari was left alone with her children but managed to make do. Later she died in her bed without pain.

'What did you learn from this life?' I asked.

'I learned to grow strong through grief,' Sari answered.

ENGLAND

2003-2010

The Last Straw

Mike was admitted to the hospital under section of the Mental Health Act. He had been moved from one of the open wards to the secure special care ward, a depressing ward from 1937 which whilst it had electricity, running water and a TV, reminded one of a bygone era. Yet the staff were wonderful- they were always caring and prepared to listen. When Mike came to the ward they had temporarily moved into another unit while the old one got a new coat of paint.

Mike had been diagnosed with psychotic depression with strong suicidal tendencies. He had tried to hang himself in his room, cut his throat with a windowpane and also escaped the hospital trying to jump from a bridge onto the motorway towards Chelmsford. Mike had tried most antidepressants, antipsychotics, sedatives as well as ECT (electroconvulsive therapy). Nothing affected him. He was as resistant as hospital staphylococci against penicillin. All in all, Mike was regarded as untreatable. In the middle of this mess I was given the dream job of being Mike's consultant.

After having tried several different prescriptions I made the decision to offer Mike hypnotic regression psychotherapy. The compassionate and experienced nurses regarded me with wide eyes, but supported me fully. Never once did they show signs of mistrust. That support was invaluable.

The therapy was performed under rather primitive circumstances in the office of a colleague on the hospital grounds. Sometimes we were interrupted by screams, lawnmowers and cold winds through the half broken windows. The first thing I had been forced to do when I arrived was to clean my own office. Sometimes it was so cold when the freezing wind swept through the broken windows that I had to put in an electric heater. While I looked at the mess it hit me that nothing indicated that Mike would be able to improve.

When I look back on my annotations I realise that I took the decision to treat Mike based on a will to do good and help a fellow human in crisis. Now, 8 years later, no psychiatrist in England would take any risks such as treating a case in this manner. The risk to be reported by colleagues is much too large. The current motto is that the fewer patients you see and treat, the lesser the risk of becoming a victim of the system as a doctor. The system with excessive top down control and "management" has paralyzed the actual treatment of mentally ill individuals. Few would believe it, but staff consciously avoid touching patients to avoid any risk of being reported due to professional misconduct or even worse, violations of sexual boundaries. But in 2010 this is how far it had gone.

'What do you see Mike?'

'Green fields.'

'Are you alone?' I asked.

'No. I see an old, tall man,' Mike answered.

'What colour is your skin?'

'White.'

'Look into the man's eyes. Is it someone you recognize?'

'He knows me. He has been watching me.'

'What clothes are you wearing?' I asked.

'They are tough and heavy. Green,' he replied.

'Why has he been observing you?'

'He walks away.'

'You are getting closer now. Ask him what he wants,' I urged Mike.

'He's ensuring that I am good,' Mike said.

'What are you doing?'

'I'm going back to the people.'

'Which people?'

'The ones in the houses.'

'Who are you?' I now asked him curiously.

'A boy. I'm 7-8 years old,' he responded.

'Who was the old man?'

'An old soldier. He carried a sword and an old coat as a disguise.'

'Have you left your mom and dad?'

'Yes. He says that it is not easy to follow him.'

'Does he become your teacher?' I asked in an attempt to understand the context.

'No. He just looks at me,' Mike said. I instructed Mike again to look on the digital board with numbers that were rolling backwards from 2003. He replied without any doubt. '1429. I am hiding in the fields. I look at the people in the houses. I am 7-8 years old and do not want to return there. He shows them to me, it's where I came from.'

'Why do you leave your home village?' I asked.

'My parents shouted at me. They did not fight,' Mike said.

Mike proceeded to tell of a life filled with cruelty and violence. He served in the Spanish army whose conquistadors conquered South America through a river of blood. Mike said he was a mercenary. Often they were given orders not only to kill natives men but also women and children. After years of killing in the name of Christ he returned to his home country. He wandered, with his actions weighing heavily on his shoulders. His fate, his karma, had become the life upon life to either kill others or to die by his own hand. All the violence towards others and his ego created a nightmare for his soul.

Mike returned to his inner light. His body relaxed and his occasionally violent movements were exchanged by a tranquil peace.

'You are in the light now Mike. Are you there alone?'

'He is kind,' he answered cryptically.

'What does he say?'

'That you are not alone. You know what you should do.'

'Who is he?' I asked.

'I am the one you will become,' he said.

'What will you become?'

'Myself.'

'Is anyone else there?'

'Yes, other people.'

'Can you see his eyes?' I asked.

'They are very clear,' he said.

'What does he say?'

'Stay here. Keep breathing.'

I was suddenly hit with worry that Mike might have hidden something. That maybe after all he was still considering suicide. That I had missed something crucial and that we were on our way to a catastrophe. 'What happens if you kill yourself?' I asked slightly worried.

'You will not become me. Work hard with life,' Mike said suddenly.

'Why do you have to go through this?'

'Your son is strong. You will find joy. You were good before you became woeful. You must be strong and remain,' Mike said enigmatically.

Mike continued to arrive punctually for his hypnosis and he started to slowly lose that melancholy and gloom he seemed to carry over his shoulders. At the ward I never saw him smile or laugh, yet the nurses reported that slowly and steadily he seemed to improve even though his medication was phased down. They could not understand how it was possible–Mike who had been so extremely self-destructive. At the start of July 2003 he told me that he had started redirecting his inner wrath outwards instead. On some occasion it had actually affected his fellow patients.

'What do you see?' I asked.

'My middle brother who is 18 years old. He is drunk and is with my father. I stand by the door and feel miserable. My brother has hit my father in his face and then jumped out the window. My dad picks up a knife and is going to cut him. He is in the kitchen with the knife. Dad is restrained by an uncle and another man. It makes me upset,' Mike replied.

'Where is your mother?'

'She is in the living room. She knows what has happened and that my older brother has left us.'

'Does everyone fight each other?'

'Yes, I have locked myself in the bathroom since I am alone. I hit the door and think about killing myself.' Mike started to quietly cry. The tears rolled continuously along his cheeks without him making a move.

77

'Is there anyone to support you?' I asked.

'Aunt Kitty. She says I shouldn't worry. Mom and dad never married. Her first marriage was a failure. She got a son out of it,' Mike said.

'What have you learnt from all this?'

'That you can forget your family. Hate and love are so close.'

'What will you do?'

'I must leave my family to find peace. To be alone. To live. My sister who is 18 has met my older brother, and my mother refuses to let her come back. The first thing I got to hear of her was that she lived in a house with a criminal man with weapons. Mom told my brother not to meet his sister. Her partner and another man took amphetamine. It carried on for a week. Suddenly one night my sister called. She was crying. She said that my brother was involved with horrible people. We went there and broke down the door and took my sister from there to a gypsy camp where she was safe. I talked to mom about letting her come back. It took a few days but in the end she was allowed back. A few days later the man she had lived with hung himself,' Mike finished. As difficult it was for Mike to talk about his life when conscious, as easy it was for him to talk about everything in his life when under hypnosis.

'How is your sister today?' I asked.

'She is happy and has two wonderful kids,' he replied.

'What have you understood from all of this?'

'They live their life and I live mine. They have used my intelligence. I left for anywhere. I cannot return home. I have done all I can. You have to stop hating each other, the violence must stop. Parental violence,' he responded.

We seemed to slowly move closer to the core of his problems, yet I had no clearer leads than that it involved family and violence throughout several lives.

***

It was now June 20 and Mike had made huge progress. I suspected that he was getting close to the end. There was a whole life ahead of him, and I told him that when he felt ready he should let me know a few weeks in advance that he wanted to finish.

'What are you doing?'

'I am in my room fighting with my brother, mother and father. My brother wants to emigrate to America. Mom and dad don't want him to. He's their youngest son. We had an agreement that he would stay and I would go.'

'How old are you?' I asked.

'21 years old,' Mike said.

'How are you dressed?'

'I have a white shirt, grey trousers and boots.'

'What does your brother want to do?'

'Start a new life.'

'Can you not go with him?'

'I can't. I have to stay to keep the land and the farm.'

'Walk around in your house. Try to find a calendar. What year is it?'

'1890,' Mike replied without hesitation.

'When you look into your mothers eyes, who do you see from this life?'

'Grandma.'

'And in your father's eyes, who do you see?' I asked.

'My grandfather,' Mike replied.

'How many brothers and sisters do you have?'

'Only one brother but three sisters. David, Katie, Patricia and Moreen.'

'What is your surname?'

'McCarthy.'

'What is the name of the place you are living at?' I asked.

'Curraghtown.' It was difficult to make out what he said.

'Is it close to sea?'

'No, it lies inland.'

'Have you been schooled?'

'No, I'm the eldest son and must stay at home. I'm not happy.'

'Did your brother leave the family?'

'Yes, he couldn't take it. I never saw him again. He worked in the fire service. My parents got letters from him.'

I took Mike to the most crucial moment during this life in Ireland. It would hopefully reveal the decisive turning point in his self-destructive life. 'What do you see?' I asked.

'A few men come to my home. They want me to look after something for them. It is a box,' Mike answered.

'Who are they?' I asked curiously.

'Irish nationalists. The box contains weapons.'

'Do you get anything for the trouble?'

'No.'

'Where are you parents?'

'My mother is alive but father is dead.'

'How old are you?'

'40.'

'What happened afterwards?'

'Two tractors came – the British army. They didn't just come to my home. Someone had tipped them off that there was weaponry on the farm. They have a chain between the tractors and pull the house down.'

'Your house?' I asked.

'Yes,' he replied.

'What happened then?'

'There is nothing I can do. I hung myself,' Mike said suddenly.

'Why?'

'It was the last straw.'

'What happened to your mother?'

'She lived with my sister.'

'What did you learn from the life as Thomas McCarthy?'

'That I should have changed things.'

'What did you discover in your own light after death Mike?'

'That it was a terrible thing to do.'

'Why did you get to see all of this?' I asked.

'They want me to stop the cycle…'

From this moment something dramatically changed with Mike. His involuntary commitment had ended and he took advantage of this to discharge himself from the hospital. During the ensuing contact he used mood stabilisers for a short while before also quitting those. In the end he became completely free from medication without relapsing. When I called him one year after his treatment he had very good news. He was living together with a woman and they had just had a baby boy. Mike had also secured a full time job in the NHS, not far from my own workplace. From that moment I considered Mike as completely recovered.

For the staff who had been involved it seemed mystifying as to how he had improved and that he never again needed psychiatric care. From the perspective that we as souls carry unprocessed conflicts and suffering from one life to another Mike's recovery was of course nothing uncommon. Mike had forevermore stopped trying to kill himself.

And today in June 2014, I have finally checked if Curraghtown exist. It does, and it lies in Ireland.

The Crying Policeman

Brian O'Toole was an English police officer in his thirties. He had Irish roots but grew up in my catchment area. He wanted to become a policeman from a young age. He wanted to help people and he perceived wrongs and injustices as difficult challenges. After several injuries in connection to arrests and car chases he had finally been forced out of the police force under the guise of being signed off with health problems. The underlying issue was conflicts with his superiors. Others remained silent where Brian stood up and spoke his mind, something that did not go unpunished.

'If someone points a gun at you, the whole station will come to your recue. If someone points a finger at you no one will help you'.

He had been referred by his GP diagnosed with depression. Brian had a wife and two wonderful children. He was a very loving, strong and good person, but he also carried a very heavy inner wrath. He naturally became easy prey in a world full of loyalty, protection and favours. Brian did not have a single superior who would defend him, and that made his fall. Finally he broke down of anxiety and depression. At the same time his sister and her husband had borrowed £25,000 which they never paid back. Clouds were gathering upon his horizon.

When I met him for the first time in Rochford he was put onto anti depressive treatment. During our second meeting it became apparent that there was something more deeply underlying-feelings of abandonment and isolation. Since he would have to wait several months for treatment he was put onto my waiting list. At the start of May 2003 he lay down for the first time on the blue couch.

He expressed some apprehension, but had an easy time relaxing. After twenty minutes I saw his eyes showing REM-activity. 'Brian, what do you see?'

He began to cry and sighed heavily several times. 'I... I am completely alone. The street is completely silent and deserted.'

'Where are you?'

'In front of our house?'

'How old are you?' I asked.

'11... 12 years old...' Brian said.

'Are you at your parents' home?'

'Yes.'

'Do you have friends?'

'No.'

'Do your parents care about what you are up to?' I asked.

'No, they are too preoccupied with themselves,' replied Brian.

Later Brian found himself on a small field with his family and an uncle he felt very fond of. Again he expressed feelings of loneliness and sorrow. He had no friends. He cried. When he rose from the couch he was shaken, stiff and tired.

'It was so incredibly real. I stood behind myself on the street,' Brian said.

***

As usual Brain walked into the clinic with a light smile on his face. During the past week he had, not unexpectedly, had much difficulty sleeping. The process had started. He described the first session's experiences as relatively limited pictures in regards to field of vision, but at the same time very intensive and real. He told me that his favourite colour was blue.

'Brian, what do you see?'

'Young children. My friend is having a birthday party. I am 4-5 years old,' he replied.

'Are you eating or what are you up to?'

'I watch the children.'

'Where is mom and dad?'

'I don't know.'

'How does it feel?'

'Different. I want to be like all the other children.' Brian started sobbing again. He seemed lonely, empty and abandoned in a way that I couldn't understand, so therefore I took him into the state of absolute relaxation and light. I urged him to return to the starting point of his current suffering. Brian travelled back with ease.

'What do you see?'

'An old village.'

'Where?' I asked.

'In England,' he said.

'Is the landscape mountainous, hilly or flat?'

'Flat.' He then received the instruction of time with digital digits that rolled back from 2003 on the board. '1...4...5...3,' he read slowly.

'What clothes are you wearing?'

'Worn down ones.'

'Are you male or female?'

'Male.'

'How old are you?'

'40.'

'What do you work as?'

'I just wander around.'

'How do you get food?' I asked surprised.

'I pick it up when I find some,' he responded.

I then let him see the illusionary globe. It was created easily before his inner eyes.

'In what country do you see yourself wandering?'

'England and France.'

He now got to return to the most important moment of this life. Something strange and unexpected began to happen. 'I see a man who puts down his sword.'

'Has he used it in battle?' I asked.

'Yes, for a long time,' Brian said.

'Look him in the eyes. Who do you recognize?'

Brian started to moan and gasp. He seemed to really suffer guilt and anxiety.

'It… it is me.' He shouted while almost struggling to breathe.

'Are you a warrior?'

'Yes. He did not want to kill anymore,' Brian answered with flowing tears. I had to spend several minutes calming and reassuring him that he was witnessing all of this from the outside, that even though it was extremely important it belonged to the past.

'Brian, how did you die?'

'Of disease at old age,' he said.

'Did you have family?'

'No.'

'What did you learn from that life?'

'To do things for my own sake, not others.'

'So you were really a very loyal soldier?' I asked.

'Yes,' he replied instantly.

'Now you can see the reason for why you're a police officer. You want to maintain order. You want to help and create justice, but you fail. Your sadness and emptiness does not only stem from the present, but also from a lifelong past.'

When he left the clinic he was in some way relieved but also shaken. Like everyone else he consumed an enormous amount of energy during the session. To claim that an effective session represented a normal intellectual conversation felt completely misplaced. I repeated over and over to my patients how painful, energy consuming yet rewarding all of this could be. It was energy and time consuming work, but it was worth every single calorie and second. Often I had to assert the importance to release the intellectual control, that this was a primary process not unlike a child's direct experiences of the world. Here and now, no then or tomorrow. Everything present and real.

***

'What do you see?' I asked Brian the first Friday of June 2003.

'Dark faces,' he said.

'What are they doing?'

'They are wearing black masks with eyes cut out. Their eyes stare vacantly.'

'What clothes are you wearing?'

'A heavy leather belt, loose red clothes. I have dark hair.'

'What is on your head?' I asked.

'Grey,' he responded awkwardly.

'What do you see?'

'Sorrow. People are sad. People are getting hurt.' While Brian was speaking he started to slowly moan and sometimes turn. It was as if he was experiencing something extremely unpleasant and frightening. Repeated instructions telling him that he was only watching passively and felt no pain had no effect. Brian was experiencing hellish visions and emotions.

'Brian, is someone dead?'

'Why? I think it was me,' he responded.

'Are there soldiers?'

'Yes. We move quickly. We kill a lot of people. I have a sword. They fight me. They lived there.'

'Where?'

'They don't speak English.'

'Are you fighting the soldiers Brian?'

'Yes,' he said.

I instructed him with the time-orientation method and he replied faster and more confidently than ever before.

'It's 1427. The soldiers are laughing because we won.'

'Are you wounded Brian?'

'It isn't my blood,' he said.

'How do you feel?'

'Strong.'

'How old are you?'

'30.'

I gave him the instruction with the globe. 'Where are you?'

'Near the coast. In the Mediterranean. Bicain… France, but not France,' he replied.

'What are you fighting for?'

'I don't know. For money. I have a lot of money.'

'What do you do with your money?'

'I have a lot of coins in my pockets. I buy women, food and drink.'

'Do you have a leader?' I asked, curious about his officer.

'The commander has a crucifix. It is about religion,' Brian said.

'Look in the commander's eyes. Take your time.'

Brian started to breathe heavily and toss on the couch.

'He is a liar. He wears a mask,' Brian replied while gasping for air.

'You travel in the light of yourself. You can now see the commander remove his mask, alone in his room. Don't be afraid. Look in his eyes. Who do you see Brian?'

'He looks away,' Brian responded.

'You can see his face better now. He cannot see you. Who do you see?'

'… Oh…. my… it is myself!'

'Are you the commander?'

'Yes. I know that it is true. The crucifix. The soldiers are fighting in the name of the cross. I get money and I use the cross. It is wrong.'

'Why are you wearing a mask?' I asked.

'It is another face. He enjoys battles and killing. I am good at it,' Brian answered. Brian started to twist and turn while groaning deeply. He started to sweat. 'Oh… I can see the faces of all those I have killed. My face is different. I sit quietly.'

'Where?'

'Under a tree.'

'Are you alone?' I asked.

'People move around me. Soldiers. I drink,' he said.

'Why?'

'It is battle. We are going to fight ordinary people.'

'Why attack them?'

'I am drunk now. I stand up, ready to fight... Oh...'

'What is happening?'

'I am in the front rank. It isn't right. We kill everyone.'

To spare Brian yet more dreadful scenes I took him back to his childhood in order to try and find an explanation for his life. He was 7 - 8 years old and living in the town of Dunn. 'Can you see mom and dad, Brian?'

'Yes,' he said

'Do you love them?'

'No.'

'Are they nice?'

'They cannot see me.'

'Brian, do you recognize anyone in your father's eyes?'

'Different,' he answered.

'Your mother?'

'A teacher I liked.'

We went forward in time trying to localise a breaking point. 'You are 13-14 years old. What are you doing Brian?'

'I wanted to leave my family,' he answered.

'Why?'

'I was 7-8 years old when I left them for the soldiers.'

'Weren't your parents angry?'

'They didn't stop me. They were not angry anymore. I started training early.'

'Did you learn how to read?'

'Yes.'

'Were there other children with the soldiers?'

'No.'

'Then why you?'

'I just followed them.'

After nearly 90 minutes I took Brian into the afterlife. For the first time he seemed peaceful and a smile spread across his lips. We had never discussed the possibility of guides or helpers on the so called "other side". 'You're resting in the light Brian. Do you have a guide?' I asked.

'Yes, someone,' he replied.

'What is his name?'

'James.'

'Ask him if what you have done is of importance?'

'You know this.'

'Why all this suffering, Brian?'

'In order to live you must change,' he responded.

'Are you ready for a change Brian?'

'I must be,' he answered.

'How will you succeed?'

'I can if I try.'

'What does James say?'

'Continue to live.'

'What do you see?' I asked.

'I hide in the shrubbery,' Brian said. He was wearing brown clothes made from animals, and he was out deer hunting, carrying a spear.

'Brian, what do you look like? What is the colour of your skin?'

'It is dirty and light brown. I am tall and have long hair. I have nothing on my feet,' he answered without hesitation.

As always he moved anxiously on the couch. It was as if he participated in the hunt with his body. Sometimes it was difficult to receive an answer from him.

'The water is blue and the continents brown and green. What country do you see?'

'An island. My God I'm happy. I return with food,' Brian said abruptly.

'Why are you so happy?'

'It is a large deer. I've killed it.'

I took him to his home and let him describe the area. 'Do you have a wife?' I asked.

'One. I am looking for Agath,' Brian said.

'You can now see Agath before you. Look in her eyes. Is it someone you recognize from your current life?'

'Oh, Cathleen, my daughter.'

'What happens to her?'

'I lost her. She was killed,' he says with immense grief, his voice trembling.

'Who killed her?'

'A woman.'

'Why?'

'She was angry. She was my favourite,' he replied miserably.

'How did she die?' I continued.

'She fell from the cliffs.'

'Which woman did this? Can you see her?'

'Acia. It is so painful.'

'Look into her eyes, is it someone you recognize?'

'Oh, yes... my grandmother.'

'What happened to Acia?' I asked.

'I killed her for what she had done,' Brian said.

'How did you kill her?'

'With my hands.'

'So you strangled her?'

'Yes.'

'Brian, what happened afterwards?'

'I am so miserable,' he sighed. I once again used the digital time board, and Brian confidently identified the numbers as they rolled back from year 2003. '3392 before Christ.'

'Are you sure?'

'Yes.'

'Did you have a son?'

'He was young and happy. He came from the outside. I like him.' I now took Brian forward and instructed him to see what would happen together with his adopted son. 'I have been depressed a long time. He gives me his spear. We are hunting deer,' Brian said.

'Does something happen?' I asked.

'Yes. I died.'

'How did this happen?'

'The animal killed me. It was a large deer, I was too old and too slow.'

'What did you learn from that life?' I finished.

'He hunts. He was the strongest. It was a good son,' Brian answered.

I then moved Brian into the light, where he met his guide James again. 'Ask James why you went through all of this! What was the meaning of it?'

'You were good before you became depressed. You will find joy. You must be strong and remain,' came the quite enigmatic reply.

One week later it was Friday once again. Clouds of worry were gathering on my mind when Brian never showed up for his appointment. No cancellation. No telephone call. Nothing, just silence. I must admit that I worried that everything had become too big and deep for Brian- that he simply could not cope. My secretary could not reach him. I kept worrying throughout the weekend. Was Brian dead?

The following Friday he arrived punctually as usual. He was deeply regretting that he had not left a message. The reason that he had not turned up was purely that he felt he needed time to process everything. To contemplate in peace. He told me that he had been a bad person. That he had a bad reputation as a womaniser. That he had cheated on his ex-wife several times, and that he treated women badly.

Brian confided that he had started to change. He had needed to escape the therapy for one week. One moment everything was real to him and he believed more in his experiences than anything else. At the same time doubt tore at him and in the next moment he tried to convince himself that he had just imagined all that he had gone through.

'I can feel the rough clothes against my body. Everything is so real. I feel sceptic but everything is so real. I am proud that I am doing something about myself. Things change, and for the first time in my life I feel shame over how I have been,' Brian said. With tears in his eyes he told me with an unsteady voice of how he once had assaulted a prisoner in handcuffs. 'How misguided and devious I was. I am ashamed' Brian said.

He was absolutely certain about one thing. He had started to change and become something he could really appreciate. He had never had a thought about suicide – he had left that solution behind him. He looked towards the future. Like other patients he said that he would take the decision about finishing when he felt ready. He decided to finish therapy after just two more sessions.

Brian recovered completely and never again had any contact with the mental health service. He left the police force and created a whole new life. His wife and children stayed with him and his marriage improved. From having been a young and angry policeman he had now become a loving and forgiving person.

'Before I shouted and raged at everyone. If someone made a mistake I could easily become violent and unpredictable. When a woman drove onto my driveway the other day I surprised myself. I had no anger left. Instead I give her a friendly wave and said that it was fine to turn around on my drive. Before when I drove my car I only used to listen to heavy metal, but yesterday I discovered that I appreciated hearing Mozart on the radio. I have changed so much,' Brian finished.

Elizabeth I's Tax Collector in Wesby

'I am sitting in a Tudor house in a large forest. I think it is north England, possibly the village of Wesby. We are a few gentlemen sitting around a table drinking mead. There is a fireplace and next to it something like a shield with the insignia of a sword or a crucifix. When I look at the clothes of the men it looks like late 16th century, possibly 1560. These men seem not to notice me, and one of them is named James Hickoc. It is me,' Said Tony.

'What does James Hickoc look like?' I asked.

'He has a wide hat and a big moustache, and he is around 36 years old.'

'What does he work as?'

'He is a tax collector for the Crown. He is quite pleasant, he was never rough with people. He wasn't married, but had a woman in each village.'

'Does he own any property?' I asked.

'He has a large farm where his employees take care of the daily work keeping cows and pigs for slaughter. They also hunt wild boars in the forest and the mead was quite tasty,' Tony continued with great detail.

'Where do you keep all the money you have collected?'

'Good question... hmm, it is quite clever. James hides the money in a secret compartment under the pigsty. No one would think to look in such a place. After he has deposited money there he puts everything back so that no one can discover that the money is there,' Tony replied promptly.

'And how is the tax collecting arranged otherwise?'

'Every six months James Hickoc travels to some kind of law or tax supervisor. Then he has to declare his work in detail.'

'What would happen if you kept some of the money for yourself?'

'They would cut my throat.'

I now asked Tony to look if he could find a book over James' accounting. 'Can you see any dates in the book that are current?'

'I can see May 1560,' he replied quickly.

'Tell me Tony, as to how James Hickoc's ended his days?'

'James is an old man with a long white beard. He had no heir that could inherit his possessions, so he made the unusual decision to split his property into different parts. Each piece of land was then given to his employees. His right hand man Jacob received the main building. It was a very unusual decision which meant not only that the people inherited land and money–they also became free independent land owners.' He expressed that James felt great joy over having made this arrangement. According to Tony, James died around the 1600s.

During the time that James Hickoc lived England was experiencing perhaps its greatest golden age. Henry VIII's daughter Elizabeth became the Queen Regent 1558 and until her death in 1603, England grew as an empire not only in Europe but throughout the world. Tony later checked these details and reported that they seemed to be correct.

The Woman with the Apocalyptic Dreams

Faith would forever become unique to me. She was markedly different from all the other patients. Faith lived slightly east of London in the relatively well-off area Benfleet. One day in January 2003 I knocked on her door in order to carry out a domiciliary visit. Her GP had referred her to me based on her distinctive and highly frightening apocalyptic dreams of the future. He had not found any real evidence of mental health issues, but at her request he decided to send her on. By coincidence or the strands of fate her case landed on my desk. With wonder I read about her terrifying prophetic dreams. According to my colleague they all had a recurring theme. We would all enter an age of difficult strife. Many people would die in the larger cities and the world would change forever.

The door was opened by a young, slim and beautiful woman in her twenties. She wore an elegant black morning gown. Around her neck she had an amethyst blue necklace with Egyptian symbols. Her large black eyes, hair and dress made me immediately think of ancient Egypt. I dismissed the thought and introduced myself.

Faith's history was exceptional and unusual. When she was 10 years old she was, according to her own account, visited by an astral projection of her then living grandmother. Terrified and alone in her room she listened to her grandmother explaining that she would die the following day. She was not certain but believed the reason would be a heart attack or a brain haemorrhage. She calmly told Faith not to worry. It would happen around 13–13:30 and her dad would become very despondent. Faith said that out of fear that they would think her crazy, she never told either of her parents.

While the family was having lunch the next day the phone rang. Someone from the hospital reported that the grandmother had died from a brain haemorrhage at 13:30 and it had been very sudden. Faith's father became very sad, but Faith herself understood that she could see something that others could not understand. She only told her aunt about the event but became disappointed when she wanted to pull her into all sorts of magic thinking, something Faith had no interest in. The aunt told her that the family had always had someone with strong medial gifts, and that Faith did not need to be afraid. Faith regarded the aunt as always having been untrustworthy and their contact thus never evolved any deeper.

During the next few years Faith despaired at the discovery of her special skill of predicting when someone would die. The whole thing made her miserable and she constantly fought with the fear of others' prejudice. Sometimes she even thought people died as a result of her precognizant dreams. In the end she told her family, but her parents never believed her. However according to Faith, her brother was also spiritually sensitive, but not to the same extent as herself.

Faith obtained very good results in school, and no one ever regarded her as mentally ill. Just as my colleague I did not find any initial evidence of mental illness, although I could not rule out hidden borderline psychotic experiences or a multiple personality disorder. However Faith gave a much too composed and serious impression for this to be likely. She had no kind of substance abuse or addictions. None of her relatives had a history of mental illness and she lived in a socially highly-ranked family.

Faith was a mystical young woman. Her warmth and radiance made me feel true inner joy, but at the same time her suffering touched me deeply. I asked myself why precisely this frail and attentive woman would experience a global catastrophe in her mind. There was no sign of early life trauma, and she was an unusually charismatic and wise person for her age.

Faith became my first English patient and would forevermore come to change my perspective of health and sickness. An invisible and indistinguishable slide. Vaguely, elusively a divergence formed from the norms and knowledge base of the outside observers and assessors. Could she really be a precognisant?

Faith's apocalyptic dream was often well composed regarding theme and content. Over and over again she would experienced the approach of a great war. She said the people never understood the danger until it was too late. The war would come as sneakily as a thief in the shadows.

In the major dream it started with limited battles in the Middle East. Successively the battles intensified until more and more countries got involved. According to Faith she saw the use of chemical weapons, and that people underwent biological changes. They mutated. The animals fared better because the chemical weapons had been developed to kill humans, not animals.

'The younger people live in the cities. They want to continue their ordinary lives, unperturbed by the imminent dangers. They form gangs and dedicate themselves towards clothes and parties. In the end the larger cities are destroyed by nuclear weapons. I see distorted people. Grotesque faces. Mouldering arms. Stench and decay. Destruction. The majority of the population dies. I have seen repeatedly how we live in enclaves in north Scotland. I am around 40 years old. I live together with my boyfriend, my brother and my father. Mom is not with us. I think she is dead. Oh, it is as if one was a vast morbid dream,' Faith said.

'But how can you go north when all transportation has been destroyed?' I asked her straight, but with some degree of doubt.

'We have horses. Lately I have seen how I go to an abandoned shopping centre. I collect a few things we need. I use a tent.'

'Is the electricity out? Is there any source of energy in your dreams?'

'Yes, we have smaller diesel and petrol generators. I see myself listening to music with a petrol fuelled generator.'

'But how can you be sure that this is not from the past Faith? Something that you may have experienced earlier in this or another life?'

Faith looked at me with her big, serious eyes and continued:

'There are destroyed cars everywhere. So much is destroyed. The old civilisation is destroyed. Something new will come instead. What frightens me greatly is that I know I am not crazy. I see things others cannot, and I know when those dear to me will die.'

'Do you have an example?' I asked.

'Yes.' She was breathing heavily and took a deep breath before she could continue. 'I have a good friend, Adam. He is homosexual and together with a guy I'm dead scared of. This guy drives his car inconsiderately and fast. In a dream I have seen how Adam travels with his partner along the motorway. The car is driving at incredible speed. Suddenly they hit a car in front of them. All four in that car die instantly. Adam is wounded in one of his shoulders and becomes stuck in the wrecked car. His boyfriend runs away from the spot nearly unhurt, leaving Adam alone in the car. I feel Adam's fear, it is dreadful. Then through Adam I feel the smell of petrol and then both cars explode and Adam dies. I can feel the agony of his death.'

'Have you tried to warn Adam, or perhaps to get his boyfriend to drive more carefully?'

'Yes, but Adam has asthma and has been unable to get his license. His boyfriend just laughs and continues as usual,' she said.

Faith did definitely not want any medication, and she did not need any either. After great hesitation I made my decision. I did work in England within a great public organization, and there were reasons not to do anything that could be construed as unscientific or unserious. But as long as the patients wanted and approved my decisions I felt safe. I decided to treat Faith with deep relaxation, by method of regression and perhaps also progression.

Faith relinquished control over herself in complete confidence. She relaxed and showed signs of quickly entering deep relaxation. She later told me that she had often meditated at home. The first session passed without complications. Faith told me that she did not walk on the beach I described. Instead she flew as light as a bird. She described colours, light and even a long fish. Pleased but surprised she declared herself comfortable with making her first journey in the light to the past. She left my clinic in Runwell full of delight.

The second session took place on a day at the end of February 2003 when crocus and snowdrops were already flowering outside my window. The green fields reached towards Southend-on-Sea. The sky was blue. The blackbirds chirped brightly. No consciousness could escape the earth's spiralling life force.

Faith was going ever deeper, but when I asked her what she could see in the light I became confused. 'Oh, there is only darkness. I cannot see anything. Oh, my feet are stuck. I cannot move them,' she said without me enquiring. I noted that she was twisting her body lightly. Her face was grimacing. Something was not right, but I could not understand what.

'Don't be afraid! I will not leave you. Everything you see you have experienced. It can no longer harm you even if it seems frightening. Yet you will be able to understand. I will stay by your side. Now go further back in this life. Look around. When I have counted to three the light will have taken you there. The light dims and everything becomes clear and precise… What do you see Faith?'

'Green fields. They sway in the wind. There are trees,' she answered. She was sure the year was 239 AD along the France border. She was 9 years old and living in a round house with a colour she described as dirty clay.

'Go into the house. Is anyone there?'

'It is dark. Yes, I can see my mother and a baby. It is my little brother,' Faith said.

'Look into your mother eyes! Is it anyone you recognize?' I asked.

'I do not like her eyes, they are so mean. She does not like me.'

'Your little brother, do you recognize anyone in his eyes?'

'No.'

'Go to the most important moment of this life. What are you doing?'

'People are standing in a circle on a field.'

'What are they discussing?' I asked.

'Chickens,' she said.

'How old are you?'

'14.'

'What else do you see?'

'Oh, my mother's callous eyes. There are several people. They put me in a bag and she watches. They throw me into the water. I'm... I'm drowning. It is dark, and I cannot escape... My feet are bound...'

'What happened with your mother?'

'She continued her life as usual,' Faith answered.

Her face was warped by fear, anxiety and discomfort. She started twisting her body on the couch, and I became really worried. Rapidly I did my best to calm her. It was then I remembered Elisabeth saying that her experiences intensified when I once had touched her hand. I decided to carefully put my left hand on top of Faith's hands which were resting on her stomach. 'Why are you touching my forehead?' she burst out.

'I have not touched your forehead. My hand lies on top of yours,' I said surprised.

'You have now experienced your terrifying death in this life. You are now in the afterlife. Nothing can harm you any longer. You are free, you are in the light.' Impulsively I suggested that someone she liked would come to her.

'You will not be alone anymore,' I said.

'She says that she killed me because I was stronger. She understood that I knew more. She could not handle it. But she could not kill my soul,' Faith responded.

'Who is saying that?'

'Eleanor of course,' Faith replied with a great smile across her lips. She giggled and I was dazed by the sudden change of scenery. 'Eleanor is my guide. She is a very old soul. She says that you are also very old,' Faith addressed me.

'So what does she think about what we are doing here?' I asked, perhaps because my mind glanced over the possibility of a split personality.

'It was about time. When you have finished your life on earth you will also become a guide for people. Eleanor says that she have several others which are her guides there,' Faith said. We had started the session at quarter past three in the afternoon. When I asked Faith what time it was she thought it was half three.

'It is quarter to five.' She was astonished and could not understand where all the time had gone. She walked unsteadily when she left the room. The session had been intense and completely drained her of energy. The journey had begun.

***

The next sessions were natural and easy. 'What do you see?' She remained silent. 'Are you alone?'

'No, I don't think so. I think I can see many people.'

'Are they wearing clothes? What are you wearing yourself?' I asked.

'I cannot see that.' She was breathing calmly and her eyes moved back and forth under the eyelids. She seemed preoccupied with something. I lightly touched her forehead and hands, and it seemed to deepen her relaxation.

'They are in a great cave, walking about and talking,' Faith said.

'What are they talking about?' I asked.

'They are discussing the augmented offspring. 'At first I had some difficulty understanding what she was talking about, so during this session I was often forced to repeat my questions. I felt confused. 'They are breeding different types of humans.'

'Who is doing this Faith? What do they look like?'

'They look like humans but are much taller,' she answered with a smile.

'Do they come from Earth or space?'

'Yes, from Earth, but some from space.'

'Why are they refining the human species?'

'Humanity is greedy. They can destroy everything. But they are too valuable that we can allow their destruction. They must be controlled.' Faith spoke at great length, almost as if someone was educating through her. It was impossible for me to keep up with taking notes of everything she said. I shook my head in frustration that I did not have any recording equipment. The few tapes I had were of very bad quality. This was the time I made the decision to make a change by purchasing a good quality audio recorder.

'When did all this happen? Faith, can humanity really survive?'

'Yes. They came long before the emergence of man,' she responded.

'Did they come from space to protect us?'

'No. They came from different places in the universe before they came to earth.'

'What is their goal?' I asked.

'To create order so that they might continue,' Faith said.

'When did all this happen?'

Faith smiled as if she recognized something. It felt like I was on the outside of a conversation she was having with someone else. 'Oh, I thought it was longer than that. It is 60,000 years ago' she said.

'How did it all happen?'

'Some offspring were mixed with human women.'

Faith again described how the spacemen were taller than the humans. I started to lose the thread and my questions became somewhat unfocused. I kept considering the dimensional aspect of my patients' inner journeys. Were there energies that we perhaps could not understand, could it be possible to move outside room-time to a non-space-time dimension? Did everyone possess the ability to acquire their own total knowledge? Freud called it the subconscious and Carl Jung the origin of the ego in the collective unconscious.

'Are they pleased to meet you? Is it possible as a patient to travel back in time? Is not all of this just an illusion?' I fired so many questions. Yet, the answers started to get increasingly detailed, especially considering that the source was a girl only twenty years old.

'Yes, they tell me I am very welcome. Physical beings register time through events. Souls are outside the time aspect and can therefore travel freely. They use spiritual energy in order to travel,' she explained.

'How will normal people be able to understand all of this?'

'You use spiritual energy. This energy must be mastered, and it will never run out. It is eternal. This is twisted in the material principle. They say that they all unite and they project themselves and their ships from on state to another,' Faith continued.

I grew progressively more astounded. What was this, a young girl educating me in spiritual drivel or advanced hyperspace physics? 'What advice shall we give people?' I asked.

'That they are descendants to the enhanced race. They have locked away their knowledge and the force has since long been forgotten,' she answered.

'Why have I been chosen to convey this?' I asked almost childishly and naively.

'You have not been chosen, it is part of who you are. You will meet strangers on the street that you do not know. Your eyes meet but don't look away because you have knowledge of each other on a subconscious level. You recognize each other's existence. There are a lot of heirs to the noble race, but their teachings have been forgotten and their intentions have not been accomplished. They hoped that their implantation and enrichment would create a hybrid human where the mixture of different forces would make the offspring greater. Their intention is that we shall become like them.'

Faith took a deep breath after her long speech. I got the impression that the process was draining in energy and that she herself sometimes had difficulty forming the words necessary to describe her mental experiences.

'Do they come from God?' I asked inanely.

'They come from an eternal force. A great spirit, which has been divided into smaller parts. God does not control everything,' she said confidently.

'Why not?' I asked.

'Humanity created God to achieve control. They have ignored the gift. God is a construct.'

'Do they come in ships or how can they control us?'

'They look at us like children. They ensure we fare well. They keep coming back. Sometimes we don't discover them. They have knowledge of the past and what is most likely to come. Humanity threads a path to its destruction if we cannot master our energy.'

'Can we avoid a final war?'

'Yes. They visit the descendants and try to ensure their strength. Humanity has no great influence, yet the progeny will acquire it,' she said.

'In which way can one augment the energies that make inner journeys possible for my patients?' I then asked.

'The technique should be used as often as possible. The strength increases according how frequently the method is used. Those who have the gift will automatically recover faster—they have a greater inner strength. Our children's strength is much greater than humans without this genetic inheritance. Keep doing what you are doing. You descend from our offspring,' Faith answered. 'Meditation enhances the ability of the spiritual energy's ability to unite with itself.'

'Should you visualise the present?' I asked.

'Yes. Through meditation your guide can take you through the tunnel to a garden where there are other people. This is the meeting point of all. This is the common room for our offspring. Take my hand!' Faith's request confused me. Her hands were in the air, seemingly occupied with something.

'What are you doing with your hands?'

'They are holding them. I am filled with energy.' This was the point of no return. Regardless of my beliefs I had to take her hands. An independent observer would probably consider Faith psychotic or having a split personality. She spoke softly yet confidently, occasionally correcting me mildly like a child by a teacher. I found myself in a situation that I no longer had any control over. I took Faith's hands in mine. She effortlessly held them in the air for a long time.

'What are they saying?' I asked her.

'You will find that people will look at you more. They are likely part of our children. Do you feel the energy?' she asked. There was no immediate strong reaction, no overwhelming experience.

'Ask them why you are having dark dreams of a terrifying future,' I asked after removing my hands from Faith.

'They fear that their descendants have failed. They do not want it to happen. If humanity disappears only their children will remain. It is our duty to save them. A part of the human spirit exists on a spiritual level. A part of the spiritual energy is connected to the Earth. The Earth is in equilibrium with the spiritual energy. If the energy is disturbed the living conditions will change,' she calmly continued with a smile. Her eyes moved visibly under her eyelids indicating a REM-like condition.

'If Earth is destroyed, what would happen to the humans?' I asked curiously.

'Then we would have to find another place in the universe,' she answered.

'Why did you come to Earth, whoever you are talking through Faith? What was the motive?'

'By maintaining life the spiritual energy can grow. Within this a higher consciousness is contained,' she said.

'What can mankind do to improve the conditions?' I asked.

'They can ensure our offspring unites, after which they can project their force unto others. All our children have the same gift, it can be noticed in their eyes.'

'What is the gift?' I asked.

'Many humans are far from spiritual. They are greedy and violent. United the force of our offspring can be multiplied. The coupling of two of our offspring creates a hybrid. The force must be returned. This occurs by infecting humanity with this energy,' she said.

'But why do they visit us in their ships if this is how it is?'

'It takes a long time to transfer the energy to humans. This is why they have been visiting us during the last centuries. They are collecting as much energy as possible.' She started to seem strained, and her face twisted occasionally when she spoke using words I had never heard her use.

I was unsure how to handle all of this. Faith spoke as someone extremely knowledgeable in a subject far beyond my own understanding, or as someone who had prepared before the session. She was mild, kind and continuously had a greater smile on her lips than her usual self. I tried to remind myself that I had observed no signs of either psychotic symptoms or a personality disorder. Faith was an unusual wise, talented warm young woman, but perhaps she had a big imagination.

I remembered what I had learnt from, in particular, the murderers while working as a forensic psychiatrist. No matter how despicable a crime might have seemed to me as an outsider, the golden rule was to condemn the crime but not the individual. We all have our lives and our struggles, and to denounce others is too easy. It is much harder to forgive and show true compassion and love. This separates the wheat from the chaff.

I thought back to an extremely dangerous patient in the secure forensic ward at Säter in Sweden. He once asked me how I dared to enter his room and sit by his side. 'I feel compassion towards you and can understand your suffering. Why should I be afraid of you? Sure, you could kill me, but to what use? Do you also know karate?' I asked him.

He looked at me and I felt an intense connection towards him. He showed me finger karate and how easily you could take out someone's eye using the middle and pointer fingers crossed over each other. For the uninitiated this might have been frightening, but to me a door had opened into a person's mind. A bond of trust had been created when I left my fear outside the door. From that moment there was a friendship between us that no one was able to understand. This event lay as a mental foundation in my mind when I considered the similarity to Faith's experiences. Did my doubts stem from fear and worry of the outside world, and more so, if I left them behind would I begin to understand?

'Why are you telling all of this through Faith?'

'I was already there when all of this began. Today all of this has been made available to you and Eleanor. There are also guides for our offspring,' she replied without hesitation.

I noticed how time had run away. Almost 1½ hours had passed on that late Friday afternoon in my colleague's office at the hospital in Runwell. Where had all the time gone? I realised it was time to finish, but I still wanted to take advantage of the situation for Faith's benefit.

'What is the purpose of seeing when people will die? Why can a few people foretell this?' My thoughts wandered to Elisabeth. She had precisely predicted her mother's and father's deaths. At the end of 2002 she foresaw the death of a good friend who was in complete health. She told me this and expressed her grief over the knowledge and being unable to change anything. She was completely convinced that her vision would be fulfilled. A few months later she was dismayed to read his obituary in the local paper.

Faith's answer was cryptic and general. 'They know when they will go. The body goes to the earth, and the spirit is united with the energy. Everyone is born again. There is no death for the spirits.' She then proceeded to discuss humanity's history and blood. 'Originally the infection of energy was not a result of breeding, but some had to be mixed through combining blood. By exchanging blood with the offspring humanity was infected with energy. Mankind's stories of vampires and blood come from them. They gave people life through the blood. Something that slowly makes them stronger. The spiritual energy exists partially in the blood and the heart,' Faith said.

'Do they mean that blood transfusions are wrong?' I asked.

'Not at all. They are reparations.'

'Is there any truth in the fact that some people who have had heart transplantations from another person experience that they have undergone a personality change?'

'Yes. The heart contains spiritual energy.'

I had to end the session. I was slightly worried that I had completely drained Faith of strength and energy. She returned slowly to her body. She felt stiff and it took a while before she stood up.

'Strange. I feel stronger now than when we began. Why is that?' she asked.

'I don't know. Perhaps you were given some form of energy.'

When she returned the following week she said that she had told her parents everything. It had felt good and they had listened. Faith had slept for two hours after getting home and felt completely drained of energy, yet she had felt true inner joy. She smiled radiantly towards me, and I had difficulty understand why she was so happy. She told me that once at home she had realised that the cave she had visited in reality was a spacecraft. Faith denied any interests in books about abductions. She had only watched the series "Taken" that was running on BBC2 for half an hour before turning it off.

'I hate everything to do with the 50s. I could feel their smell in the spaceship. It was as if they had eaten fruit. Their skin was soft like a child's, and their clothes reminded me of velvet, or perhaps more like a second layer of skin. I had nothing on my feet. They told me that I needed to gain knowledge. It seemed like it took an hour for you to catch up to me,' she said while smiling at me. 'They noticed your presence through me, and they were frustrated they could not show you what I saw,' she finished before leaving my office.

***

'Faith, what can you see?'

'I am with him again. He is pleased. Each time I return the energy level will increase, which releases knowledge and emotions,' she answered. She often spoke in longer sentences. She made me feel as if I was chasing her, as if I was disturbing her experiences. Yet she never showed any irritation or anger. She always answered the questions, and often the person she was talking to addressed me directly.

'What is needed for me to see what you can see?' I asked.

'You need a lot of energy. You must meditate and go to that place where the spirits are resting,' she answered.

'How do you get there?'

'The spirits will take you through meditation. You must calm your mind,' Faith told me.

'Can people connect to each other in order to increase the energy level and perhaps project mental images or experiences in the room?' I asked Faith. My thoughts were occupied with questions about projective mechanisms. No one would question a projector's ability to clearly project an image on the wall. Most psychologists would also accept the presence of primitive projective mechanisms between people, such as feelings of conscious and subconscious rage projected towards someone else, people's experiences of discomfort and confused communication, an everyday occurrence in a world full of violence, greed and immaturity. Would people be able to understand the possibility of parallel connections to each other in order to amplify the mental abilities? The possibility of transforming the mental signal processes from streams of electrons and cerebral fluids into conscious projections from the mind towards the external world? Likely not.

'This can only happen if the people are part of our offspring. Everyone who is, they know instinctively, subconsciously, from birth that they are part of this whole.'

'Are you inside the spaceship now? What does it look like?' I asked.

'The lights are off. It is night,' she said.

'Why?'

'They are sleeping.'

'What food do they eat?'

'Fruit but also meat from animals.'

'Why do they eat meat Faith?'

'Because their bodies need it. When they project themselves they require a great amount of energy.'

'Is humanity part of the cosmos?' I asked when dwelling in my inner thoughts.

'Everything is. Humanity knows instinctively that cosmos exists. But humans are still not a true part of this cosmos because of fear.'

'Why has humanity been equipped with fear?' I asked.

'It is a natural instinct,' she replied doubtlessly.

'Do they like you dread confronting fear and death?'

'No, not like mankind. They do not fear death. However they are frightful of ignoring their souls. They fear fragmentation.' She kept talking without me asking any questions. She made me feel like a student at a lecture, it was a strange feeling. 'Lower souls are ignorant. This creates fragmentation that on a greater level creates negative energy. Some spirits have issues and this affects the Earth itself. There must be balance, which humanity is harming.'

'Why is Earth important to them?'

'It is similar to their own. It lies millions of light years away,' Faith answered.

'In another dimension? Is it corporeal?' I asked.

'It is physical but very spiritual.'

'How many civilisations are there in the cosmos?'

'Thousands. Most are more advanced than yours. Your greed impedes you,' Faith said but yet through something else.

'But how did Homo sapiens come to exist?'

'She was born here, it was planned. Everything depends on where a specie is suitable. The adapted specie is part of the Great Spirit. They become a part of the planet.'

It would have been easy to dismiss Faith as having severe mental issues when she was in this state of deep relaxation. I considered that many would probably see that as a suitable solution, that in relaxation her normal identity would fall to the side, her psychological defences weaken, and she would fall victim to dreams and fantasies. The problem was that Faith never displayed any such behaviour. She was always controlled and kind regardless of whether she was fully awake, or deeply relaxed. She never hesitated with her replies, and showed no signs of changes in her state of mind during the relaxation.

'How many lives have you lived before?' I asked.

It took a while until she replied with a scowl '3000 lives. Not all were completed.'

'Which was the most joyful?'

'The beginning. We were happy. We had such great hopes.'

'Faith, has the continent of Atlantis existed or is it fiction?'

'They were another species, similar to mankind,' she said.

'Did they work with energies?'

'I do not know.'

'Why did they disappear?'

'They needed rest. They left before anything happened. Through the passage of time their seed has disappeared. They left Earth in their own ships.'

'How long ago did that happen?'

Faith took ages before replying. She frowned and I got the feeling that perhaps my questions were unnecessary. '45 000 years,' she replied undoubtedly.

**

It was 28 March 2003 and outside my window the fields swam in greenery. The trees were budding and I could not help but watching a blackbird with wonder. It had been singing constantly throughout the previous session. As soon as Faith began to speak it picked up its song again. 'He comes towards me and wishes me welcome. He does not call me his daughter like all the others did, because I am human. Strange, he is not as tall as before.'

'Why do you return to the ship?' I asked.

'They want to teach me to help people become more spiritual. We have to understand that there is no God, and that we must abandon our independence based on false premises. We have to reclaim self-awareness,' she responded gently.

'What is his name?' I asked curiously, with a hint of cynicism.

'Nyadomyn.'

'A strange name.'

'It exists in their culture.'

'What do they want to teach us?' I asked.

'There is still so much liberation needed. Many lessons to be learned,' she replied.

'What do we need to learn?'

'To control our power.'

'How can I see what you are seeing?' I asked in an effort to understand what was happening to her.

'You must relax your mind to obtain knowledge. You need someone else who can take you to this place.'

'Why are we reincarnated?'

'We are trying to increase the number of descendants. We need more people who master the energy, to help others. The descendants are connected and must increase the force that helps the humans. More need to gather,' Faith said.

'Must this happen now?' I asked.

'It does not happen instantly, rather within 100 years. If not, then we fail.'

'Have they attempted this before?'

'They have made many hybrids before, and they accomplished their tasks. They have never encountered a species as different as humanity before. They have never seen a species as greedy and violent,' Faith said with sadness in her voice.

'How did life emerge?' I asked as I tried to understand if Faith was simulating or if she was in a trance when she unconsciously portrayed another person.

'Nothing created life. It just is. Spirituality is part of the universe's physical form which includes the characteristic that the spirit coexists with the environment. We can see this in even the simplest of life forms,' Faith concluded.

'Have other species been greedy?'

'Yes, but we have been able to guide them.'

'What is the energy characteristics of greed?' I asked.

'It is negative and destructive,' she said.

'Are thoughts powerful?'

'The thought creates what it wants. One must understand how to vanquish the negative. One must free themselves from the body and become pure energy. Greed comes from the body and partly from the human spirit.'

I tried to remind myself that Faith could be a fraud, that she might be trying to fool me consciously or subconsciously. At the same time it hit me that a doctor should always consider a patient's story as true until proven otherwise. Who dares to deny headaches, just because you have never suffered it yourself? I decided to carry on with Faith but to keep my mind open for all possibilities. It was therefore important to return to her core issue. At the same time, I also needed some kind of checkpoint. 'Why are you having apocalyptic dreams, Faith?'

'I will have them maybe a few more times. They remind me of who I am and at the same time increase my inherited spiritual strength. I need to be reminded,' she replied peacefully.

'What should we do?'

'Become more self-aware and powerful. Together the descendants can come out.'

'Why do they not come here and help us?' I asked.

'It is physically dangerous. Humanity fears the unknown. Our kind might be perceived as something bad. When you awake there will be hope,' Faith said.

'Have different species visited Earth?'

'Yes, they have a need to ascertain that we are not a threat.'

'What are they afraid of?'

'The destructive power of mankind. We strive to destroy everything and create disorder.'

'Is this satanic?' I asked.

'No, it is a creation of the mind. There is no devil and no God. There is only good and evil,' she said.

'Oh really. Do the spirits wage war on each other?'

'The spiritual elite have no need for war. They are above that state. No one uses fear to rule.'

'Faith, does Nyadomyn show you anything?'

'He points towards the furthest part of the ship and shows me different directions. He takes me to the furthermost point. He shows me a landscape,' she continued. 'There are bushes, flowers and trees.'

'Inside the ship? Why do they have those there?'

'They need them in order to live in the trees where their homes are.'

'Why do they live in the trees?' I asked.

'They feel safer in the trees than on the ground. It is a primitive instinct from their distant past that remains. It gives them a feeling of security. They can see animals. The flowers produce food and fruit. They also eat animals. A mixture of substances for their bodies. The houses in the trees are made from dead trees. In the large spaceship they have created a natural balance,' she responded.

'Where do they get energy from?'

'From spiritual energy. The spirits are light.'

'Do you and I have the type of mind required to understand this?'

'You are born with it.'

***

I was growing increasingly concerned about Faith, but at the same time she showed no signs of mental illness. I was convinced that no colleague could possibly disagree with me on this matter. But then, why all of this? 'What are you doing?'

'I am in my room...' She started describing her room. I became perplexed and thought that Faith had not entered deep relaxation. There was one thing that distinguished her from many others, something that she could not change. She had very weak REM activity under her eyelids, something that I considered an important sign that spoke against the genuineness of her inner experiences.

'What do you have in your room? In which country are you?' I asked.

'A cat. England,' she said.

'What year is it?'

'2005. I thought we were going back,' she said spontaneously.

'What are you doing?'

'I am painting the walls. There is a single bladed sword above my bed.'

'Are you seeing a psychiatrist nowadays?' I asked.

'Not my best,' she replied.

'Where is he/she?'

'He is on vacation.'

'Was he able to help you?'

'I feel whole now. Oh, now it is shaking. I should not be here. It is time to leave.' I brought her down deeper in relaxation. I calmed her and assured her that nothing would disturb her. As always she lay completely calm, with no hint of worry. 'There are so many faces, both young and old. They have the same velvet-like fabric as before. There is a forest further away. The people take me to the forest and hold my hand,' Faith said with a calm voice.

'Are you in the spaceship again? Inside or outside?' I asked.

'Not on Earth. It is where they originally came from.'

'Any water?'

'Oh yes, it is clear.'

'What do the houses look like?'

'They are in the trees. They are circular, quite cute. They have the same brown colour as the trees. Older trees make more greyish houses.'

'What is the name of the planet?' I asked now starting to get really curious.

'Kuplasina,' she said.

'Why are you there? Is Nyadomyn there?'

'We must finish what we are doing. It isn't dangerous. Yes, he is here.'

I still had my doubts and questions. I thought I had to test her with a difficult question. 'Ask him what cellular memories are?'

'A type of copy. Part of the role cells play. They always remember. If one is hurt, new ones grow with the same memories. They all have different tasks. The memories must be opened, but it is very difficult. It is tough for all species to conquer what they fear the most,' she replied.

'Is the term cellular memory incorrect?'

'No. Man always runs away from fear of living in terror. He must confront this. Creatures like us do not have cellular memories. We live above this. It is wrong to hurt, you must live in peace. It has taken us thousands of years to become a higher species.'

'Does cellular memories cause cancer?' I asked.

'Cancer of the body is genetic information resting in the DNA. Cellular memories are both something physical and spiritual. Some people still remember pain. Cancer is part of the physical. Genetic coding causes tumours. Part of this relates to overpopulation. The species controls itself to live through epidemics. People are nervous of imbalance. To not have children means death,' she said while I raised my eye brows. She was so incredibly gifted with knowledge in this state. How was that possible, I thought?

115

'Why do you go back in this way?' I asked.

'It creates security to return to where you belong,' she answered.

Faith wanted to stay in this condition but I decided to remove her from there. She had spoken of Egypt several times and because of this I randomly decided to ask her to return to another life. If there was a life in Egypt she might return to that one.

'It is a large room. There are many valuable things here. There are statues of Anubis and Isis.' She sounded completely changed. She did not sound as intellectual, but rather young and more childish.

"What place is it?' I asked.

'It is not a temple. It is something big and important. People walk around the place,' she said.

'Can you read anything on the walls?'

'There are incantations protecting against those wishing to disturb the harmony of the room.'

'Who lives in this place Faith?'

'It is someone's room. She is not here now. I can't see her,' she replied.

'What year is it?'

'7592.'

'Who are you?' I asked.

'I am the daughter of an important man. This is her private room. If they found me here they'd execute me instantly,' she said with her breathing getting faster.

'They cannot see you. No one will find you. You can remain calm, I have sent you to this place. Can you see anything of importance?'

'There is something like a witch's altar. She is one of the descendants.'

'Is there any technology in the room, anything unusual? Look around carefully, take your time,' I instructed her.

'Yes, some plants I recognize from Nyadomyn's ship. They are medicinal herbs. You cut the leaves straight into water,' Faith said.

'And then you drink it?'

'No, you just smell it. It is used against headaches.'

'What is the name of the city you are in?'

'I don't know. It is part of the royal palace, not far from the Nile. She has painted the hieroglyphs on the walls herself. She has also put in place the wards. She wishes for a child with Pharaoh. She has great strength of will.' Suddenly Faith said something that greatly shocked me- she started to talk about me. 'Your execution was last week. You were a priest and helped her with your spiritually healing power to get pregnant. She knows from where they came originally' she said without me asking.

'Is she angry over what has happened?'

'Very. She implored the Pharaoh to spare you. But he was weak, and that is why they only killed you. Otherwise they would have also killed her because of the child.'

'Did she give me anything?' I asked.

'She put a golden scarab on your body. You were buried under the temple. Today you lie under the sand. She participated in the ritual binding of you, and chanted incantations to protect your tomb. Only your spirit can find this place. You can find the location through hypnosis,' she said. 'Are you certain that they can't see me?' she asked.

'Yes, you do not need to worry at all. How will I find the tomb in Egypt today?'

'The current government has to disappear first. It takes many years until this happens.'

'Can you describe the scarab?' I asked anxious to get more details about an object that Faith could have no previous knowledge of.

'The scarab is reminiscent of the past. It contains a secret. It is not solid. She was very clever. By opening it you can access the plant inside the scarab.'

'How did I die?'

'You were killed on the palace courtyard. It was a somewhat snobbish execution. The very rich received tickets and my father had got some. You stood in the middle surrounded by spearmen. They killed you with the spears.'

One week later when we were summarising part of our work, Faith told me that there had been a negative experience in the Queen's chamber. In the chamber she had seen statues of Anubis on the right, and Isis holding oil lanterns on the left side of the Queen's bed. Faith described how she could see my hands tied, and 20-30 people standing around me in a ring before the execution, all staring at me.

Faith had no more apocalyptic dreams during the past 4-5 weeks leading up to the second to last session in April 2003. One thing was certain however. Faith was imaginative and easily influenced. A new lady had started at her workplace. It turned out that they had both been born at the same time at the same hospital, and that they had both originally lived in the same small Welsh village. Faith took this as an important sign. The relaxation itself was becoming more difficult and it took longer to take her down sufficiently deep. Faith first saw her brother crying in front of a mirror, and then her mother. She never really understood why they were crying, but felt that it had something to do with herself.

'It is something that will happen. It hurts,' Faith said.

'Where?' I asked.

'I don't know. Lee is also here. He sits in the kitchen with another friend. It is another accident. People look at me. They seem sad.' Faith then returned to the state of rest in the light before she chose to return to the spaceship and Nyadomyn.

'He shows me the past. Where I come from. It was a good life.'

'What did you do?' I asked.

'Danced,' she said.

'On Earth?'

'Yes, it was the first place I met him at.'

'How long ago is this?'

'300 years. It is during the middle of the 1760s. We are part of the offspring.'

'What country is it?'

'England.'

'Which town?'

'Leicester.'

'Why is he showing you this?' I asked.

'It is important with context. Dyron… danced at the court. Everyone danced,' she replied.

'Did you marry him? Did you get any children?'

'Yes. Five survived and two died at birth.'

'What is the name of your husband?'

'Jonathan Bromby. My name is Sue Ellen.'

'What is this all about?' I asked slightly puzzled.

'That we have been together in past lives. Paths cross and you know them from back then,' she responded.

I left the subject and moved her on to the subject matter of light and science. No matter if she was making things up or telling the truth, there was value in studying her mind. 'Does thought travel at the speed of light?' I asked.

'Thoughts travel with the speed of the soul. The spirit is the speed,' she said.

'You mean that it travels faster?'

'Yes. The spirit frees itself of the body. The mind must be open, because then it is easier to accept. While time passes our species tries to enlighten mankind. The more sensitive, the easier it is,' Faith replied as Nyadomyn.

'Is it dangerous?' I asked.

'No. We must return to the physical world. Back in the spiritual world the body dies. We have studied this for years,' Faith answered.

'What advice can he give?'

'That you are alone and learn more.'

'What are you doing now Faith?'

'Exchanging blood. My body is somehow also in the ship, I have a physical presence. Recognizant connections are created so that I can return,' she replied.

'How do you return?'

'Sound, something relating to frequencies. The body recognizes the sound which releases the time travel during the relaxation. The music is calming.'

***

Faith lay down relaxed for the eleventh and last time. We were in a new room at the hospital and, after a dialogue evaluating our previous experiences, Faith disappeared once again into the world she loved so greatly. The world where she was in focus and had to carry the race forward. As usual she returned to the spaceship, a fact she had herself commented on in our discussion. 'Nyadomyn shows me the past. People and places I have known.'

'Me?' I asked.

'Yes,' she said.

'Where?'

'Egypt and before on the ship.'

'Why do we meet again Faith?'

'To remind each other of our bonds. We need more,' she said.

'Why is it important for Nyadomyn to tell us?' I asked.

'I have not had any previous lives with Mel.' Mel was Faith's new boyfriend after she had broken up with Kai. He was increasingly present in both her conscious and subconscious mind. 'He is a new acquaintance. I have shared a life with Kai before.'

'You have given me much knowledge Faith, and I am pleased that you no longer suffer from your apocalyptic dreams. If I may, I would like to give you some simple advice. Of course, it would be wrong of me to judge or look down on your experiences. They are uniquely yours, and no one can take them from you. However, I still perceive that you have a great imagination and involvement, and the important thing is that you master this force. You are talented. But you should take care not to lose yourself in dark arts and witchcraft. You must live in the present. I wish you the best of luck.'

I felt that Faith listened to my well-considered criticism. She trusted me, and during the transfer of emotions I noticed that she understood what I meant. You cannot make up past lives. Imagination is markedly different from the sharp truths that are seemingly delivered from the "fifth dimension". When Faith left, we hugged as good friends. She had taught me the importance of also listening with a critical mind. Her experiences were vastly different from all other patients. Yet, how did she have knowledge of my life in Egypt as a priest at the temple of Karnak?

A Cycle of Rape

Rochelle was a 33 year old mother of four who had been referred by her GP due to very severe anxiety. She had been given anxiety reducing and anti-depressant medication without any real effect. She remained sceptic towards medication herself. She had grown up during relatively stable circumstances in a Jewish family. Her life had changed dramatically when she was brutally raped at the age of 16. Only when she was in the seventh month of pregnancy did she dare tell her parents the truth. Rochelle gave birth to a healthy boy, but she came to have mixed emotions about love and considered putting him up for adoption. She never told the truth to her son about his father. Her husband, who she had three younger children with, did not know anything either. All he could see was his wife suffering from sleeping troubles, severe anxiety attacks and fear.

Just like most psychiatrists would have done I referred her to psychotherapy, but the waiting list was 6-12 months. She would only get an assessment and then be put onto another waiting list. Rochelle was given stronger anti-anxiety medication which she stopped taking after a month due to side effects. Her attitude towards medicine was naturally growing more and more cynical. In the end I decided to offer her the possibility of regression and deep relaxation. I understood that the underlying trauma could of course not be treated with only medication. My own conviction of the strength of the therapy made myself have more faith in that rather than the prescription pad. Society could benefit greatly from the improved recovery rates, but would anyone care?

'What are you doing Rochelle?'

'I'm with my family. I am 6 or 7 years old. I have two sisters. Mom says "Stop that". She does not like me,' she said with a soft voice.

'What are you doing now?'

'I'm in my room. I'm reading "*The lion, the witch and the wardrobe*" by Lewis Carroll,' she replied with precision. I moved Rochelle forward in life to her graduation. She moved mentally and spiritually with unusual ease. 'I graduated. I have worked hard, but mom does not care. She says nothing. She just says that dad will be happy.'

'Where is your dad?' I asked.

'He's at work,' Rochelle answered.

'How old are you?'

'11 years.'

'Do you have any friends?'

'Yes, Caroline. She lives around the corner.'

'How are your relationships with your sisters?' I asked.

'They are always fighting with me. Emma is terrible. She destroys things. She has cut into the sofa and blames me. Mom doesn't believe me,' Rochelle said.

'Do you hate her?'

'I don't know. She's my sister after all. I wish dad was here. I told him, and told him to talk to Emma, but he doesn't care.'

Rochelle had told me she did not have any religious faith, and had never had any interest in spirituality. Because of this she was an excellent patient. My base hypothesis was as usual that it was completely irrelevant as to which faith you adhere. The method worked excellent regardless.

'Rochelle, you have now left your family and dwell in the light. Do you have a guide?' I asked, certain that she had never encountered this branch of theosophy. I presumed that she would reply "no".

'Mba,' she replied briskly with certainty.

'Mba, who is that?'

'She smiles,' Rochelle said.

'Ask her if you will be able to recover.'

'She doesn't want me to speak. She wants me to smile.'

The following session was challenging. I had to take Rochelle to a hospital ward to try and find an empty room, and once in the room with my equipment we were continuously disturbed by noises from outside the room. Patients were talking loudly while the clanking of plates and cutlery could be heard. Music was played and doors were slammed. To summarize, the external conditions were close to impossible. I asked Rochelle if she even wanted to make an attempt. Even though she had expressed that she had no faith in anything and no previous spiritual experiences, she was more interested than before. I started to calmly and methodically chant as the music played in the background and candles were flickering around us. She once again entered a REM-intense stage, which could be described as a hypnagogic state–the fourth state after sleeping, dreaming and being awake, a state in-between awake and sleeping. Yet there were clear differences. Rochelle was completely conscious and there were no signs that she was tired or drowsy.

Rochelle became Peter married to Sarah. They had no children. Rochelle told me that Peter was dressed in a pair of trousers and a t-shirt. His brother Peter hated him/her, and when she looked into Peter's eyes she recognized Steven.

'Oh… It is… It is Steven.'

'Who is Steven?' I asked since I knew nothing.

'I have never said his name. He is the one who raped me,' she said.

'What year is it?'

'1912,' she responded in the blink of an eye.

'Where are you living?'

'Hampstead, outside of London.'

'What do you work as?' I asked.

'I'm an office clerk,' she answered without a hint of doubt.

'Why does your brother hate you so much? Do you hate him?'

'He wants Sarah. No, I do not hate him.'

I asked Rochelle to go to the moment just prior to her death. 'What year is it?'

'1914.'

'What is happening?'

'Such pain. I have terrible chest pains. It came so sudden,' she moaned.

'Do you get any help or do you take any medication?' I asked.

'I take some pills,' she said.

'What happened to Sarah?' I asked.

'She died.'

'She died? How?'

'She was strangled on the heath.'

'Why did you die Rochelle?'

'Because Sarah died.'

I asked her to look into the murderers eyes, but she could not recognize him and everything was muddled. 'But you can see into Sarah's eyes. Take your time. Who do you recognize?'

She gasped and replied 'Oh, it is Simon.'

'Who is Simon?'

'Simon was my great love in this life, but it did not work out between us.'

***

Rochelle was quiet and reserved. She had suffered more anxiety and felt hopeless and downhearted since the last relaxation. She also told me that the headache that she had had for a week had disappeared after the last session. She came back to her great need of control and how she had no belief in a life after death. Rochelle expressed scepticism towards her friends who talked about psychic powers, and carefully distanced herself from all sorts of faith's beliefs in other dimensions. I encouraged her, and expressed my approval.

'It is good that you don't believe in anything of all this, it makes you a more believable candidate. My experience is that someone's personal faith matter very little, it still works no matter where they come from. By the way, do you have any relatives or dear friends that have passed away?' I asked.

'Yes, my grandmother and grandfather. Oh, and my friend Lucy passed away last year in childbirth. She was only 32. Why do you ask?' Rochelle asked me.

'I'll tell you later. Let's begin,' I replied, careful not to push Rochelle into any specific meetings.

'What do you see?'

'Lilies. Mm, it some type of room.'

'Can you look out?' I asked.

'No, I cannot get out. The flowers are so beautiful,' she replied.

'Can you see anyone?' I asked.

'Far away.' I moved Rochelle closer and asked her to describe whoever she had seen at a distance. She describe her grandpa in a brown cardigan and grey trousers. She told me how sorry he was that things was 'messed up' with Matthew, and that he asked to marry her.

'Who is Matthew?' I asked.

'He was my husband, and he wasn't kind,' she answered.

'Can you forgive your grandfather?' She went silent for a while and then responded 'yes'. 'Does your grandfather think it's good that you have gotten help?' I asked. The reply was surprising and told me that I had missed something when Rochelle first came to the clinic.

'He says he got me to come here today. He asked June to call me. She got me to go. He says that enough is enough, and everything will sort itself out.'

'What does he want you to do?' I asked.

'He wants me to believe him,' she replied.

'How is your grandmother?'

'She is happy.'

'And Lucy?'

'She is currently getting help.'

'Is there anything that June wants to show you?'

'She wants me to show her son pictures.'

'Ask your grandfather as to why you have such a need of control?'

'Because I am afraid. I must learn to trust people.'

'Does your grandfather trust me?'

'He sent me here.'

'Is there anything he wants to show you?'

'He shows me his home. How strange. He shows that he looks after me. He's leaving now.'

***

When Rochelle returned to the clinic in the beginning of May she expressed doubts and worry. During the past week she had suffered bad nightmares. Time and time again she had been raped by Steven. Hundreds of pictures had passed by in her dreams. She also said she had been avoiding June since the last week's events. She was still fighting with all her strength in order to not abandon her false reality of suppression and a long list of other psychological defence mechanisms. It was not difficult to see that she spent a lot of energy just fighting all the truths that lay waiting for her just around every corner. We were sitting in the hospital's therapy department in the main building. Slowly tears started to roll down Rochelle's cheeks.

'I only cry here. I don't even cry at funerals otherwise. And I keep fighting with pretty much everyone,' Rochelle said.

'It is good. Don't fight it. Let go. You don't need to believe in anything. Affirm your experiences. All your dreams have been awakened through this work. Sure, I have a responsibility for this, but the pain is in some ways necessary for you to become whole,' I said with a calm voice.

'Can you mentally develop bruises?' she asked suddenly.

'What do you mean?'

'One morning I awoke with the same bruises I had after Steven had raped me and beaten me badly.'

'There is something called stigmata, and during hypnosis some people can develop skin damage. Let us call it a psychosomatic reaction. Yes, when it concerns very serious trauma it is possible,' I said.

'Steven assaulted me after the rape. I went to a good friend. I lied to my parents. I've lied to so many. During four years I wouldn't even speak to my dad. He was a higher up police chief and how would he be able to believe that I had been raped?'

'Has your son never asked about his father?' I asked.

'No,' she said.

'I've written a letter that's in safe-deposit box. But I got frightened when my son's teacher told me that he'd played his role excellently in a serious drama leading up to his exams. I shouldn't have, but I read his script. He played a wife beater. It chilled my bones. After Steven I moved in with a Muslim filled with misogyny and wrath. He was the very last kind of man my parents could have wished for, yet I chose him. Can you understand? He kept me locked in the apartment with my son for six months. And I who come from a Jewish family,' Rochelle said with anger in her voice.

Rochelle was pouring her heart out, and the fact that she came from a Jewish family increased my curiosity, but did not surprise me. Rochelle carried so many secrets that she was ready to psychologically explode. She sighed heavily and cried quietly as she started to realise the importance of truth–and the risk that her son might one day find it out from someone other than his own mother.

'Do you love him?' I asked.

'I don't know. One moment I wanted to keep him, and the next put him up for adoption. Are you sure this isn't harmful? You're awakening so much in me,' she said.

'I cannot give any 100% guarantees, but I can promise you one thing. I will do my very best and I am convinced that you will be able to recover. You are talented and you have no mental issues, but you suffer from difficult anxiety and depression after all you've been through. You chose this yourself after I had fully informed you, and even though we carry out this work together I am accountable.'

Rochelle went quiet. I was uncertain if she would accept my answer. When she eventually relaxed and went down into the state of subliminal or subconscious knowledge everything happened rapidly. Rochelle became a 12 year old girl living with her father. The mother had died during her birth. 'What country are you living in?' I asked.

'France,' she answered, almost a tad offended. Her voice was lighter and a little bit childish.

'Do you attend school? How many years have you been there?'

'Yes, for four years.'

'What year is it now?'

'1872.'

'Do you have any buddies or a best friend?' I asked.

'No,' she said.

'What are you doing?'

'I'm helping my dad.'

'Is it heavy?'

'Yes.'

'Describe the house you live in,' I encouraged her.

'There are seven rooms. In the kitchen there is a table, a stove and six chairs. There is a bucket for water,' she said.

'What is your name?'

'Alexandra.'

Suddenly she mumbled something in French. Thinking it might be amusing, and having no knowledge of Rochelle speaking French, I said 'Parlez vous francais?' ('Do you speak French?')

'Oui, je suis française.' (Yes, 'I am French.')

'Ca va?' ('How are you?')

'Ca va bien!' ('I am well.')

I realised I had lost control. I had only studied French for three years at high school, and even if my grandfather spoke seven languages fluently, my French was quite poor. Rochelle on the other hand spoke fluent French, with not the slightest hint of an English accent. It was flowing out of her as she asked, 'Qui est tu?' ('Who are you?')

'Je suis docteur Suedois. Pour Rochelle et bien pour Alexandra.' (I'm the Swedish doctor. For Rochelle as well as Alexandra.')

'Why doctor for Alexandra?' she asked in flawless French. It was occasionally difficult for me to understand. I was clearly in over my head.

'Yes, because. Where is your father? Are you eating?' I asked in French.

'Papa, est dans la cuisine. Non mangous pas.' ('Dad is in the kitchen. We aren't eating.')

'What do you study in school?'

'Dans l'ecole je travaille un peu avec francais et matematique. C'est tout,' she replied. ('In school I study a bit of French and mathematics.

That is all.') She kept speaking French and seemed irritated that I could not explain what I was doing.

'Where is your mother?'I asked.

'Elle est mort.' ('She is dead.')

I couldn't handle any more French. Thinking that she must speak fluent French when awake too, I moved her to the most important event with her father. 'What do you see?'

'My father is hitting me. He isn't happy. He says that I killed mom. He undresses me. It hurts. I'm bleeding,' Rochelle said.

'How old are you?' I asked.

'Eleven,' she replied. I asked her to look in her father's eyes to see if she recognized anyone. 'Mm, it is him.'

'Who?'

'Steven.'

'For how long does he hit you?'

'Forever.'

I asked her if she ever got away from her father. She moved away from the farm and left her father. She was living for herself and helping poor children through the church. She died at the age of twenty-two, following a fall in the house, leaving no children of her own behind. Suddenly she went back to speaking French again. I could not understand everything but it was something about the church. 'Prais eglise moi,' which could have meant something about church and prayer.

'Where did you die?' I asked.

'Ecole par l'eglise' she replied. ('In the church school.') 'Par les un peu l'eglise,' she said again. I did not understand so I ended by asking for her father's name.

'Philippe.'

When Rochelle woke up it was the first time she had difficulty remembering what had occurred. It seemed as if she had been in such a strong regressive state that she had completely forgotten her current personality, or that she had been in a very deep hypnotic state. The latter could explain her troubles remembering. She said that she mostly just saw faces in front of her.

'For how many years did you study French in school? I asked.

'I didn't do French, I studied German,' she answered.

'How much French do you know?'

'Just hello, good day and a few other words, that's all.'

'Really. Well today Rochelle, you spoke fluent French as Alexandra.'

She looked at me with wide eyes as I explained what had happened. After this session I decided to get my own audio recording equipment. I considered how unbelievable this would look to outsiders. There was some pre-existing literature, but often the work had not been performed by doctors or qualified scientists, and the credibility had always been negated by the critics. In my case they could of course not doubt my qualifications, but they would still likely refuse to acknowledge me and my patient's experiences. How would they explain the patients' recoveries? Perhaps suggestion with a large dose of modern mesmerism, combined with a wishy-washy work based on non-science and unevaluated experiences. Well, at least my patients keep sending letters to the management as they recover. I'd just have to wait and see whether I'd find myself with a pay rise or a pink slip. As Rochelle walked to her car I thought she looked happier, but I could have been imagining things.

The following week turned out to be one of the worst in Rochelle's life. After the session with the life in France all dams had burst for her.

'I have had massive flashbacks, and I have had more experiences of the life in France. I haven't slept properly during the whole week. My mind refuses to accept it. There cannot be any life past death, but the more I fight it, the greater the intensity of the experiences. I don't understand what is happening,' she said with a desperate voice.

Her husband was away on a conference and she had for the first time in six months been forced to go out shopping alone. She sighed heavily. At the same time there was something positive in her suffering. It was like she was slowly moving towards a point where she would realise that fighting against the truth would only cause her more pain.

'It seemed so easy when you said that I should consider what it would entail to tell the truth to my son. He played the main role as a wife abuser in the school's drama class, and I was shocked by his performance. The other mothers cried, but not me. When two other parents congratulated him on his performance I could not say "I'm proud of you" or anything else to him. I just stood there. No, I cannot tell him, because then all the lies I've told others of how I came to have him would start to unravel, and it might affect him. What would he believe?' She sobbed softly and looked at me.

'How many languages do you actually speak?' I asked.

'Decent German and Italian. I'm currently studying Spanish, but I've never learnt any French,' she answered.

'But you have a French name?'

'Married into it. Originally my family comes from Poland–we're Jews.'

I made great efforts to reaffirm Rochelle and give her time to talk through her anxiety.

'I know it is painful, but your suffering won't be for naught. There is a purpose to even the darkest moments in life, believe me. You're a very talented woman, and I noted your denial of all this with great pleasure. That you believe death is final, that we are nothing more but flesh and blood. I respect it. It nurtures and strengthens the treatment itself. Nothing will make me happier than to cure you. I warned you that there was no return. You could leave of course, but I will help you as much as I can and stand behind you on your journeys.'

'I only cry here. No one else knows all that you know now,' she said.

'I'm grateful. Let us begin,' I replied. As usual she relaxed incredibly quickly. Her complete journey into the depths of the oceans of her soul lay as a paradoxical counterpoint to her strong mindful defences.

'You will return to the origin of your suffering. Today you will understand, you've been through enough. What do you see?'

'A room. Steven's.'

'What is happening?' I asked.

'He threatens and hits me. He says that it is my fault,' she said.

'Does he force your clothes off you?'

'Yes.'

'Is it his apartment?'

'No.'

'Where is this happening?'

'In his parent's house. They aren't home.'

'What happens afterwards?' I asked. Everything took such time. Rochelle moaned and twisted, and I repeatedly instructed that these were just memories, that she was only observing without physical involvement.

'You're seeing this in order to understand,' I instructed her.

'It hurts... he's hitting me. He ties me up and cuts my breasts with a knife.'

'Look deep in his eyes! Do not be afraid now, I'm behind you. Look carefully. You will see things that you recognize. You will understand,' I prompted her.

'He is pitiful. He needs help,' she responded.

'But why does he come back to torment you? France, England 1912 and now in this life. Why?'

Rochelle sighed heavily and started to mumble, as if she was fighting herself, until she quietly said: 'I stabbed him to death.'

'Stabbed him? Where?'

'A long time ago in France. He has returned for revenge?'

'What year was it?'

'I do not know.'

Before she returned to the present, I instructed her that she would have a lengthy and deep sleep at home. Sleep is always an important ally. Perhaps the strong REM-activity was one of the explanations of her sleeping issues. As soon as she entered this phase in bed, it would activate her since long past slumbering memories. When Rochelle returned to herself she remembered all the details. Something had happened. Regardless of her fierce opposition of life after death, she admitted that it felt better. 'It is logical,' she said with her intense eyes wide open.

I peered at her with surprise: 'You will recover.' Of course, some therapists believe it is unprofessional to say so. However, I believe that I need to make myself a part of the treatment, not just sit and coldly analyse, awaiting intellectual revelations. Rochelle needed all the comfort and warmth she could have, and in the end it doesn't matter if I'm riding a pink elephant, as long as she recovers. Perhaps one day it will be discussed why we so strongly opposed our true existence, I thought.

***

During the past week Rochelle had slept more than usual and my instructions seemed to have helped her. She had a lengthy letter with her. She looked at me and said: 'I want you to read this letter.'

'I will, of course, but not right now,' I answered before I carried on with the methodical instructions. She was helping her father and she was a fourteen year old boy by the name of John. He was dressed in brown trousers and a white shirt. John didn't attend any school but instead he was taking care of his family's horses. John had no siblings and he complained about life being horrible without food and having cold weather. It was 1513. His mother was in the kitchen whilst he was looking after a mare. For no clear reason Johns mother just left.

'Your dad then, do you like him?' I asked.

'He is kind,' she answered

I took her to the most important moment in this harsh life. Everything to speed up the process. 'What are you doing?' I asked.

'I'm dying,' she replied with a very deep breath. Rochelle was sitting up in an armchair since it was an on-going struggle to get a room with a sofa. Her head fell forward and she seemed to feel the physical pain of her death.

'Where do you live?' I asked.

'I have no home. Mom and dad died of fever,' she replied.

'A week, a month, a year ago?'

'A few months.'

'Where are you?'

'At the same place by the fields. I have been stabbed in my back.'

'Who did this? Look him in the eyes, don't be afraid. You're just observing. You can feel no pain. Everything belongs to the past,' I softly instructed her.

'I saw him… with Rachel,' she said.

'Did he hurt her?'

'He raped her. It is… Matthew.'

'Who is Matthew?'

'He is my ex-husband.'

'Did he hit you?' I asked.

'Yes,' she said.

'And finally you left him?'

'Yes.'

'What did you learn from this tough life?'

'To give trust.' She then proceeded to speak a bit more spontaneously. As many other patients she seemed to experience so much more than she was able to express. 'There are others there. You were one of them,' she exclaimed.

'Me? What was I doing?'

'You came to the main house. You were a doctor. My master was ill,' she said.

'Was this the first time we met?' I asked.

'No. You need to know, they are saying,' she answered.

'Does it have anything to do with the book?' I asked to see if she knew anything else about me. I had never told her anything about my past. The only thing she knew was that I was writing a book about my patients, and my passion for my work.

'No, I don't get to find out.'

Rochelle returned to the present more easily than before. She remembered most of the session-an important part of the process. The greatest gift she gave me turned out to be her letter which she agreed to have published as a part of this book.

Rochelle's Letter, May 2003

There comes a time in everyone's life when enough is enough. Whether you are having too much of a good thing or you are in the middle of something you can't get out of, you generally know when it is time to get off of the carousel. The problem is that some people can jump off unharmed whilst the others need lots of patching up after they hit the ground. This is my time to be patched up.

If someone had told me a year ago that I would be looking at the world through my window and not actually be taking part in it I would have taken a drag on my cigarette, downed a tequila and laughed in their faces. Only they would have been right and I'm not laughing anymore.

I thought it would be easier as I got older. The longer you suppress your memories the easier it was to forget them. I had developed a great gift for the ability to forget and have no recollection of my childhood at all. I write a diary. As a child I wrote one for my mother's benefit and the other for mine. As a youngster you expect your motivation for doing something to be questioned; as an adult you expect to do the questioning. I have questioned and been questioned all of my life.

I have never had a confidante, someone that I could trust. It has, therefore, been easy for me to justify my lies to those who could not be trusted.

My plan has always been that if you home life crumbles, throw yourself into work. Whilst you are successful you are untouchable and above questioning. When the unthinkable happens and your work life begins to crumble then the flaw in your plan becomes apparent. In my arrogance I never once questioned my success. That was my downfall. The dominoes started to fall. The next thing I know I end up in the doctors' surgery, contemplating suicide and having the worst feelings of my life. I'm back on the carousel unable to get off for fear of being hurt worse still. Sensing my desperation the doctor calls in a 'crisis team'. They come and see me and tell me I'm knackered. No shit I'm knackered, thanks for your help. Anti-depressants are prescribed and I'm left alone with my turmoil. I don't take the pills and stop going out.

The doctor tries again. I'm sent someone else. A man, that's all I need. I don't need any help. My friend stays and helps me to tell this man the truth, only she doesn't know the whole truth. He talks to me and I have this overwhelming feeling of safety when he is speaking. All that he says makes sense and he hugs me when he leaves. The first time any man has spontaneously hugged me in my life. It feels strange.

I visit him at the hospital and he tells me (rather abruptly I thought) that I should visit him at his consulting rooms at the other hospital. He makes the appointment. He has no idea how much courage it took for me to leave the house to visit him this time and I'm not sure I want to go to see him again. The problem is that again I feel drawn to talking to him but I can't explain why.

So here I am. Through all of the feelings of pain and anxiety, I am as headstrong and opinionated as ever. I need reference books as proof as to what I am being told and what I'm about to go through is real enough. Only there are no reference books and yes, even the manifestation of the Lord Himself will not convince this woman of the facts that stare me in the face.

For the first time in my life I have met a person that I am completely transparent to and, for all my misgivings, I trust implicitly. These feelings are both liberating and claustrophobic. I am to find, as time goes on, that what happens when I am with him gets harder and harder to justify. He wants me to let go, to lose control and be open to the suggestion that what I go through every week will help me to overcome the increasing problems that I am facing. For the first four weeks that was never going to happen. I have lost count of the number of times that I have gone to pick up the phone during the week to cancel my appointment on Friday. My justification being that there were obviously lots more people that need his help than me. Who am I kidding? I need help. I desperately want help but find it incredibly hard to ask or accept it. I know that he can help me and something sends me back every week.

I don't need psychotherapy to tell me that what has happened to me is not my fault. I know it's not my fault. Only now I am starting to wonder. If this entire Karma thing is to be believed that 'what comes around goes around', the problem is that I now have to try and justify the rest of the crap that has happened in my life. How many people must I have murdered to have endured the torture of this life?

Even though I trust this man more than I could possibly explain, (another thing I can't explain) years and years and years of hiding the truth is not easy to break down in a month, No one on this earth knows what I have been through and I really, desperately want to tell him. Only I can't. I start to and the words don't come out. He says that he won't judge me or consider me to be a bad person. I consider me a bad person, not for what happened to me but the route my life has taken since.

From the age of 12 I was sexually abused by an older male cousin. He never had sex with me, he didn't need to-he would find other more sadistic ways to pleasure himself. He would find objects to put inside me. He used them as a scientific experiment he said. To see how far they could go in. He always measured the object then put his hand in me. After that he would either make me have oral sex or would masturbate over my face. This always ended in him crying, cleaning me up and leaving me alone until the next time he babysat. He left me alone for good after going to University. I was 14.

Two years later I was raped by the son of a very good friend of the family. His father and my father were in the Police force together. He knew I could never tell anyone. He took me to his house while his parents were away. He tied me to a hook at the head of his bed and raped and buggered me for 6 hours. He too put other things inside me but he did it to see how long it would take me to scream in pain. He dumped me in a field 4 miles from home. I went home 3 days later after staying at a friend's house. He taunted me in phone calls and his father and my father are still friends. He is now a serving police officer.

So here I am, if I am to believe the last few weeks the man that raped me is following me from life to life to exact his revenge on me. How much of this can I believe? I suppose more to the point, how much of this do I allow myself to believe? I don't know which way to turn. Nothing is getting better for me at home. In fact I'd say I was worse. I have been told though that I am acting less like an egg!

It's like I'm in the middle of a maze. I can see the way I came in but I can't get out that way. I can't see the way out but I know it exists. It is a feeling of hope and hopelessness all together and consumes my every waking moment.

Through all of my experiences so far I have learned one thing. You can control what you say even in another state of mind. I see things that I don't share.

After my first experience I had incredibly bad headaches all week and was concerned that they would never go away. I could justify my experience that week as it was a childhood memory and I told him this on my return the following week. Even so I was disturbed and couldn't see the help in the whole thing. It still took me 20 minutes to coax myself into the car to go and see him for a second time and the panic attacks about being late still sent me close to the point of going home. Then he spoke to me and all was well.

In my second experience I was a man in uniform, living in London with my wife in the early 20ʰ century. The rapist was there as my brother and I recognised my wife too. I didn't tell him that though. My wife died young and so did I just before the war. I had a heart disease. My justification for this one was also fairly easy. It was probably a story in a book that I'd read. I went back next week and told him the same. He smiled. During the week leading up to my third session I had flashes of the rapists face in my dreams. Not just in this time but as all sorts of people. I didn't tell him that either for fear of being locked up as a loony. The other problem that I was having was that I could start to feel the presence of other people coming to me also, mostly at night but also if I were daydreaming. It was scary and I didn't tell him this due the same fear. The difficulty was this then breeds a sense of guilt as I then felt that I was repeating the pattern of dishonesty that had been my life to that point. I went with the intention of telling him during week three but it didn't happen.

And so it goes on. Week three could be explained away as this was just my relatives. I would have known what they would have said to me if asked. I go home completely exhausted and have a horrible week. My grandfather comes back to me during this week, nearly every night. He brings others with him and I am given messages that I don't understand. I fall asleep more quickly than I have done for years this week. But I feel like I haven't slept. I see hundreds of movie reel images. I see flashes of images of people that I know but not looking the same as they do now. My trusted doctor also appears. I need a rest. Bruises that I can't explain start to appear on my thighs and my wrists. This is not a good week for me and I'm on the verge of jacking the whole thing in. Then something odd happened. I went to pick my son up from playgroup and a woman that I haven't spoken to before started to talk to me. She seems convinced that we've met before. After a little while it becomes apparent that we can't have, coming from different areas, so she smiles and collects her son saying "It must have been in another life" and goes to her car. We haven't spoken since and just exchange smiles.

I go back for my fourth week and tell him about the movie reels but not about my grandfather. I feel an urge to tell him some more and we spend a lot of the session talking. Then he offers me therapy even though he is to miss lunch to do it, I really want to say no but equally want to say yes too. I want him to help me and feel incredibly close to him this week. I am more relaxed than ever before during this session but what follows is incredibly weird.

I am a young French girl called Alexandra and I am speaking to this man in French. I am being abused by my father (the rape perpetrator again). I don't speak French. I could probably get by asking for the toilet and the menu and that's about it. I am extremely freaked out by this session and cry for the first time on my way home. I get home and cry at night. The first night I start to go to sleep and I have horrendous flashbacks of being that little girl in France. Only it seems that my father was not the only one abusing me and there are lots of pairs of eyes there that I recognise in the ensemble of men my father has collected. I cannot sleep for the rest of the week and even go to the drastic measure of calling my GP and telling her. She offers me sleeping tablets and anti-depressants. I decline her offer and decide to phone and cancel Friday's appointment. Just as I went to the phone it rings. It's his secretary changing my appointment time. I tell her how I've been this week (not the whole truth of course) and she gives me the option not to come. Yes, I have a get out clause, I have a bone fide way out only I find myself saying that I'll come. I put the phone down and plan my leaving speech.

Friday comes and this time I have to tell him. I have to tell him everything then I have to walk out. We start a conversation. I'm waiting for the right time to tell him and then BANG, it hits me. He's right and he appears to have seen through my soul again. He hits the nail on the head. It would take more than god Himself appearing in the room to convince me. I want to scream, cry and thump him. He makes me so mad. He wants me just to open my mind to the suggestion that all this is helping and that I stop controlling everything and everyone around me. I want to be able to lose control, to go mad. I want to be able to look good and lose weight but of course I can't. I want to be able to walk out of my front door with the ease that I used to. I want to be able to love my children like a mother should, not control their lives. I want him to make it easy for me but he doesn't. I hate him for that but I love him for his complete faith and respect him for his persistence. And then it's time to go back. I see several scenes before reaching the one in this life that we are going to. I'm being raped again. This time I feel a great sense of distress whilst watching the scene. The first time ever I am afraid. Then grandfather arrives and takes me on a journey to show me how I murdered the rapist. I have immense feelings of anger and sadness. I come back to the room that I started in. I go home. Not crying this time.

I've slept for longer periods this week and with much more peacefulness, I still see things and they've started to manifest themselves as mini premonitions. It could just be déjà vu.

I'm sure that I'll get better. I left my house on my own to go shopping this week for the second time in 6 months and it didn't take me so long to get out. I'm sure I'm going to resign from my job soon. My husband and I are having some problems and he has informed me this week that I am not only fat but neurotic too. I can't get angry with him.

I'm sure my life will never be the same again and I'm sure that I've been found by this incredible man for a reason.

I'm lost in the maze and I want to get out. Do I believe? Maybe I do, maybe I don't but surely it's more important that I am learning to trust what I see. I feel as if I was travelling this life alone until he found me. I will get better.

Rochelle Lamére (Pseudonym)

Lessons of Love

The vacation in Sicily gave me so much strength. The clear ocean. The high mountains with breezing yellow fields and carefully placed stone walls. The endless rolling of waves towards the beach below our rented apartment outside of Pozallo. Everything had been a perfect framing for the future. My energy had been recharged. At the same time I had continued my studies of quantum physics. Several pieces of the puzzle had fallen into place regarding the connection between elementary particles, dimensional wormholes and photons as a carrier of information between a world and a mirror world. My theory of the true quantum brain had started to form. It had been more than two weeks until I once again saw Rochelle at the clinic.

Rochelle sat melancholically in the corner of the sofa. She had lost a very close friend in a car accident on the M25 just two weeks earlier. She was sad and quiet. At the same time there was strength, a life force, which was slowly but surely becoming more prominent in her appearance. Truly, she seemed to be on the road to recovery.

'How are you?'

'I'm not as bad now. My anxiety is not as bad and my mood is less chaotic. I had a horrible fight with my sons last week. My thirteen year old pushed me down the stairs. I became blinded by rage and grabbed his throat and pushed him up against the wall.'

'Why do you think this happened?' I asked.

'My husband and I had a discussion if we should send him back to his father,' she said.

'You know what is best for yourself, of course, but may I suggest that you let your husband into your life a bit. Many things could get easier.'

***

'Where are you?' I asked.

'Inside a tent. I am being prepared' she answered enigmatically.

'What for?'

'To meet them?'

'Who?'

'Your master. He is Rohden.'

'What clothes are you wearing?' I wondered.

'A white dress. Nothing on my feet, but wedding gold in my hair,' she answered.

'Oh, are you getting married?'

'No, I am going to die,' she replied.

'Why? I asked, taken aback for a moment.

'To be united with them.'

'Are you alone in the tent?'

'No.'

'Who is there?'

'The ones preparing me.'

'What country can you see?'

'Denmark but… no, Denmark is not quite right.'

'What year do you see?' I asked.

'922,' she answered decidedly.

'What is the name of the location you are at?'

'Mudden.'

'How old are you?'

'17 years.'

'Why have you decided to die?'

'Because they asked me,' she replied.

'How do you die?' I asked.

'She kills me. The angel. She brings death. I am held, and she cuts my throat. I can't see it.'

'What do you do just before you die?'

'I visit other tents, so they can show him.'

'What?'

'Love. In each tent they take my body like a man takes a woman.'

'Are you scared?'

'No.'

'How many tents are there?'

'Seven.'

'What is the reason for all of this?'

'Love,' Rochelle said.

'Do you love life?' I asked.

'Yes, it makes him happy. Worship of Odin – faethin.' Her words were difficult to recognize.

'Look at all the faces around you in the tent. Do you recognize anyone?'

'Yes, Jane. She's my sister. There are no men, only women in the tent.'

'What is Jane's name as the woman in the tent?'

'Freyn.'

'Has this happened in this location before?' I asked.

'No. It occurs out of love,' she answered.

'Why do you choose to die?'

'To save her. She is my sister. She is so beautiful.'

I took Rochelle to the moment after her death in a life where she was sacrificed. 'Do they bury you?'

'No, I'm on a burning boat that is sent out into the sea.'

'Why?'

'Journey,' Rochelle said.

'Where?' I asked.

'To the other side.'

'What happened in the afterlife?'

'I was greeted by them… the teachers.'

'Are you happy?'

'Yes. They planned everything.'

'Why?'

'To teach about love.'

'What do your teachers say now?' I asked.

'Man is cunning without love. With love he is wise,' she said.

'What must you do in order to understand?'

'Things are wrong. I have to find it. I must learn to trust and love others. It is taking too long.'

'And what should I do?' I asked on an egocentric whim.

'Time is to see far. You will find more. Your thoughts are correct. It is true.'

The following week Rochelle told me she had been haunted by strong memories of how she was killed. 'They tied ropes around my neck, my feet and my body. I saw soldiers with shields standing in a circle around the tent. I was then almost garrotted before I was pulled and torn by two horses. It was about showing love through the one you killed. It was disgusting. All of this is threatening to completely consume me,' she said.

I realised how important it was not only for Rochelle, but for all of my patients to share their vivid experiences. Rochelle had an enormous unmet need of conveying everything she had been through. It showed me once again that I was only told a fraction from that timeless dimension where my patients existed in joy, sorrow, hate and suffering. Rochelle had a strange ability to increasingly and easily disappear into the relaxation's non-physical realm. Yet it was with jealousy, and sometimes real nagging, that I tried to get some answers. For each patient I was becoming more and more aware that I was constantly playing catch up. Assumptions and speculations were often incorrect, and it was becoming all the more important to ask questions that made a real contribution.

***

'What do you see?'

'People.'

'What clothes do you have?'

'A pink dress and pink shoes,' she replied.

'How old are you?'

'39,' she responded instantly.

'What year is it?' I asked per my usual instructions.

'1616,' she said just as confidently as before. The session was as natural for her as reporting back from a party in her real life.

'What are you doing?'

'I'm at a wedding. My daughter is getting married.'

'What is her name?'

'Flora.'

'What is your husband doing?'

'Waiting.'

'Look into your daughters eyes. Do you recognize anyone?'

'Kathy, my sister.'

'What is the name of the location of the wedding?'

'Bascondor.'

'Are there many guests?'

'Yes.'

'And your husband, where is he?' I asked.

'He has gone outside with the lord,' she said.

'Who is your husband?'

'The Duke of Wookingham.'

'How many children do you have?'

'Two girls.'

'What is the name of your husband?'

'John Trenskand.'

'What is your name?'

'Edith.'

'How old were you when you married?' I asked.

'17 years,' Rochelle said.

'Are you wealthy?'

'Yes.'

'Have you ever travelled outside of England?'

'We have been to Umbria in Italy. We travelled by boat and horse.'

'Did you ever go back there?'

'No. I became alone. John left me.'

'Did he die?'

'Yes. Four years after the wedding. I never remarried.'

'Look into John's eyes. Anyone you recognize from your current life?'

'No.'

'Is your daughter happy?'

'Yes.'

'Do you have music?'

'Yes, very beautiful music.'

'Are you dancing?'

'Yes, we're dancing quartz.'

I took Rochelle to the moment of her death. 'What do you see?'

'My family,' she replied.

'What are they doing?'

'Saying goodbye.'

'Are you ill?'

'Yes, I have been sick with flu for a few weeks.'

'Are you scared?'

'No. I want to be with John. I say goodbye to my daughters.'

'What is the name of the house where you die?'

'Bascondor.'

'What did you learn from this life?'

'To not fear separation,' she said with a calm and firm voice.

I then moved Rochelle to the light. Her voice became very quiet, almost inaudible. With my usual folly I asked her if she knew how the work with the book would end. 'Who are you with now?' I asked her.

'Higher beings.'

'What are they saying?'

'You can only finish when it is complete. The book is published in many countries. You are too worried. You know. You are never alone. Your work is valued here. Look outside yourself. Trust yourself.'

When I researched I found a Sir John and Lady Zouche of Conder Castle who lived during the 16th century. It is unclear if it these were the ones Rochelle spoke of.

***

Rochelle was sitting with me during the last session as we evaluated our sessions. 'I feel stronger now than ever. I've gone from a mental wreck to self-enlightenment and finding joy in life. I suffered from panic attacks, I was depressed, gained weight, and felt completely bombarded by all the medication. On Saturday I'm going to a wedding and nothing frightens me anymore. But the world around me is starting to collapse. I lost my best friend in child birth. A few months ago my closest male friend died in a car accident. I have two failed marriages behind me, and now it seems like my current husband will leave me too. Do you really think that is such a success?' she asked me.

'No. Not at all. But I did warn you that there would be no return. You would grow strong but you would also be perceived differently by your surroundings. To switch from 'a mental wreck' to self-enlightenment and self-confidence represents a toll on the outside world. People arrange themselves and their systems according to weak individuals' abilities. When someone unexpectedly breaks out of the system and recovers, it takes a while before you can rearrange yourself mentally. Old friends might turn their back on you, their concern reveals itself to be selfishly planned. True friends can often be counted on a single hand. My patients never ever denied that their recovery not only changed the surrounding world's treatment of them, but they also started to discover the illusions and self-delusions. It is not easy, but you chose this path.'

'Yes, I did,' she replied after a moment's hesitation. Rochelle completed her treatment and created an exceptional career for herself. She became a student at Cambridge University and later became a college teacher. She was, and is, deeply loved by her students. Her marriage lasted and she has continued her life without medications or psychiatric care. She is and always will continue to be a good friend. In other words, a wonderful outcome for a seriously tormented soul!

Generations of Hatred

T he woman was fifty-five years old and had been referred by her GP based on difficult anxiety. It would be revealed that she had suffered recurring anxiety through large portions of her life. I initially met her in Rochford where I once again faced the challenge of a patient who refused all pharmaceutical treatment. She had been given a large variety of pills from different doctors throughout the years. Nothing helped against her nightmares, anxiety, disrupted sleeping and recurring depressions. She had two grown up children as well as a comforting and sympathetic husband. Once she had started to trust our relationship she told of how her father had regularly sexually abused her from when she was nine to twelve years old. During the past twenty-six years she had been taking Lorazepam, an addictive sedative, against her serious anxiety. Now she was taking 4 mg every day. She did not wish to tell me anything else.

She later described how her father had tied her feet to the bed and thereafter repeatedly sexually assaulted her. Sandy said she hated her father and that she would never forgive him. I assessed her as a suitable candidate and described my methodology. She didn't think twice. The following Friday she came to the hospital in Runwell for her first deep relaxation. The first session was, as in most cases, simply practise in pure relaxation. Sandy was in truth a very warm and openhearted woman. These would be her allies during the fight against the source of her anxiety. The first session proceeded admirably, even though she expressed some worry in regards to the work that lay ahead of her. Sandy described how incredibly peaceful she felt in the light. She described a yellowish shimmer. I never let her get close to either her childhood or any past lives. She still said it was a warm and pleasant experience.

She was a little bit excited by the experience, even if I had trouble understanding why.

During the second session Sandy once again exhibited an excellent ability to relax. I instructed her that she could travel to any point in the past or the present. After twenty minutes, I asked her what she could see. As in the past, I felt that I was simply a guide, a privileged fellow traveller without any ability to predict.

Sandy took me to a place I had expected least of all.

'I can see my father.'

'Really, you see your father. Is he alone?'

'No, my mother is also there. She hates me. He asks why I didn't attend his funeral,' she continued.

'What is he wearing?' I asked.

'He is nude.'

'Oh, nude... Your mother then? What is she wearing?' I asked.

'Some kind of gown that goes all the way to her feet,' Sandy said.

'Where are they? Do you see any trees, flowers or a landscape?'

'They are in a state after death but before they can pass on. They just float around.'

'And does he tell you why he did what he did?'

'Yes, he is deeply sorry for what he did. He says that he loved me, and that he slept with me because he was not allowed to sleep with my mother. Oh... he says that it wasn't an accident when he died. He wanted to die. That day it had rained, and he knew that the crane where he was working was old and rusty. When he stood on it, it came crashing down.'

Her story was surprising and unexpected. According to her, her father had really died through suicide, and not by accident as everyone, including herself, had believed. She seemed neither happy nor sad from his revelation, but her conversation with him showed a new dimension of processing and suffering. She knew that he could no longer hurt her, so she dared to ask questions and behold his nakedness. She later told me that her mother was still alive, but that she hated Sandy. They had not been in touch for a long time.

'He wants me to forgive him' she erupted.

'Why?'

'Because otherwise he cannot leave from where they are. He must have my forgiveness... oh...' She sighed but seemed calm and comfortable.

'Can you forgive him?'

'No, not yet.' When she returned to herself she told me that it had felt as if she had received a key in her left hand. 'If I forgive him I will forever be free.' She said it in such a tone that there was no room for doubt. She truly meant and believed what she was saying. I was overwhelmed by her insightfulness. Even though she did not seem educated or intellectual her knowledge seem to stem from a deeper consciousness. There seemed to be hope even for Sandy.

When she returned after the second session she was in good spirits. She had just had a grandson. Out of joy she had called her mother to tell her the news, but she had just said she wasn't interested and hung up. While Sandy's father was alive he had been extremely jealous. According to Sandy he would take her mother straight home if she as much as accidentally looked at another man on the street. 'It seemed to consume him', Sandy said.

Sandy also told me something she found strange. Her husband had told her that after the second session it was as if she had completely changed. On her own part she had discovered that she did not blame herself any longer for her father's abuse. 'He said that it was as if I was a completely different person, calm and with brand new self-confidence. It only lasted a few hours, but he said that he hoped I could become like that.'

Sandy relaxed. Her face softened and her breath became almost unnoticeable. Slowly her eyes started to move under her eyelids. 'What are you doing?'

'... My father enters my bedroom. He pulls me by the hair into his bedroom, and tears my nightgown apart. He threatens me with violence if I make any noise. He says that if I get any marks on my body it is from fighting with my sister... Oh, I cannot think. I am completely naked, crying...' Sandy said as she was moaning, twisting and turning on the sofa.

'Does he ask you to take his thing in your mouth?' I asked.

'No, he puts it up my butt. Oh, it hurts so much. Terribly painful. I scream and my sister stands outside the door and is wondering what is happening,' Sandy said.

'Where is your mother?'

'She is out shopping with her mother every Saturday.'

'What does your dad do when he is finished?' I asked her carefully.

'He takes me back to my bedroom. My body hurts so much. I just lay completely still. I hate her.'

'Your mother?'

'Yes. My dad wants me to take a bath. My sister helps me. I can't sit so I lay on my knees. There is blood in the water. Then I return to my bedroom.'

'How often does this dreadful thing happen to you?' I asked.

'Every Saturday. Every Saturday when my mom is out shopping,' she answered.

'What does your dad do afterwards?'

'He buys me sweets, but I throw them away.'

I calm her down and reassure her existence and that she in no way whatsoever is to blame for these actions. After a while I take her back again. I am hoping that she can find a deeper reason for the evils that are happening to her, but once again she ends up in her horrible childhood traumas.

'My mom is shouting and fighting. She pushes me into my bedroom and asks me if I liked it, then she hits me behind with a broom. I tell her that I am just ten years old. Mom and dad are fighting. I can hear them shouting in the bedroom. Dad shouts at mom: "You never want to have sex with me, so I take your daughter".' Sandy continued: 'Mom says that I'm a slut, and that she never wanted me and she really hates me. She says that I'm so evil that I will end up burning in hell. When I get my menstruation I ask her what it means, and she says it's because I am so evil. She shouts that I will never be married. My dad says that if I stand next to a boy when I have my period I will get pregnant... Oh, that's why I never dared to be close to any boys.'

I decide to take Sandy out of her torments. Even though she has been instructed that she is just an observer, it seems incredibly taxing on her. She seems to really suffer. I take her into the light and let her rest her mind there. After a good while I tell her that she is no longer alone, that someone will be there.

'Laureen is here' she said.

'Who is Laureen?' I ask.

'She is my father's sister. She says that she always knew what he was doing. Laureen is with her son now. She is happy. She dances with her son.'

Laureen was wearing a long black orange skirt with many holes, and she started to tell Sandy why she had to suffer so much.

'She says that the reason was that my mother and her brother were sexually insane. She says that my mother never wanted to have sex. When I was born my father took care of me. She says that he was like a mother to me. And then my mother turned him against me. My mother was very stubborn, she says. She never cared about me.' She spoke spontaneously at great length. In contrast to other patients I did not need to ask that many questions–she described things as if she was watching a movie.

'Does Laureen say anything about how your mother will end up?'

'She will die with her hate. She is bitter and she will never find happiness.'

'Will she be reborn?' I asked.

Sandy's answer surprised me. 'No. Only kind people will be reincarnated from now on.'

'But then, were will she go?' I asked a bit puzzled.

'She won't return. Neither will my father. Laureen says that she saw me as her daughter. Oh, my dad is standing behind her. She says that he wishes I could forgive him,' Sandy said.

'Does she tell you how it ends for your mother?' I asked.

'She had an operation six months ago. They removed a piece of her lung. She worked at a petrol station for many years. Laureen says that she will die in her sleep. She won't suffer at all, but she does not have it good now. She will live around three more years,' she said.

'Does she think it's good for you doing this?'

'She tells me to free my mind. There is no other way. She says that she can see how I will feel good, and that I have a good husband. She tells me that I must be kinder towards him. Sometimes I hate him. He is dirty. I am dirty. She must leave now… I will be well…'

When she returned to the real world she was astonished when I told her that she had been gone for 70 minutes. She thought it had been at most ten minutes. Once again time had simply disappeared. When she left me I convinced her that I was not disputing or judging, either her or her relatives. That everything was possible and to me the healing process was the master. It was a crooked road, and with closed minds and prejudices we could never reach our goal.

***

'I'm sitting in the garden. I'm laughing and playing and dressing a doll. I am seven and my sister is two. I look after her. She is my only friend.'

'What clothes are you wearing?'

'It is a hot summer day. I have a t-shirt. I always have the same clothes.'

'Where are your mom and dad?' I asked.

'She is in the kitchen. Dad is on his way back from work… Dad is coming… I'm scared.' She started to breathe more rapidly and seemed scared. I reminded her that she was just observing, incapable of feeling pain. She calmed down.

'Dad calls my sister. He has sweets for her. But I have been naughty. I hide so I don't get punished… I see him speaking to the lady next door… it is cold. We are sitting at the table drinking tea, but my dad pulls me out the backdoor. He's shouting. He forces me to put my hands on the doorpost as he slams the door on my hands while he's laughing. I scream and cry. I wanted him to spank me, but he just does this again and again… I have to go upstairs without food.'

'Why is your dad doing this?' I asked, despairing over humanity's capability for evil and wrath.

'I was nasty because the neighbour girl teased me so I pulled her hair.'

'Does your father often beat you this seriously?'

'Yes, if I speak back to mom. Then he beats me with his belt.'

'Do you hate him?' I asked.

'Yes... I just want to leave.' Sandy said.

'What does your mother do when he beats you?'

'She walks away. She is not in the house. She says that he is the master of the house and it is only he who beats me.'

I decided to do another experiment. I felt intuitively that Sandy had access to all the knowledge. I calmed and comforted her, and told her that after the assault she would go into her parents' bedroom. They would not notice her presence.

'You're an invisible guest. They can neither see nor hear you.'

'They are wondering why I'm so naughty. Mom says that I don't help out. Dad says that he loves me more than anything else in the world. I can see the rage in my mother's eyes when he says it. He keeps talking and says that he can't wait for me to grow up, so that he can have me all to himself. He says that he wants to have a child with me, and that he wants to hide me away forever from the world if he can't have me all to himself. Mom says that he is crazy, and she pushes him aside when he gets close to her. She cries. She asks if he's joking but he says "no".' Sandy talks for a long time and without any hesitation. All the years of anxiety and rage pour out of her. No matter how gruesome the details, she calmly describes her mom and dad.

'Why is he doing this? Can you perceive his emotions?'

'It is something within him. He is completely obsessed with marrying me. He is going to kill me if I marry anyone else,' Sandy answered.

'Sandy, can you register where your guilt comes from?' I asked, now feeling certain that Sandy would be able to become whole again.

'Yes, from my mother. She never thought it would happen. He never gets to cuddle with her.'

'Doesn't she want to leave him?'

154

'No, she loves him too much. He takes what he wants. He forces himself upon her... "You are mine, mine," he says. I take what I want,' Sandy continued, speaking as her father.

I then moved Sandy to the state of pure light. There I asked her if she could notice the presence of her father.

'He is here. He has a shirt and long black trousers, black shoes and socks. He says that he is looking after my child... Yes, I lost a child, Anna-Belle, when she was 8 months old.'

Nothing surprised me any longer, yet I was slightly astounded as I listened to her. 'How did your daughter die?' I asked her carefully.

'When I was out on a walk. She was so beautiful. She says that she wasn't normal when she was born. She was ill, that's why she died.'

'Does she want to return to Earth?' I asked.

'She can't because of dad. But she is happy, she says. Through her I can forgive him,' Sandy said.

'What is it that you must understand?'

'It was his way of showing love. He realises now that he was wrong. It is natural that he suffers, he was wrong. But he's looking after my daughter because of it.'

'If you could forgive him Sandy, what would he do then?'

'He could only go through the door into a garden.'

'Why does the door not open?' I asked curiously.

'There is no one there. The door opens itself. It knows. It does not open if you have been evil. Anna-Belle can pass through it alone. If he goes she will also go. Anna-Belle is the child we would have had together. It is his fault that she died. He wanted her to go. He never rested. He cannot let go of me. He is still obsessed with her.' It now seemed as if Anna-Belle was speaking through and about Sandy.

'Can he not let go of you from the other side?' I asked slightly worried.

'No he cannot. He is trying. He is scared and wants me to try and forgive him. He understands and he sees her joy.'

'Is he willing to pay the price by letting you go?'

'He isn't sure. He starts walking towards the door. If he gets through it then he can let go. He wants to try. Anna-Belle waits behind the door. She can walk through it. She can hear him but not reach him.'

***

It was the beginning of March 2003. Sandy had suffered severe headaches since the last session, and she also had strong "flashbacks". She told me that when she was 18 and 35 years old she had tried to commit suicide by using pills. She also confided that sexuality had always felt dirty and unpleasant–she had never been able to take any pleasure from it.

'What do you see?'

'I am five years old. Mom comes through the door with a baby. It is a girl. I am a little jealous. Mom is so obsessed and not even dad is allowed to hold her. I sit on the stairs. I can hear her say "Not another girl, I hate it". My dad has been to prison in his youth.'

As she is speaking I realise that she might be experiencing things that are completely unknown to her conscious self. During the relaxation she seems to use the ability to listen to others more so than before. 'Why did he go to prison? Did you know this in the life you've lived?' I asked.

'No, I knew nothing. He raped a girl. My mother knows nothing, but she is scared and suspects that something is wrong. She would never have married him if she knew. I can hear people speaking to him. My grandmother says to him that she's ashamed of him. She says that he will never change. I sit on the stairs crying,' Sandy continued.

I decided to increase the pace of the therapy, as closure felt imminent. I wanted a breakthrough–to get Sandy to understand the origin of her suffering.

'Go back to your father's childhood. Everything is possible. I will remain by your side and never fail you. Relax deeper. The light surrounds you, and you will go there when I have counted down from three to one. What is your father doing?'

'He plays with some other boys. He is 15. They bully him. He stands and cries. It isn't physically but with words. They just push him around. He goes home and his mother asks him why he's been crying. He replies that he hasn't cried, and his father then says that he shouldn't lie to his mother. He says that he will teach him. He removes his belt and beats him badly out in the garden. It is raining. My father gets no food or tea. His whole back is bleeding and he feels useless. His father keeps telling him to become a man and stop being useless. His father says that he will never become a man. From that moment on my dad hates his father. My dad has an older sister and she comforts him afterwards. She removes the flannel shirt and washes of the blood.'

Everything was pouring out of Sandy. I asked very few questions, and it was as if she was watching a movie at the cinema. Her eyes were moving rapidly in a REM phase under the eyelids. I asked her to go to her grandfather's death to extend the search for answers.

'He's lying in the bed on the second floor. My grandmother sits with him. It is too late to make things right. He wants to see his son but he refuses to come. My grandfather regrets all the hate. It came from the war. He lost his best friend who got blown up in front of his eyes. After that my grandfather just used people. He had so much hate. He killed people during the war, and he loved it. He regrets this deeply. He wishes to meet his son and wife, and wish for them to forgive him. My dad did not attend the funeral. Grandma is crying, and she and his sister try to convince him to go, but he refuses,' Sandy said without a question asked.

I then move Sandy into the light in the afterlife. I instruct her to, if it is possible, meet her grandfather to answer her questions. 'Can you see him?' I ask.

'Yes, he is handsome in his uniform. I can see the hole in the neck after where he was shot during the war. He says that my dad loved me and that I have to forgive myself. He does not want to see me full of hatred, he wants me to be happy. He says it is his fault.'

'Does he think you are doing the right thing now, trying to find answers?'

'Yes, at last things can be made right. No one listened. He says it is time to leave the past behind. He says he can see me happy again,' Sandy said.

'Do you have a guide?' I asked her, never having mentioned the subject before.

'Someone named Angelica,' she answered.

'Ask her why you needed to suffer!'

'I didn't choose it, my father did. He had a dreadful headache, which made him do terrible things. He completely lost his mind.'

'How many lives have you lived?' certain to hear the usual answer of 30, 40 or more.

'This is my second life. My first one was in Egypt many years ago.'

Sandy then told how she thought she lived in Egypt around the year 1104, but she wasn't sure. She had only two lives because she didn't want to be reborn. She had no children, and in her Egyptian life she died by the age of thirty when her husband killed her by decapitation. 'Look into your husband's eyes from back then. Is it someone you recognise from this life?' I asked.

'No, I have never seen him,' she said.

'What can you see in Egypt?'

'Sand.'

'What did you do in the afterlife after the death in Egypt?'

'I sat in a garden observing different people.'

'Why did you come back to this life?'

'Punishment! For everything I had done. It was horrible. I killed another woman. She was awful, but more beautiful than me. Oh... it was my mother' Sandy said with a heavy sigh.

'What have you managed to learn about hate?'

'Yes that is why she has always hated me. She doesn't know, but I know why. But it is too late now to do anything about it.'

'Is it important to forgive her?' I asked.

'No, I cannot do anything,' Sandy said without a shiver of doubt.

'Does the suffering serve a purpose?'

'Yes, I have to forgive him. I feel warm. I love him so much. I wish I could have told him that. Angelica walks away.'

When Sandy rose tired and dizzy it was as if a miracle had occurred. Her face smiled radiantly, and I felt confident that she would be fully healed. It was not important if the events were scientifically true. To Sandy all of this was true, and that was more than enough after 51 years of suffering. Finally it would give her a life of harmony and joy.

***

During the next session I realised that Sandy had returned to an earlier part of her current life. She had been working in a hardware store for four months. She described her boss as a kind gentleman. She was fifteen years old. In contrast to before, there was now also something positive in her story.

'How did you get the job?'

'I just went in asking for work. He hired me and now I work there part-time.'

'How much are you earning?' I asked.

'Ten pounds a week. My mom takes everything except one pound,' Sandy said.

'What happens if you don't give her the money?'

'Then she hits me and shouts. But I never told her I got a raise,' Sandy smirked.

I smiled to myself. There was room for a little bit of humour and survival instinct during her tragic upbringing. With a few simple instructions I moved Sandy to the most important time at the age of 15. 'What are you doing?'

'I am walking along the beach with my sister. I have met my husband. One day he drove up along the beach with his little Omni. He asked us if we wanted a ride. I had never done anything like that before. We went to a pub. I felt safe. It felt as if I had always known him. Oh, I felt needed, loved, safe and happy. I don't know what love is,' she replied.

'What is your sister doing?'

'She is with any man. Peter and I sat and talked for hours.'

'Look into his eyes. Is it anyone you recognize?' I asked.

'They look like Dougye in Egypt,' she answered.

'What is Peter saying?'

'He asks if he will get to meet me again. After a week he asked me to marry him. It was in January. I was desperate to get away from home. In March we got engaged. I told mom. The next day she threw me out.'

'Where did you go?'

'I lived with a friend. I was happy. In September we got married.'

I had to interrupt Sandy here and carefully take her back. Every session made her stronger. Everything would be fine. When she came back she was ecstatic. Her joy spread irresistibly into my soul and mind. It was as if she had been magically transformed into her true self. Sandy had found her own true self.

'If you knew how I miss Egypt. I really appreciated that life. I belonged there. I have gotten so close to my father now. I forgave him after the last week. I love him. It made me so warm, a strange feeling. He is at rest now. I saw his face. Before it was a mask. He is not in front of the door any longer. He has moved on,' Sandy said as we spoke for a few minutes before she once again lay down on the sofa.

'What do you see?' I asked.

'I see my dad. He's in a wheelchair,' Sandy said.

'Does he know that you've forgiven him?'

'Yes. It is time to give him the key now. I put it in his hand. He rises from the chair and walks towards the door. He has been longing for this. He waves, ready to go. Anna-Belle walks alongside him holding his hand. They turn around. They open the door. They have waited for me and wished for this. I love him. They close the door. I say goodbye to Anna-Belle. The door has closed. He is gone,' Sandy whispered.

'Are you sad?'

'No, happy.'

After this intense experience during which, she slid over into a calm and relaxed state. I let her for the last time make the inter-dimensional spiritual journey back to her beloved Egypt. Perhaps it was my own unspoken longing. Eons of time. Love and hate. Hidden knowledge and invisible treasures–everything was buried in the eternal ocean of human knowledge. Just like a rising Phoenix, the pain and death perhaps in the end made us all understand our beginnings and our goal. We all carried, myself included, a desire to find out our true origins.

***

'What do you see?'

'I'm sitting at a table with my husband. There is music and dancing.'

'Why are you sitting there?' I asked.

'I make people happy. My mother is also at the table. She is so beautiful. She sits in a man's lap. She desires my husband. She is a servant and fills the glasses with wine. She puts her hand around my husband's shoulder and he hits her behind. No, I'm not angry with him. I start flirting with another man. A soldier,' Sandy responded.

'Look into the soldier's eyes. Anyone you recognize?'

'Yes, it is Dougye. I made love with him. My husband became angry.'

'What happened to your soldier?'

'I wanted to be with him, but my mother told my husband who tied Dougye up and tortured him. No, they didn't kill him. His head is hanging. I hate my mother. She is in bed with my husband.'

'When did you decide to kill her? I asked.'

'As soon as they took her away. She destroyed my life,' Sandy said.

'How did you kill her?'

'With a dagger. I have it behind my back. She lay on the bed and I stabbed her in the back. She screamed and called me witch. My husband sees the dagger and I hate myself. He says that no one else can have me. The guards took me away. I did not want to live if I could not be with the soldier. My husband killed me. He decapitated me.'

'What was your husband's name?' I asked, moved by the bloody tale.

'I can't hear the name. It is very difficult.'

'When you were at the table with all the guests, where in Egypt were you?'

'There are so many temples and lots of sphinxes. They form a large circle. The temples and buildings are so beautiful. There is lots of sand,' Sandy said.

'Can you see the name of the city?' I asked.

'Mm, yes, I can see a name… Caro. The king and Queen lives there.'

'Do you see anything else?'

'Soldiers. They fight but I don't know why. There is a lot of trouble. Someone has taken land that does not belong to them. There is a market. I am in the background and I can hear people speaking to each other at the marketplace.'

'What do they say?' I asked.

'They are talking about how much they like the king. The women talk about how they want to work as servants,' Sandy answered. She never used the word "Pharaoh" during the session.

'Can you hear anything important?' I asked.

'I hear men talking. Can they see me?' she responded.

'No, you're hidden behind a screen. No one can see or hear you.'

Sandy seemed scared. I did not understand why until she said:

'The men are saying the king will not be king for much longer. He will be killed. It will happen very soon.'

I decided to spare Sandy any more unpleasantness. With ease she returned into the soothing light. 'Are you alone? Do you have a guide?'

'Yes, I have Angelica. She tells me to be happy and to take care of myself. "Follow your heart," she says. I should do what I want to do.'

When Sandy returned to her conscious self she stayed for a few minutes in my office. 'I have started to grow strong again. I must stand tall and forget. I must love even if I have been mistreated. I feel satisfied. This would not be possible through any other treatment method. I am free and don't feel afraid any longer. I can forgive. I am happy,' she said before leaving my office.

Sandy had encountered several different opinions from different doctors in regards to her anxiety medication. Someone had abruptly cancelled her prescription with the argument that she had come to abuse the medication. Another one had continued it as usual. I encouraged

Sandy to very slowly start reducing the dosage. Taking six months to a year would be absolutely fine, because otherwise the withdrawal symptoms might become too difficult. Sandy was eager to start something she had always feared. She said that she no longer needed the medication. Before Sandy left she wanted to give me a gift. She was not sure if I would accept it, but she said it was important to her.

'I need nothing. The salary is good, but the greatest reward is seeing you and all my other patients improve. Nothing can compete with that. The greatest gift is to see someone recover!' I said.

Sandy handed me a few simple notebooks, a pen and a black tie with a green dragon. The most beautiful of her gifts was in an envelope. There were written the lines that I will always remember:

'Thank you for giving me back my life!'

Buried Alive

Jo was referred to me by her GP. She had lost her husband a few years earlier in a tragic workplace accident. She was now single with two young girls. Jo suffered from depression and difficult reoccurring anxiety. She had been treated with several different anti-depressants without any result. Now she was sitting glumly in front of me in the examination room. Her youngest daughter suffered nightmares, and sometimes spoke of seeing her dead dad and other spiritual entities. It was obvious that Jo was in a very bad mental state. Jo came to have a total of 15 sessions with me. Some of these would prove to be revolutionary not only for her, but for me as a doctor, fellow human being and spiritual seeker.

Jo was describing herself sitting under a tree with her dead husband by her side. She described him as funny, with a great sense of humour.

'He's laughing. He really did draw the shortest straw when he died, leaving me with the girls,' she said.

'Why do people normally not remember their past lives?' I asked.

'Because people would grow hungry for revenge and the world would become a catastrophe. "The others" block your memories before you return to earth. They block memories of when you will die and of life in general. The spiritual life is far more wonderful than the physical. But we need to decrease the pace. From the slower pace in a human body we gain the conditions necessary to learn important life lessons.'

'Why did Ron die so early in your life?'

'He had decided to die at that stage even before he had been born.'

'And what can a person learn from regressing back to the spirit world?' I asked.

'As a soul the person can see everything clearly and learn through the guiding of the therapist, although the therapist needs special skill in this work. Otherwise they could cause severe damage,' said Ron through Jo.

The session continued into a more intense phase. Jo seemed far off in another world.

'My name is Jo. My father's name is Arthur and my mother's Eliza. I have two brothers, Jonathan and Freddie. My father is a very wealthy man. He never seems to do anything, even though he always travel. My family has several hundred servants. We live in Surrey, England. I will not reveal my surname, it is a secret. I love riding my horse. I have boots and a green riding jacket.'

'Do you have trousers?'

'Ha ha… women don't use trousers!'

'Do you know anything about the world outside of England?' I asked.

'I know of Ireland. It is a small country. I have heard of London, but I have never visited a large city,' she replied without any doubt. Her eyes moved intensely under her eyelids as her life in Surrey continued.

'Do you attend school?'

'I have a governess who teaches me Latin and sewing,' she replied.

'Tell me of the most important event in your life,' I encouraged her. Suddenly she started breathing quickly and gasping for air. She moved up and down in the reclined chair, apparently under extreme duress. It took a good while before she calmed down again.

'Oh… my fiancé has been shot by some men. They continue to chase me and I try to get away, but they keep closing in… They shot my horse. These evil men took me and buried me alive. The attack happened in the forest. I remember trying to flee around the trees…'

'You are calm now. You feel no pain. You are looking back at everything just the way it was. What do you see?' I asked.

'My father found me dead… he was very upset. They never found Bill,' Jo said.

'What do you do after your body has perished?'

'I stay by my horse. My guide Tuah is close to me. She supports me. I stop by the fields. I refused the assistance of my guide and instead stopped by that field... waiting by the tree... a place of serenity. But since I had seen the rampaging horses the place had become inhospitable to me. A barren and cold place. When I think about it the trees have no leaves. Mud everywhere, like everything has been trampled down. There is fear. It is a place of loss. A place to leave and try to forget. All this created a fierce rage that I carried within my soul. I lost my life as a warning to my father. A mild warning since he would have reacted, acted, if the boys had been attacked,' Jo said.

It turned out that Jo stayed by the fields of death for many years. When I studied the case closer to see if she had had a life during the 18th or 19th century, it seemed that she had stayed in spirit form by her dead horse for 100-200 years.

'How long is a hundred years in the spiritual world?' I asked.

'Only seconds,' she quickly replied.

'How did you get back to the light?'

'A higher being came to collect me. She delivers lost souls. I go with her into the light now...'

It turned out Jo had an exceptional ability to not only convey information about herself and her past lives, but also regarding the spiritual world's structure and form. As the first client who had spoken of some kind of angel, or higher being, who located lost souls, it presented an excellent opportunity to study the subject further.

'Where do lost souls go?' I asked.

'They are not always found by the masters... there are so many,' she answered.

'What happens then?'

'They cannot return... they can be reborn but are often haunted by fear because they have no guides.'

'What happens if they are reborn without guides?'

'Plants can sting and animals can bite. Guides notice the lost soul.'

'Are people without guides bad?' I asked.

'Of course! If they ignore the guides and make their own plans. They become selfish and unkind. They keep to themselves. The guides want to tell them that they make their own decisions,' Jo said.

'Do the masters search for evil souls?'

'They know where they exist and use them to help others. The masters can use the darkness in their plan... struggle... a challenge for other souls.'

'Is there really a meaning, a higher purpose?' I asked.

'There is a higher order and a higher purpose,' she replied.

'Does that mean souls try to meet on Earth? That advanced souls try to meet in the physical form?'

'They ought to.'

'Why?' I asked.

'Because it is like... a collective knowledge and wisdom. I have survived you and you will survive me. It is a constant cycle,' she replied.

'How do we people look like from the perspective of the spiritual world?'

'You can't see us, but we view you kind of like turtles...'

167

The Wise Master

Is it possible that the knowledge which Jo shared with me came from a Master with the knowledge to free lost souls? It seemed natural, especially considering Jo's horrible death where she was buried alive.

This conversation departed from the point when Jo had been buried alive and stayed on the plains together with her dead horse. After a short moment in the afterlife, which passed as 100 years here, a liberator of souls arrived. I never had the intention to speak to a master, this was something that Jo herself mediated. During the session it grew increasingly clear how the spiritual process created information and healing in a mutual manner.

'They come here terrified,' Jo said.

'Who are terrified?' I asked.

'Those who have just passed.'

'What do you mean?'

'They come to the light. They must see something they recognize. They are strangers and I have to calm them and stop their fear.'

'Who are they and where do they come from?' I asked.

'They are earthbound souls,' Jo answered.

'And where does a soul come from?'

'The light. Souls are energy, light energy. When you look up into the sky you see the light and feel the strength.'

'And what is light?'

'Light is energy. They are very old... they are masters but sometimes they come here... for only a short while...' Jo said.

'Is it possible to create a new soul?' I asked.

'Yes. Not many souls are new.'

'And who decides that?'

'The Masters. They are curious about your questions!'

'Where in the body does the soul exist?'

'The soul is not in the body. It is easy to think that-it makes everything smaller. We are closer. Picture an image of a globe with a light inside. Inside that light is your body... the soul is not bound by anything in life... you must visualise... we need to see.'

'A need to see what?' I asked.

'Only a part of the soul is here. The other part is with the prophet of souls...' Jo said.

'Do souls incarnate in animal bodies?'

'Yes, to get experience.'

'Do we go back and become animals again?' I quickly asked.

'No, because the animals are limited. When you first come down everything passes slowly. The learning is slow. You can only learn a little as an animal,' Jo answered.

'Have the Masters also been animals?'

'Far, far back...'

'Do you travel to and get born in other worlds?'

'Don't want to... but sometimes...'

'How many dimensions are there?' I asked.

'How many do you want? There is no limit. There is a dimension of hate and fear. Some souls can go to an old battlefield and experience pain,' Jo said with a smile.

'Does hell exist then?'

'The mind is beyond the physical realm. One can create one's own hell. There is no real hell. Only darkness and loneliness without meaning. The nature of the soul is not loneliness.'

'Can the mind travel into other dimensions and then return to the physical world?' I asked.

'You cannot and it may not be used. It is too dangerous. If one returns here one has no need to travel back. It has already been done,' Jo said.

'By whom? Aliens?'

'You are an alien to them. They are surprised over how slow humans are.'

'Are there spaceships in the universe that uses different waveforms to travel?' I asked.

'There are different sources. Earthbound,' she replied.

'Will we get to know them?'

'What makes you think that they do not know you already? They have a purpose, just as you have yours.'

'Do they also communicate with the masters?'

'They do, in their own way. They are closer to the masters.'

'And why can't we see you?' I asked.

'Would you let your children know everything? You would not fulfil your purpose!' she answered with a firm voice.

'Why do you seem to travel so much faster?'

'You move too slowly... You get stuck... you can separate the physical form from the spiritual, but without a physical body you are lost. There is no balance.'

'Is it dangerous to look into the future?' I asked.

'No. Souls can be in many places at once. Some souls move in advance,' Jo said.

'And what purpose does that serve?'

'You are running before you can walk... you must slow down.'

'Is there a plan for each and every one born on earth?'

'Yes.'

'Can one influence the plan?' I asked.

'You can change small things, but you do not have the power to change the name,' Jo responded.

'Is it then possible to give one's life for another person?'

'No, it is not a part of their plan.'

'But if you die while physically saving another person?'

'It is the plan then...'

'Can one decide for themselves as for which life they want?' I asked.

'You do not ask them. They tell you that you can do this or that. You have choices as like on a menu,' Jo answered.

'And which choice did I make?'

'You chose emotional pain. You cannot change it even if you wanted to. If you had no demons you would not be able to help them… it takes time to explore ones inner self. Look inwards, it is the strength. It gives you strength. You think you are weak because you are strong. Every strength knows its own weakness… you use much energy for searching… all too much… worry less… believe in what you are doing… they give me strength to give to you, in your heart. It strengthens your heart. The soul can be in two places at once. The soul is in the light, always. You can reach it through yourself and it matters not where you are. The place exists within yourself,' Jo told me.

'Why must the souls live physical lives?'

'They get bored. They cannot be guided right if they do not come down. They are given tasks. The souls exist everywhere, nature continues. The nature's beauty is humanity. They are our strength.'

'If we gave this treatment to all humans, could we then not heal the entire world?' I asked.

'It is not allowed, since some people must suffer in order to learn,' she replied.

'But I wish to convey this work to all of humanity.'

'It is easier to prove your faith. People need proof. You must go back to earlier lives in order to get proof from earlier records. You correlate the information and the records. Never look towards a failure.'

'What is it that I do not see?' I then asked.

'Fear. Her fear is weaker when she knows the strength. She stands in the wind and feels the strength of it. The wind can move the waters. The calm water becomes stronger. Never be afraid, you only have to bring the soul to a special place,' Jo said.

'A special place?'

'You have a garden. Jo must feel that she has a place. Take her there, but I think that she is by the sea. She sees when they arrive, she sees dark waters…'

'When she sees what?' I asked a bit confused.

'The devils. Take her then to calmer waters. The fear stops her from hearing you. You are like a window cleaner, you have to scrape a small hole through all the grime…' Jo said.

'Who can help Jo?'

'The masters. You never lose contact with them. Your soul, they always know if you will not manage to learn. Then they bring you back.'

'Can a soul be destroyed by pure evil?' I asked.

'Energy can be changed. Such a soul has less light energy. Such a soul can be transformed into something else. Sometimes guides make mistakes. That can pose a danger for the soul since it does not receive any help,' she said almost like a lecturer.

'Do all souls have guides?'

'Yes, and you have four greedy guides... all guides show themselves in the manner you want to remember them... two are usually enough... You have four who offer assistance when you need it... you receive strength because you are a beginner in this work. No one knows everything. She knows that you wanted to change. She won't stay. She goes back because she has no other choice. Everything is a part of the plan, and there is nothing you can change.'

'Does a person know when he or she should die?' I asked.

'Yes, because they have a gathering... with their spiritual friends,' Jo answered.

'So they have to attend this gathering?'

'No, the gathering comes to them. They ensure that you get back properly.'

'Is it harder to die or to be born?'

'To be born. It is unsuitable to enter a baby. You become slow. You have to start from the beginning again. Jo was born before the midwife arrived... she wanted to get it over with. When you die it is also difficult since you have to leave people behind. You see your soul mates and they will perhaps not come back at the same moment in time. For them you have perhaps only been gone an hour...'

In the middle of the session the master suddenly asks me something through Jo.

'What is it that calms you?'

'Nature... the blue sky. What helps me live is the sea-its strength, its purity.'

'Change your wrath's energy,' said Jo.

***

Jo recovered completely and never again had to find help from the psychiatry in England. Her past lives and communication with the masters was an unforgettable experience during years of hard work. The contact with Jo also demonstrated a basic phenomenon within psychiatric/spiritual healing—the understanding that the process between therapist and client is not one-directional as consistent with the traditional belief that the therapist heals and the client recovers. Contrarily, each client's recovery seems dependent on the deep inner contact which is established and in its own way also heals the therapist.

The Canadian Indian Tribe

Before Laura started describing her life in Austria as the girl from Berchsteig, she spoke of a short but pleasant life as a Native American in Canada. You will read about this life in the next chapter. Laura had been referred by her GP due to unexplained anxiety and depression.

'My name is Faya and I'm nine years old. My mother is Toma and my brother Sky, but I cannot remember my father's name. We live with an Indian tribe in Cananda...mhm... It is 1630 A.D,' Laura said with ease. During the session it seemed she was back with her tribe again, free and deeply loved by her brothers and sisters.

'What are you doing?' I asked.

'We are skinning animals. My mother is skilled at crafting things from the skins. She shows me how to transform skin into shoes, and how to make pearls from the bones, especially pearls ribbons that go around a man's chest. My father has a ribbon around his head, without feathers on it. He uses a spear when he hunts and a knife to cut open the carcass. The skins from the animals must be stretched. My brother was taught by our father how to use a bow and arrow, but he was never especially good at it. My father thought his problem was that he never could pull back the string enough for the bow. There is a stream close to our tents where I'm sitting with my parents. I love wolves, but my parents say I have to keep away from them. Babies are put in a back carrier (papoose) that is put on the back of the women.'

Laura was speaking with such vividness that you could think she was reading aloud from a book. When I looked closely I saw intense REM-activity under her eyelids.

'Are you getting married when you grow up?' I asked.

'My father will decide who I am to marry later. I am quite good at cooking, and I like making strings, belts and bootstraps from skin. I cut patterns into bone with a small knife and I make circles of horses, arrows, trees, lakes and mountains. We all share what we make,' Laura said.

'What do you wear in the winter?'

'I have a double pair of moccasins turned inside out because the skin on the shoe protects me more. I use strings around my coat. During the winter I am taught to get water from the snow and how to fish. I am laughing as we catch fish.'

The years passed and I moved her to when she was to marry.

'My husband's name is Handful. I recognize him as Uncle Jim. My Indian father was my grandfather in this life' Laura said.

'Tell me about Handful,' I encouraged her.

'We are happily married. He is good at inventing things and keeps thinking that he is skilled. We have a healthy daughter named Sharma… when I look into Sharma's eyes I see my grandmother Blanche. The life in the Indian village is relaxed and filled with patience and compassion.'

'Do you have a faith?'

'Oh yes! All Indians believe in a life after death. Animals like the black bear, the falcon and the eagle are very important. If you see the white bear which is the spirit of all bears, it is proof that you believe. The spirits are very helpful.'

'How does your life end?' I finally asked.

'I think I am around 30 years of age. The tribe is out hunting buffalo. Suddenly the herd turns and comes straight towards me. I die… it is a pure accident.'

'What happened then?'

'According to the tribe's customs I was cremated. They believed that my spirit would then rise to the heavens. The tribe called the place where we lived Gwnith or Gyeneth.'

The Girl from Berchsteig

'Read slowly and tell me what letters you see. It is the name of your village. Take your time,' I instructed Laura.

'B E R C H S T E I G...'

'Any more characters?' I asked.

'Berch... Berchsteig.'

'Berchsteig. That is good', I said reassuringly.

'Home... It was my home,' she said like a child.

'What is your name?'

'My name is Renni... It is so beautiful... Snow covered mountain Alps... we have a beautiful horse and we live by the water... in Austria.'

It was as if her age and life made her naïve to the evils of the world. Like a small child she wanted to tell me everything.

'Dad has a suitcase,' Laura said with an almost German accent.

'Excuse me, what? Sprechen sie Deutsch?' (Do you speak German?)

Even though Laura spoke no other language than English when conscious she replied without hesitation: 'Nein. Mummy ich nicht. Papa... mama... He has wool samples in his case...'

I instructed her to see the digital numbers to see what year she was referring to.

'1...9...4...2...'

'Do you attend school?' I asked.

'No, because I help mom with the wool and the animals,' she replied gently.

'What is your mother's name?'

'Eloise' she replied.

'Is there a war?'

'Yes, there is war. Ba... bangs... and explosions... and men in uniforms... yes.'

176

'Do you have any siblings Laura?'

'Yes, a brother named Reinhart.'

'Is Reinhart a soldier?'

'No,' Laura answered confidently.

'Tell me about Laura's most important moment from her life in Berchsteig!'

Laura continued to speak as a young girl, filled with anxiety and worry. It was as if a child was suddenly put in the electric recliner. 'Terrible men come to the village by car. They have symbols with swastikas on their clothes. The soldiers destroy things.'

'Where is your brother Laura?'

'I cannot tell. It is a secret.' I convinced her that she could fully trust me. 'Reinhart is in the resistance movement against Gestapo and the Nazis. The soldiers take my parents with them. I get scared and run out. I sit down by the water in the dark and wait for my parents for several hours. Then the soldiers return. They pull my hair. One soldier shouts at me to stop... oh... I am so afraid.'

'You cannot feel any pain Laura. You see everything clearly now. What happens?'

'The soldiers take out their guns... I run... suddenly I die... my body is filled with bullets... oh... I fall... I am dead... why? The soldiers throw my body in a ditch before leaving the place. I do not want to die? Mama... Papa...' she moaned.

'What happened to your mom and dad?'

'The soldiers executed them... it was so terrible...'

As the 55 year old Laura was describing this it was as if it was all happening again. She screamed as a young, innocent and terrified 12 year old girl, meaninglessly slaughtered by the Nazis in an Austrian village. Gone was the idyllic joy. Laura's trauma had clearly been carried over into her new life. Laura cried and snivelled like a child. It was a remarkable transformation from a middle aged English woman to a young, worried, confused and scared girl. Was it the Germans who had so completely terrified her? I was forced to view Laura as the young girl she had been when she was killed by the German soldiers. I had to try and imagine the evil that she was reliving again and again on a spiritual level.

'This is your home. Yes, everything it alright. I am right behind you. Do you like your brother Reinhart?' I asked.

'I love my brother,' Laura said.

'That is good. I'm going to do something special for you, something I don't do very often. And you will stay there because I am your guide. I can take you anywhere you want. Now you take my hand and hold it. Together we will go visit your brother Reinhart. You will be happy because I take you to Reinhart. But he won't notice you. Not as a person, however his soul will register your presence. You are safe and secure because now I take you to Reinhart so you can see that he is okay. Breath in and out slowly Laura...'

I chanted gently as Laura's breathing gradually calmed down. Steadily she grew safe and calm. 'What do you see?' I asked.

'A burning fire. A beautiful fire. Warm,' Laura said.

'Warm? Is it a big house?'

'No.'

'Can you see Reinhart? How old is he?'

'83' she replied confidently.

'83 years. Is he alone or married?'

'His wife has passed away.'

'Does he have any children?'

'Two, and grandchildren too...'

'When you look around Laura, do you see any pictures of yourself?'

'Yes, he has some.'

'Now he's looking on the photographs, and he feels something strange because you have the ability to affect his mind and tell him that you have it good. That you have come to look after him,' I said boldly. It clearly had a calming effect.

'He has pictures of mama too... in her wedding gown with dad standing behind her. He has his hand on her shoulder... papa... mama...' she said almost childishly as she started to cry.

'When you look around Reinhart's house, can you see if he's still living in the same village?'

'Oh, no, he's living in France.'

'It is alright Laura. You are outside the house. You are moving towards the sign with the name of the village. This is where he lives. Go closer. You can see the sign and slowly read what is written.'

'B e l t u s t o n,' she replied slowly and vaguely. The name remained uncertain. 'I can see the shops. They are cute.'

'Is the village far from England?' I asked.

'It is a town in west France. I can see "la Boulangerie"...' she answered surely without having been asked.

'Did Reinhart marry a French woman?'

'Yes, he did. He is still suffering...still suffering...'

I then instructed Laura that she would stand in front of Reinhart's fireplace while her mom and dad came to visit. It worked surprisingly well.

'Papa... stands in front of the fire... mama sits in an armchair crying. Reinhart is sitting by the table... he has a book. He looks at photographs of his wife and children. He has only a photo of me... and it is so small. He has a small photo of me... the corners are frayed. He always carries it... in his wallet... the photo is so faded,' she said, sobbing.

'But you can still see the face. Is your face familiar?'

'She has blue eyes... and cute long hair...'

'What does your parents tell you? Take your time Laura. Are they saying anything?'

'They know... I know... they say that I should never have been abandoned... not there... not so young... they are sad... they are sad that I only touched... only graced the Earth for such a short time.'

'And then you died?' I asked.

'And then I was pulled back in such a cruel way,' she responded.

'You can always tell your parents that you forgive them, that they did nothing wrong.'

'No, they didn't.'

'Would it be a good idea for you to travel and meet your brother in the real, physical world?' I asked curiously.

'No...no...no...no. They say nothing can be accomplished with that,' Laura answered with an almost anxious voice.

'Nothing can be won, that is true. It is very important we respect that, and maybe it would break his heart.'

'He is old… he smiles… he has wonderful long, white curly hair. Grey eyes. Like a movie star… he has experienced joy… he has two beautiful children… three grandchildren… and a little girl… she's skipping… she has blond hair… and blue eyes.'

'What kind of job did Reinhart have?' I asked.

'He was a baker. He made bread in… the big oven… with a long bread peel… patisserie…' Suddenly Laura said a few words in perfect French. 'A la patisserie…'

'Why did you have to return at such a young age of twelve? Was it part of your plan?'

'It was part of God's plan… for me.'

'And what did you accomplish with such a short life?' I asked.

'I learned how to love… and to be loved. I like… my parents… such good parents. But I also knew hate… hate… how can people have so much hate in their hearts… for other human beings?' she asked.

'Are they going to return to life before you leave it, or are they waiting for you?'

'They will be there. Their task is done. Papa says they have done their assignment.' When I proceeded to ask the parents through Laura if it is useful for Laura to go to the doctor to heal her heart I am given some plain, friendly advice.

'She says that is not good to be too rushed… you must proceed slowly… she says that you must have patience… I am slowly becoming like papa… she thanks you… I can see a cat, a red-haired cat. It is Reinhart's cat. It sleeps on his bed. Oh dear…' Laura burst out. 'I can see the light… intense…white light… it comes through the window… white… sent from above. A light force… such power in it. Sends energy. Energy that gives me strength… to do what I know must be done… help from them… to go and do what must be done… Reinhart…' Laura continued.

In order to assist Laura I take her to my personal favourite spiritual place, the garden of souls.

'I'm sitting in the light... it gives me strength.'

'How did it feel to die as a twelve year old?' I asked.

'Sad...so sad... so much to do... never did it,' Laura said.

'Where did you go after your death?'

'I went to a garden.'

'Did anyone come to meet you?'

'Yes, mama and papa... they had also died...'

'Killed?' I asked.

'Yes.'

'What did they say when you arrived?'

'They said everything was alright. We were all together again.'

'Did anyone tell you why you had to die?'

'No.'

'Did you later go to the place for re-orientation where other beings told you that you were okay and that you shouldn't be shocked over having been killed?'

'Yes.'

'And who took you there?' I asked, now more curious.

'A master. The master of the universe,' Laura said.

'What did he tell you?'

'That there was unfinished business... that I had to return.' Laura seemed to speak about the time for her reincarnation as Laura in Austria.

'Did he give you different possibilities, different lives?'

'No.'

'After the place of reorganisation, did you continue to a spiritual learning centre Laura?'

'Yes,' she said.

'What did you do there?'

'I met some people. A Japanese man... mandarin... Li Tan... Indian woman... Azaria... and Broken Arrow... I met him... He is a strong man.'

'And what did you learn there?'

'I had to learn to trust again... because they had killed me' she asserted.

Laura became very emotional and started crying again. Slowly I instructed her to follow her guides to a higher spiritual level. Naturally she preferred to stay in the spiritual garden to gather strength. Gradually a clear change occurred in the way she spoke and answered my questions. I realised that it might be possible to ask her guides directly to get around her fixation on her life as a twelve year old. Almost like a medium who conveys messages from the other side, a brand new type of information started to flow via Laura.

'Philosophers…philosophers…guides…' Laura said.

'Who are the philosophers?' I asked.

'They are my guides.'

'What do they want to tell us?'

'That you should… sometimes listen to… to what is in your heart and not in your head. Follow your dream!' Laura said.

'And what is that?' I asked.

'Whatever you wish for in your life, follow your dream!'

'How many guides do you have?'

'Three.'

'May I speak with Broken Arrow now?'

'What is the issue with Laura? Why did she forget to work with animals?' I asked tentatively.

'Passed into the wrong life… and the wrong path,' Broken Arrow replied through Laura.

'How will she find the right path?'

'Through being strong with our support. I give her strength.'

'How long have you been around her, Broken Arrow?' I asked.

'Many years,' Laura replied.

'Have you been on Earth?'

'Yes.'

'Why don't you return?'

'No need. Evil. Evil. Humanity is evil.'

'Last time, Broken Arrow, you told me that I was a brown bear. Is that correct?'

'Brown bear because you have the strength.'

'Which strength?' I asked.

'The mental strength,' Laura replied.

'Why can we not share it with Laura?'

'Because first she has to seek it.'

'How will she do that?'

'Be helping more of those less fortunate.'

'Who are they?'

'The master's creations.'

'Yet Laura seems to have accomplished incredible things during just four lives. Is that true?' I asked.

'It happens,' Laura said.

'How often?'

'Seldom.'

'So we could say that Laura is a rare character, a rare soul?' I suggested and asked.

'Yes,' Laura said.

'Are you unhappy with what she has achieved?'

'She is too trusting. She trusts the wrong people.'

'How was she able to accomplish so much from so few lives?'

'Because she has... a special soul.'

'What kind of soul?' I asked.

'An angelic one,' she said.

'What does that mean?'

'Loving...trusting... trusting the wrong type of people.'

'And why has she chosen to work with animals?'

'Because their souls don't... they are never different... they know no evil... they kill for survival... not for pleasure...'

'And your other guide Laura, has she lived in India?'

'Many hundreds of years ago.'

'Where?' I asked.

'L i g e... wrong way. She is an Indian lady. She wears a green sari... with gold... beautiful belt... green and gold... parts over her chest. She has ...a... yellow stone... on a string... I cannot see her hair...' Laura said with a smile.

'What does the stone symbolise?'

'I don't know… it is… it is the colour of the light… yellow… gold…'

'And what colour is her soul?' I asked.

'White with gold around it,' Laura answered.

'What colour is your soul?'

'Blue.'

'And what does blue represent?' I asked.

'Blue is the colour of healing. The darker the blue… the greater the healing power,' she said.

'So how dark is your blue?'

'Sky blue.'

'Does that mean you need to reach a darker colour?'

'Mmm.'

'If I speak with you now, Azaria, what is the most important thing for Laura to accomplish in her life?'

'A goal… must put up a goal,' Laura answered.

'What kind of goal?' I asked.

'To see… she needs… what she needs to achieve… what she aspires to achieve she can do through us.'

'And why did she forget it?'

'She never got the chance… it was taken.'

'And why did she never get the chance?' I asked.

'Because a man took her life before she was able to do it,' Laura said.

'And what must she do now?'

'She is expected to care for… the master's creations…'

'And why did she forget that for 50 years?'

'Circumstances. Her life took a wrong turn. She was persuaded by others to do what they want her to do.'

'Is it possible for her to get back on track again?' I asked.

'With help. She knows I am here to help… to push her…' Laura replied.

'And you probably help her more than I do?'

'No. You are the physical assistance… we are the mental one.'

'So in a state of higher consciousness something different is realised?'
I asked.

'Mmm.'

'So to sum up Broken Arrow, Azaria and Li Tan, what is it we must give Laura so that she can heal herself?'

'Time.'

'And will she be able to?'

'Of course!'

***

Laura never attended school as a twelve year old in Austria and it is therefore perhaps natural that she had trouble spelling her home village. She repeated "Berchsteig" so many times that it often sounded like Bergstein. There a place with such a name. Bergstein lies in Völkermarkt in south Austria, straight north from Ljubljana in Slovenia. In a postcard a few years later Laura wrote the following:

'You are the only person to ever really have helped me. Now and then I still suffer darker episodes when I cannot stand being close to other people. I live my life in a quiet and secluded manner…'

Laura seemed to be able to cope without medication or continued psychotherapy. Of course her traumas were very difficult from a spiritual perspective, but it is my absolute conviction that her hypnosis was the decisive step towards the recovery of her soul. In the middle of all human suffering the supreme goal is to stop circles of evil karma that otherwise tends to repeat in life after life. To process the pain and putting it behind us becomes a basic necessity to evolve as a person and as a soul.

How many psychiatrists and doctors would accept the working model that difficult traumas can be carried over from one life to the next? If we could manage to defeat our own intellectual doubts, dogmas and prejudices, we could reach deeper to heal all frayed souls.

The reward of all those loving "thank you" cards from my clients have always overshadowed that doubt, scepticism and hateful jealously that the health care system occasionally has poured over me. Not a single client has raised an issue with my methodology. However the system has sometimes threatened not to only destroy my work, but also myself as human being and doctor.

When I met Laura again at the end of April 2010 she had contacted me and told me that she once again had suffered anxiety. I gave her an appointment at my private clinic without really knowing what was ailing her. At the same time Laura promised to give me opinions from the other side regarding their views on the book, which was now largely finished. When she came to my clinic she had an astonishing surprise. She had suffered a relapse of anxiety, but I knew little of its cause.

'1986 I met a strongly medial woman and artist. She painted a very beautiful lady from the other side name Azaria. I did not know then that she was my guide,' Laura said.

During the session Azaria and Li Tan came back to Laura.

'Azaria is saying that my son has it good now. He has no pain anymore. The book became good but you shouldn't remove any chapters like you have done. Everything needs to be there. The book will help people in their lives. It will be translated into several languages... There is a funny man here I have never seen before. He is jumping up and down,' Laura continued. She started laughing as she sat in her chair.

'He asks if you have ever had any experience with a royal jester?' Laura asked me.

'I'm not sure I understand,' I replied.

'He says that you have a slightly dry sense of humour but that he has helped you to get some funny sections in your book. He has a hat with three dots. One black, one red and one green. There are three bells in his hat. When I ask him why, he says that three bells are funnier than one.'

When Laura returned to normal consciousness she told me that her son had died of cancer 5 May 2008. Laura said that for the first time she had received a message from her son, and that she was so happy for her husband. He had been completely devastated when her son passed away. Now she felt she finally had something to give him that might give him hope and peace.

Report from the Western Front

'Tell me what you're doing and what you look like Jenny,' I encouraged the lady sitting in the recliner.

'I see trees...oak trees...I have a brown hat, a white shirt, a vest, trousers and brown shoes with clasps. I am playing with my sister Isabel. My name is Charlie and I am 13 years old. I live in the countryside outside of Coventry in England.'

'What does your family look like?'

'My father is a blacksmith and my mother works at home. I have three sisters. Isabel, Victoria and Daisy, as well as three brothers, Albert, Ned and Thomas. I am the fourth child.' She moved with joy through her past lives and the level of details she relayed was astounding.

'Do you attend school Charlie?' I asked her directly.

'No, it stopped. I never liked school, because I wanted to be with my father.'

'When you look in the eyes of your parents, who do you see?'

'When I look in Charlie's father's eyes I see my own father, and when I look in Charlie's mother's eyes I see my own daughter.'

'What do you like the most, Charlie?' I asked.

'When my father is shoeing horses,' Jenny said.

I then took Charlie to the most important moment in his life. What occurred became an unforgettable eyewitness account from the frontier in Flanders during the First World War.

'We came here six weeks ago. I joined the army but I lied when I said I was seventeen. I am only fifteen but will soon have my sixteenth birthday. There is a constant exchange of fire, but I have to keep going with my donkeys and the horse. One of the donkeys has been shot and doesn't want to get up. I have to bring ammunition to the frontier, but I cannot get him up. I have to unharness him as bullets fly around me. No one helps me. I can't do this. I just want to run away.'

'What happens then?' I asked.

'I hide from my own and the Germans. I am tired, cold, and I have nothing to eat. I walk off and I see many wounded, but I don't care about them. I keep walking, but then I stop and decide to turn back. I need to find the corporal, and I cannot find my regiment. I went back to my donkeys. I don't want to die. I decide to try to unharness the dead donkey. I took the only horse and tried to concentrate my efforts on it. I wish I could go home. It seems the fighting has ceased but I'm still crying. The wheels on the right side of the cart have been damaged. Tommy comes up to me now, he's the corporal. He can see that I've been crying but do not say anything. I feel relieved. He tells me to go back and he's out of sight now. I unharnessed the donkey and I am back. I'm fine but everything is chaos and there are dead soldiers everywhere. I just want to eat and sleep. There are lights on the sky and I am given something to eat.'

I was completely astounded by Jenny. Her story continued as if she was reporting as a war correspondent. You could almost smell the gunpowder and the stench from the filthy trenches. The only difference was that she was lying in a recliner in front of me and reporting back from her latest life at the frontlines in France during world war one.

'I was wounded, but I survived and went home in 1917.'

'What happened then in your life?' I asked.

'I became a smith and started a family business. I had three children. I served in the Home Guard during the Second World War and I died in 1946,' Jenny said without any trace of hesitation.

I've thought about all these young men who died in the trenches many times. For the first time in history more soldiers than civilians died. Most of them were young soldiers who had barely left school. During a few years a whole generation of young men were wiped out in the European trenches. Charlie was one of the few lucky ones who were able to return to England without grave injuries.

I met Jenny again a few years later. She was then feeling very well and had no more contact with the psychiatric field.

188

Enzo - The Japanese Monk

Enzo was a barely 40 year old woman who came for help with her melancholy and existential anxiety. She had a great interest in Buddhism and spirituality. Enzo free-lanced as a project manager in anything from IT to health care. What I didn't know was that Enzo, like many other clients, not only came to heal, but also to deliver a message. It would take several years before I accepted these synchronous meetings between the doctor, who only thought he was healing, and the clients who in reality contributed to a slow, irresistible change of the doctor.

Enzo wore that black habit which represented the Soto Zen School Nagasaka-machi at Kanazawa. The temple was built in 1261 by the feudal lord Togashi, and had at first served as the Shingon cult's temple. In 1283 the temple welcomed a priest from the Soto Eihejii temple, and the Soto Zen School was thus born. Enzo knew well that cast of Buddhists who had deserted the path of peace and donned a warrior's cloak. They were feared masters of the sword and ninjutsu. Their discipline and tough life reflected two sides of the perfect Zen circle. A circle symbolising the passing between life and death, emptiness and the whole.

Enzo sat outside the shrine watching as people struggled up the hills towards the cloister with heavy wagons.

'I think that I am passing through solitude. I wonder why they struggle so. But I am not a part of it,' she said.

'What is the reason of your solitude?' I asked.

'To achieve purification...'

'And did you?'

'Apparently not...I thought I had. The others came with food to the cave where a fire was burning,' Enzo said.

'What did you achieve?' I asked.

'Release from the shackles of earthly needs…it seems pointless… I have a feeling that I never understood women.'

The sky was brilliantly clear. The Japanese monks entertained themselves with the search for medicinal herbs by the river bank. Enzo was thinking of how he had been taken to the temple as a young child. He felt a chill in his spine as he thought of when his parents handed him over to the monks. He felt great sorrow, but he smiled as he thought of his most cherished memory–his girlfriend.

Suddenly dark clouds gathered in the horizon. It was time to return back to the temple hidden in the distant mountains.

The catastrophe hit upon their return. Enzo had tasted forbidden fruit. He had fallen in love with the beautiful wife of a young warlord. He had even made her pregnant. Holy and unwritten rules had been broken, and the cloister was beyond salvation. Without warning the warlord attacked the temple with his soldiers. He did not only kill his wife, but also her children.

When Enzo heard and caught a glimpse of the slaughter, he terrified ran away from the temple through the forest. Enzo described how ashamed he felt of himself. He had lost all dignity. To find the answer to Enzo's suffering I decided to take her to the Council of the Elders.

Enzo's Council of Elders

'Yes, I stand before the Council... I can see you sitting on the left side of the Council. You have been permitted to listen. There are around 40-50 beings in the Council. Around the chairman's neck hangs a medallion... I cannot understand the symbols around the medallion, but in the middle I see three tears connected to a wheel... I don't understand...' Enzo said.

'Did the Council give you the option to choose your gender in your current life? Did you choose this life?' I asked.

'I understand that I chose it without realising... I asked for lessons... but I appreciate that I do not need to learn about life... I stand outside of it. There is a privilege that nothing is a privilege,' Enzo answered.

'What was it that was important for you to learn from coming back as a woman this time?'

'To come back in that form where I would be overwhelmed by emotions... it is like walking through fire... I need to find a teacher here... there will be teachers there.... I know who the teachers are when they present themselves... and I need to trust in that the teachers will come to me,' Enzo replied.

Suddenly Enzo told of how the chairman of the Council pushed the medallion through her soul's energy.

'What is happening?' I asked.

'Mm... to discover a higher level of consciousness... so that it will be easier for me to find the teachers... and so that I will be able to more easily communicate and understand the lessons I have already learned... so they gave me a bit of the past. The chairman of the Council asks me to be more open... that I should allow myself to venture into the reality of life.'

Enzo later realized that the medallion was the ancient symbol for trinity-the triskele. She was stunned when she realised its true meaning–a symbol representing three aspects of the dependent conditions which create all functional relationships.

Firstly, phenomena exist based on cause and effect. Secondly, phenomena are dependent on the connection between the whole to its parts and attributes. Thirdly, and most pervasively, phenomena are dependent on meaning, mental intention, attribute or designation.

Enzo later told me that she had received an important message, and that the "Triskele" represented a part of her life and choices.

The Fireman's Fear of Death

'I started at the fire service to help people and to be a good citizen,' Jeff started his story. He had suffered from anxiety for many years. Now he sat in my office at Southend-on-Sea after a referral from his GP. Therapy, counselling and medication had had no effect. The anxiety often gripped and tormented Jeff. He had trouble sleeping and his wife was worried about his mental health.

For many years Jeff had worked as a fireman. He had been at the frontlines of several larger accidents. Jeff was at the site of the Moorgate tube crash 1975 when 43 people lost their lives. During the King's Cross fire of 1987 Jeff helped injured and carried out the dead. This session was the first time Jeff relived the disaster. Previously he had only had flashbacks. Now it was deadly serious once again. Jeff was back at the site of the calamity.

'Everything is as real as the day it happened at Moorgate. I walked down the stairs to the tube station with a colleague. He faints as we get closer to one of the cars. There are dead people everywhere and we have to carry them onto the platform. I carry a young Asian woman. She is dead. There doesn't seem to be one unbroken bone in her body. She is like a doll. Another woman is hanging dead with her hand caught in a handle-strap. Others are standing or trapped in steel. I count up to 45 dead bodies. I walk towards the driver and try to pull him out but can't. The train hit the wall at full speed yet the driver doesn't look hurt, but he is dead. We work in shifts of ten minutes each.'

In order to give Jeff some peace I took him to the garden of souls.

'I walk through the garden. There are beautiful red, yellow and blue flowers. I'm sitting on a bench with my father. He looks just the same as when he was alive… he tells me that my mother is well. He doesn't say much. Now he's leaving…' Jeff said.

In the middle of his career Jeff was haunted by all those deceased that he had been unable to save. He was convinced that most accidents could have been prevented. In particular he was haunted by an accident where two men and a woman expired after their car had gone straight through a railing and ended up in a lake. He was frustrated that the local firemen and policemen had arrived at the accident site without trying to save the people in the car. Jeff used his oxygen tank designed for smoke diving in order to try and save them. After the incident Jeff felt deeply frustrated and angry. There was no offer of any crisis counselling. To find clues of the cause of his anxiety, I introduced Jeff to a few of his previous lives.

'I am dressed in strange clothes, weird trousers and a very old fashioned type of shirt. I am sitting by the fireplace in my house with my wife Elizabeth. We have two children, Jaime and Sheryl. It is 1685 or 1687. My wife is very loving.'

'You now stand at your own gravestone. What does it say?' I asked.

'Redhan or Glenhan. I was born 1664 and died 1728,' Jeff said.

'How did you die?'

'I was run down by some horses. When I was dead I felt disappointed and sad that I had died so early.'

***

Our sessions continued searching for the original trauma, which I suspected being the root of Jeff's anxiety. Where was it? The only thing I knew was that the client would find their goal when he or she was ready. There was no reason to rush something dark and inaccessible. During Jeff's tenth session I tried to reach what I described as a "great loss" in Jeff's past through especially deep hypnosis.

'I am a young boy. My name is William. I am lying on the bottom of a boat in a beautiful lake surrounded by pine trees. I am visiting this place with my parents during their vacation,' Jeff said.

'What year is it, and where are you?' I asked.

'1805 or 1905. It is Canada. We live in a simple house that we all share.'

'You look into the eyes of your father. Who do you recognize from your current life?'

'My father!'

'And your mother in William's life?'

'She was not my mother in this life.'

I moved Jeff forward to the most important moment in his life as William. I asked him to describe what had happened.

'My parents are gone… I do not know where. I feel terrible. There is nothing left to live for and I decide to hang myself… I have done it…' The experience was so real to Jeff that he literally tried to rise from the chair. He then fell back into the chair, liberated with the knowledge of his anxiety's origin. We then continued to the garden of souls in order to give Jeff some peace and counselling.

'I am meeting my parents from William's life. They say that they left me intentionally because they did not believe that they could provide for William. I forgive them,' Jeff said.

Jeff thanked me again and again. It was as if he had suddenly realised the paradoxical truth, that he time and time again tried to save lives even though he once had not been able to save himself from suicide. This revelation made him subconsciously try to repay an unpayable debt. The solution was to forgive himself and his parents. Before Jeff said farewell to me and continued his life, he had a life-changing encounter with his father in the garden of the souls.

'You won't believe this doctor! My father is meeting me in the garden. He says that the woman two doors down from me have cancer in her leg… It is true that something is wrong with her leg and I know that she has been to the doctor, but I don't know what is wrong with her. My father says that it is some type of skin cancer, but that she will recover. He also tells me to tell my wife to stop smoking as it is affecting her health.'

Jeff was so changed by this experience that he himself in the middle of the session suggested that he should ask his father about his daughter's diabetes. His father said that his daughter would be alright and that Jeff shouldn't worry.

When Jeff returned a few weeks later he had positive news. He told me that he had visited his neighbour and found out that she had been diagnosed with skin cancer in her leg, but that she would be okay. He couldn't believe his ears. Jeff stressed that he had never had any religious faith, but that the sessions had changed his perception of spirituality completely. Jeff recovered from his anxiety. He stopped his medication and was able to live a life free from his lifelong anxiety. He regarded the treatment as exceptionally successful.

The Premium Bonds

J ake had been referred by a colleague due to his difficult anxiety and prophetic dreams. Obviously this was a somewhat unusual referral. Jake's mother had been a strong medium, and he had received a part of these gifts. At the same time he had trouble with alcohol, and the picture was therefore complicated. Jake had loved his mother more than anything else on earth.

My secretary had put him down on my relatively long waiting list, but Jake's father had both written and called my secretary, insisting that Jake should be moved up. One day he called me and asked me to see his son as quickly as possible.

'I will pay, but it can't wait long now.'

The old man seemed very keen but yet wonderfully compassionate and pleasant. There was something in his voice that made me relent-I saw Jake the following Saturday.

***

'Last year I saw my mother die in a recurring daydream. I became more and more anxious, restless and filled with guilt. And then she died... I knew then that I had seen the truth... That I had been given time to prepare,' Jake said.

'And what is your problem now?'

He looked at me intently with his blue eyes, and we both knew that it was time for the truth. My colleague had only heard half the story.

'Oh, it is so difficult... Now I have visions of my father dying, but he is in good health and still lives in the house after my mother passed away. He is a wonderful man.'

During the first session Jake met his mother in the garden of souls. She warned him and reprimanded him for his smoking and drinking. She said: "Use your father's premium bonds to pay for the treatment". Jake left the clinic with a sense of inner strength and protection. Three days later Jake called me, weeping.

'Do you know what has happened?' he sobbed.

'No. You sound so sad, Jake. Has something serious happened?'

'My dad died unexpectedly Tuesday morning… Only three days after my session.'

I was stunned. My gut feeling when Jake's father had seemed so extremely insistent had proved correct. In the end Jake came to use the money just like his mother had said. Within two years of losing his mother and father, Jake's only brother also died. Jake was now all alone. Just days before his sudden death, Jake's father had written the following email to me:

Dear Dr Westerlund

Thank you so much for your email, Jake was overjoyed when I called him this morning to tell him that you had agreed to see him. Like I said to him, make sure that this is the beginning of end of all horrible thoughts and torments.

My wife passed to the other side in July last year, and I know that she will watch and help, much as she did during our 59 years long marriage.

My sincere thanks,
(Name omitted)

Nigeria 1883

The nearly 20 year old woman had sought help for her compulsive thoughts and actions. As a child she had been diagnosed with Myalgia Encephalitis (chronic tiredness). The young woman was intelligent and she was studying at a local university.

During the first session Meg found herself back in Spain, 1873, where she was kept in a castle to be sexually abused and eventually killed by a cruel and disturbed man. She was kept prisoner for several months before she was allowed to die. Meg described the time after her violent death: 'I stayed there for a while to take care of the boy, but later a bearded old man came to save me. He took me into the light... we are flying through the clouds... then we lie on the beach. I must go to the place of healing... There is a lady there who takes me to the place of healing. I just saw mom and she looked at me... continued... she thinks that I should go back to 1883.'

'What is so special about 1883?' I asked.

'There are people playing cricket.... And she wants to take me there... they are posh people who just sit there watching them play cricket. Eh, I think we are slaves, really poor, they carry rags and hats and things... carry brown... and the posh ones look at them... they are wearing deep purple dresses and massive headdresses,' Meg said.

'And who are you?'

'I'm playing cricket. I'm one of those in rags. I am the one standing behind the hitter. I am an eleven year old boy. They just wanted us to continue playing but we are really tired... we don't want to play any longer. They own us.'

'And where is this?' I asked.

'Nigeria... I am a young black boy... one of them hit me in the back of the knees... with a belt... because we wanted to stop playing... I fall to the ground... he pushes my head down into a bowl of food... and drags me and throws me to the side... he is in charge... black and with a black moustache... he shouts at me and walks away. He goes out to game and orders them to keep playing. I cover my body with my hands over my head. There is a young girl who glances towards me, but if she came over to me she would be given the same treatment...' Meg said.

'When you look into the eyes of this black man, who do you see?'

'My uncle.'

'What does your guide Linda say that you were supposed to learn in Nigeria, Meg?'

'To keep fighting... because I will soon be sent off to the war... I must be prepared for it.' Meg was suddenly drawn into some battles. She spoke quickly – it was sometimes difficult to grasp where she was and what was happening.

'What is your name?' I asked.

'Nijen. Yes, he is called Nijen. He's fighting on the German side... Americans too... we are against them...' Meg answered.

'Describe the battle now' I encouraged Meg.

'We are in the trenches and there are a lot of explosions further ahead and the clouds are grey. They push me to go to the front... we need to move... and I take the bullets meant for them... in my right shoulder... and I fall down in the trench and they just run over me, but one of them sits down and rubs my face to get me up... we must keep running. He's Robbie, and he's white. They are just thinking about getting themselves to safety but Robbie helps me. We found some kind of cover... behind the other side that passed us... someone looks towards us... I think they saw us but... they kept running... so we prepare my rifle while Robbie takes his... we cooperate...we try to find the others... to enter this brick building. It is only a single room. It has iron bars across the windows... We all tried to get there, but some got shot... but I get there... and Robbie gets there too.'

'Are you fighting for survival?' I asked.

'Yes, Robbie helps me with my shoulder. He finds something... in his pocket. He shows me a picture of a woman with wavy brown hair and says that it's his girlfriend. He keeps working on my shoulder. He shows me a trick with a coin and a capsule. Robbie has a bit of bread wrapped in some old rags. He shares it with me,' Meg continued.

'Did you survive?'

'I become... Robbie survived but not me. I died in that building. I bleed out from the shoulder wound. We didn't know what would happen because I seemed alright... because I had a girlfriend and when he showed me that photo I told him about my girlfriend... Mary something... and I just spoke of getting back to her... but apparently I never did... I was 28 years old.'

'How does it feel when you realise you're dead?'

'I am saddened... because it was only us two there, and now he's alone. I felt sad because I wanted back into life. I leave Robbie even though I don't want to... I just wanted to ensure that he was okay... I was forced to ensure myself that my girlfriend was okay...'

'But she didn't see you?' I asked.

'No, I'm a spectre... it is horrible. She couldn't see me. And no one has told her but she will get a letter. Suddenly Robbie arrives. He has found her because I told Robbie about her and he visits her to check that she is alright... because he survived the war. She is upset... I wish I could be there but I know that she will get well... because Robbie looked after me...' Meg continued.

'And after all this has happened, where do you go?

'I walk up a hill. It is sunset. I sit at the top of the hill, but it is so high that no one can get there... and I... I stay there for two and a half years... Linda, my guide has come up...'

'Where does she take you?'

'To that cylinder... the place... healing cylinder... up and down in the cylinder with the circles of light through the body. I need this to restart myself. I heal my shoulder... my emotional injuries... it doesn't take long at all... she has done it... a place I have been to many times.'

'Where do you go afterwards?' I asked.

'I continue to the womb. To start fresh again,' Meg answered.

The Man from the Government

Mike was an extremely articulate and intelligent 68 year old gentleman. By recommendation he came for help with what he expressed as "compulsive thoughts that have tormented me my whole life". Since the 60's he'd had contact with a long line of therapists, doctors and psychiatrists without finding a solution for his inner suffering.

Mike was not only an unselfish and entertaining personality-he was also a storyteller with a sense for details far beyond what is common. When he depicted the life from the inside of his department, time stood still in my office. He had served his whole life as a Government official in the UK and abroad, and in his work he had naturally met with several well-known personalities during the construction of post-war England.

Since my experience was that controlling, analytical and stiff personalities sometimes had difficulty responding to hypnosis I had some reservations regarding the possibility of helping Mike. It was with pleasure during the following weeks that I noted that my misgivings had been baseless. Mike responded excellently, and he in truth became an excellent source of details. With his experience from the Government he was able to give extremely detailed and precise descriptions of his past lives, and of the structure of the afterlife. Summarily Mike was irreplaceable as a diplomat in the afterlife. We would remain friends for life.

'You are now four years old, Mike. What is your father doing?'

'He is down in the shop and the post office. He brought me, my mother and the shop's staff manager... it is because it is at the end of the war... it is night... the streetlights are lit again... they are not normal streetlights. This is where some people went for holidays before the war.

They are decorative lights down by the sea, hanging down towards the street from poles on both sides. They are kind of like beams over the street, and there are lanterns made of glass. I have never seen streetlights before. My father was very eager for me to see it. It was wonderful to see for a four year old who had never seen this before. You can see the lights going far beyond in blue, green and red.'

Suddenly the surroundings changed, and Mike had gone to a different place from his early childhood.

'What are you doing right now?' I asked.

'It is a place named Barnham about 5 miles from Bodna. My grandparents have retired and built a bungalow there. My father is no longer with us. My mother has returned to her teaching training. We have gone to my grandparents and my mother has arranged for the bungalow to be extended so we can live there. I am very much in an environment created by my grandparents. It is terrible defined by their religion, specifically my grandmothers. She is practically a Calvinist,' Mike said.

'And what does the house you're living in look like?'

'It is a rather modest house, much like those around it. Life revolves around the non-conformist Methodist church in the village. She would probably have wanted it to be in more of a Baptist denomination.'

'How old are you when you visit them?'

'Five years.'

'Why are you there today?' I asked.

'It is Sunday morning and we are on our way to the humble church. There is one preacher there. There are no crucifixes. They sing hymns and read a bit. When it is over we walk back, it is around a mile. They had meetings both in the morning and the evening... quite busy you might say. My grandmother forces me to wear this coat that she throws over my head. I had to wear it. I wanted to get out of it, but couldn't. I felt embarrassed and trapped in it. I could not get out of it because it had big ornamental buttons that sits on the back. I feel helpless and panicked. I do not like feeling helpless,' Mike continued.

Mike gradually went over to his conscious self and started describing the long line of doctors, therapists and psychiatrists he had seen. He felt that throughout his life he had always been too quick to conform to others. A colleague had once asked Mike: 'Why do you always do everything that is expected of you?'

'I met someone from the University of London and he said that things would work themselves out,' Mike said.

'And why did you see him?' I asked.

'Because I had this compulsion... I did not want to be attracted by... these types of straps... seeing coats could arouse me but sometimes be extremely repulsive.'

'And did you need to use a coat or other things to get sexually aroused?'

'No, never, but I have done things for myself.'

'And what is it that you feel such guilt for? It sounds to me like your grandmother is still standing behind your shoulders, judging you. Is that how it is?' I asked Mike.

'When my grandmother decided that I was finished with the coat she had put it in the shed. I later put it on and masturbated... everyone at church judged these kind of things severely... they condemned and spoke of hell, the apocalypse and other things...' Mike answered.

'And your grandmother had children?'

'Yes, she had two. But you always felt... that people with this type of religious conviction perhaps preferred a different type of human reproduction that would not necessitate going to bed and having physical penetration... and that type... you never spoke of it... never...'

'Why did you feel guilt about this?'

'I did attend a Baptist boarding school. I still believe that it gave the pastor a chance of hitting on my mother. Some teachers at the school said that you would become blind if you masturbated... it was of course a very shameful act...'

'Are you religious Mike?'

'No, I'm agnostic. You could say that I had an unfortunate introduction to religion. I know that what I have done is very small compared to other things,' he said.

'And all of this has grown into a compulsion for you Mike?'

'It feels like I'm perverted... and the flip side of having girlfriends was that the better the relationship was getting, the more I felt that I would have to confess my perversion.'

'It almost sounds as if you're punishing yourself Mike!'

'Very much so.'

***

The sessions continued and Mike changed drastically. One day he told me that coats no longer affected him the slightest. It was almost magical to him to be able to admit that the compulsion was gone and that his spiritual journey had allowed him to leave the guilt behind. Even through his agnostic outlook, Mike grew more curious about the afterlife. He simply wanted to find out more.

'I'm not quite sure where we are... I can see two dead friends, Debbie and Ron.'

'What are they doing?' I asked.

'Smiling. They look lively,' Mike said.

'What kind of place is it?'

'Kind of like a station... as if we had met at the station. Other people just pass us by. It seems to be a station from where you travel.'

'What are your friends doing?'

'They seem to be waiting for me.'

'Ask them to explain why they are there and what we need to do.'

'Debbie is there to support me, because I supported her so much during the end of her life. We became very close. She had cancer and didn't improve. I had cancer and recovered. For a while she worked at the same office as me. She is very welcoming. Ron was also a work colleague at the ministry, and he's someone I knew well,' Mike continued, almost like he wanted to make sure I got all the details.

'Are they surprised to see you?'

'No, they do not look the slightest surprised. It seems they were waiting for me.'

'Where do they take you?' I asked.

'We're in a pub. An old fashioned pub with alcoves. The kind of place we used to meet at. It is a really relaxed place. I don't think Debbie and Ron knew each other, although they could possibly have glanced at each other. They were from different offices. Debbie and Ron exchange a look as if they really know each other. Life was not kind to Debbie. She cared for people much more than they ever did for her,' Mike said.

'How will you Mike, a man with a nose for details, really understand that they are living on after having past death?'

'She says that it wasn't the end. They seem to be waiting for me. It seems as if they believe that I need help!'

'Ask Ron what sort of help you require!'

'He believes I take things too seriously. That I have attributed too much importance to too many things. He wants me to continue this treatment so I can find a greater peace and joy within myself. He is not worried about anything specifically. It will not be easy. Sixty years of negativity. I want to ask them "what can I do, really?"'

'Who answers you first?' I asked.

'Debbie. She tells me to start letting go of things. She speaks from experience, because her illness weighed heavily on her shoulders. She knows what it means to feel mentally repressed. When she moved department to the ministry of defence they arranged a great party. Back then it seemed like her treatment had been successful. It was a wonderful moment. Several older military colleagues made her feel like Queen for a day. The military are always good at arranging these sorts of ceremonies. At the end of it she said "We are those who survive Mike. We survive."… But unfortunately things did not go that way. She tries to say that she's finally found peace after all she's been through.' Mike was deeply touched, and went from being composed and detailed in his descriptions to emotional and teary.

'What does Ron say?'

'He was always an easy-going person. He tells me to stop worrying and to follow my interests. To not let worry and anxiety control things. He tries to use himself as an example. He was always so relaxed. He died three and a half years ago. He had obituaries in *The Times*, *The Guardian*, and *The Independent.* He asks me if it's really worth the anxiety to worry about such small things. He tries to show me a path through this,' Mike said.

'Is he surprised to exist after death?' I asked.

'Yes, I think he is actually. He smiles. He says that he has returned for my sake. He thinks that I need help.'

'Ron, do you think that Mike might benefit from visiting the council of the elders?' I now asked through Mike.

'The council of the elders, who are they?' Mike asked. I explained their role to Mike, and that Ron would know well who they were, and that they offered advice to the souls.

'Neither wants to stop me, but Debbie is more hesitant than Ron. I want to go in any case. Somehow I knew that they would remain in the pub and that I would leave them. I knew it before you said it.

'Slowly we walk towards the building where the council of the elders awaits us,' I told Mike.

'What is it you experience?' I asked.

'They are sitting at some kind of curved table. They each have a lot of space. Their faces are not especially distinct but they all seem kind,' Mike answered.

'How many are they?'

'Six or eight I think. They are six,' Mike said after counting carefully.

'Do you see any colours around them?'

'It is a room with a lot of wood. They seem to wear some type of dark blue cloaks with white shirts. We seem to be the reason for their meeting.'

'Does anyone in the council carry something around their neck? That could potentially be the chairman of the council,' I asked and encouraged Mike.

'It is strange with three on each side, and you would expect a chairman seated in the middle, but there isn't one.'

'Are they women or men?'

'I can see at least two men, one has grey hair. There are women sitting at both ends I think. On the right side there is a woman, but I cannot see their faces. He with the grey hair has an inquisitive face, but I cannot see the others clearly.'

'Is someone in the council speaking to you Mike?'

'Not right now. I can see a smile on the woman's face,' he answered.

'What does she suggest you should do?'

'Listening. They haven't really said anything. They tell me I am compulsively fixated by guilt. And that guilt is the key to everything.'

'What do they suggest that you should do with your feelings of guilt?' I asked.

'They do not tell me how, but I have to find a way to free myself from it. I have thought about this for so many years,' Mike said.

'You should be able to ask "How should I act to free myself from my compulsive fixation on guilt?"'

'First I need to have hope of achieving it. At the moment I don't. I do no longer believe that it is possible to make the past undone. I feel like I have wasted my whole life–that I have failed at all those things that have actual importance,' Mike said with a sad voice.

'But the doctor standing behind you can give you hope. If I give you hope, what can you do then?'

'Hope would give me strength. They agree to it. I would be able to be freed from a part of my guilt and my debt. I want to become free of the self-accusations. I truly want to be free from it,' Mike said.

'If you ask the council what you need to avoid doing, what do they reply?'

'They tell me to make a conscious effort to not get hung up on things as much. To recognize when I'm on my way into one of these grey, depressed states. To make conscious efforts to recognize when that is happening. They also tell me to trust you to give me hope. Everyone has been so positive and I have not been as positive as I wish I could have been. But it is because I am standing face to face with all my doubts and emotions.'

'These wise, older souls in the council know everything. They can see straight through your soul,' I said to Mike.

'Yes, they can see straight through my soul…' he responded without any doubt.

'What do you feel you've been given the chance to learn from this life, Mike?'

'It is hard to say. Very difficult. I suppose... to recognize... even if I can get angry I am not vindictive ... saying something good might sound pompous. It is more than just that, but kindness and the positive in normal people. Those people who never had any headlines. They are the threads in the network of society... It sounds terrible... sociologically speaking... but I like the idea that people are threads in something greater. Each might seem insignificant on their own, but weave them all together and you get something better. So many of those who reach the headlines are empty noise, yet common people have so many good qualities...'

'How does the council perceive your appearance where you are right now? Is it a part of the healing process?' I asked.

'They have done this many times before with many people. They are there to share help and wisdom, not to judge... perhaps that is why there is no chairman,' Mike answered.

'Do they find it selfish of you or me to seek the help of the council? Because I am physically restricted in my role as a doctor as to how I can advise you. They already know everything.'

'No, they do not deem it selfish in any way.'

'What do they think is useful when we visit the Council of the Elders?' I asked.

'It seems to be their task. They have wisdom that they wish to share. But they cannot do the work for me... I get the feeling that there is something I cannot reach,' Mike said.

'Can you ask the council if there is some sort of symbol that could give your life meaning? Something that symbolises who you really are, and what you are trying to achieve.'

'A snowdrop... ah... the first sign of spring... emerges out of the worst of ice and snow... and signifies better times to come. The snowdrop is standing in a glass before the council.'

'What happens when the council look at the snowdrop in the glass?' I asked.

'They agree to this… that it signifies hope… and that it has survived the worst weather that nature can produce,' Mike said.

'So this is you, Mike. You survive… you find hope… the snowdrop manifests itself as the return of life… the return to yourself…'

'They do not judge me at all… it is almost as if I wanted them to condemn me so that I could confirm I was just as bad as I thought… but there is nothing like this from the council. Rather the exact opposite. And yet I have to believe that this is the path I must walk… and it will not be easy, but I did not expect it to be. There is a real struggle within myself. All these negative emotions pull me one way, and hope pulls the other. But I suppose I always knew that would happen.'

'No matter what happens Mike, you carry the seed of life within yourself. Before you leave the council, do they offer you any additional advice?'

'Do not give up. There are moments when it will be difficult. You need to help me to surpass the feelings of worthlessness. So that I can work with them myself and believe it, rather than that a doctor has told me it in a letter. It has to be an inward process, even if it is externally initiated.'

'What is known can never become unknown. When you stand before the council Mike, do you believe yourself to be a young, middle aged or an old soul?'

'A lot younger than I am now, but definitely an adult soul… I am sixty-eight years, yet I do not feel particularly old.'

'You can now see a mirror in your right hand. What colours does your soul have?' I asked.

'A kind of yellow, orange hue. The middle of it is almost ocean blue, it is the core,' he said.

'What does the council advice you to do once you have left them?'

'That I should continue exploring my emotions, and that I should not be afraid to speak my mind. They insistent that I should not be ashamed of myself.'

Mike recovered completely from his troubles, but he also developed a completely new side to himself. He became more spiritually accepting, and was able to become what had always been his birth right. To be himself. In the following letter, written April 2010, Mike describes with his trademark precision those experiences he made of hypnosis and the past life therapy.

Mike's Letter

*H*ypnosis has worked for me, even if I cannot explain why. In contrast other therapists only achieved at best limited and temporary improvements, over a lot more sessions and much greater time. It seems to me that hypnosis is effective because it is an involving treatment. In your information leaflet you call it "intense and powerful". Modern terminology is also applicable— it is proactive. When you look at your list of conditions that have been successfully treated with hypnosis they broadly seem to involve experiences or circumstances that have left a remaining obstruction on the client's ability to live a happy and full life. I can only think of the metaphor of a garden hose that does not work because someone has their foot on it. Remove the foot and the water will flow. For me, hypnosis was able to remove the foot where conventional therapy failed. The method can reach attitudes which, twisted by some experiences, puts the client's life in danger. Because of that hypnosis can change attitudes and behaviours by changing perceptions.

The Role of the Therapist

*T*he role of the therapists highlights (again, in my very limited experience) the difference between the therapies. The speech therapy from "Pastoral Foundation" offered a pleasant man with the best intentions, but with hindsight I believe that the therapy had limited practical resources. There were not that many tools available, especially not something so intense and powerful. He listened passively yet attentively for about an hour. Seldom, or never, did he dedicate himself to a more definite and practical view as to the continuation. Perhaps this detachment prevented him from suggesting any practical initiatives. Yet an external initiative is what the client needs–he has gone for help because his problems are beyond his own internal ability to solve.

The hypnotherapist–in this case you–stands in distinct contrast. First you asked me what I wished to achieve with the treatment. Everything that followed was precise, focused and goal-oriented. That your information leaflet confidently proclaims that "It is unusual with more than eight sessions" indicates a treatment where experience has shown a strong focus on results. There is an intense and powerful tool that is able to penetrate down to the root of the problem.

You help the client find resources he was unaware of in order to tackle his problem. There is nothing manipulative, as some opponents insist–you keep reminding that I am in control, while I feel that I am able to end a session when I want to. Not because I want to– after all "I did invite you to refurbish the room".

General Thoughts on Hypnosis

*H*ypnosis is likely suffering from being associated with various types of entertainment hypnosis. Not only Svengali, but also performances in amusement parks. That is how I first became aware of hypnosis. It was "Festival of Britain", 1951. As an addition to more serious exhibition at South Bank there was a big carnival at Battersea Park. One of the offerings was a demonstration of hypnosis. At the theatre, volunteers were invited onto the stage, where they were hypnotised to do bizarre exercises to the amusement of all. I especially remember a beautifully dressed, rather young and attractive woman who was told that an enemy aircraft was attacking and that she had to shoot it down. She showed such real conviction and dramatization (I have since wondered if she might have been one of the female members of London's air defence during the war). The hypnotist had a sense of responsibility–compromised of a "do not attempt this at home" warning. He added that hypnosis could have a beneficial effect.

I later became of aware of a dental assistant who worked at a dentist's in Chichester that offered hypnosis as anaesthesia to calm nervous patients.

When I read an encyclopaedia entry regarding hypnosis it says: "... is known since the beginning of time". So it is a proved phenomenon. It thus seems unexplainable why advocates of other modern and current therapies either ignore or dismiss it completely. What other, more recent method can proclaim such a history?

England, 14 April 2010
Sincerely
Mike

The Return of the Queen

She moved with pride and grace in spite of worry and anxiety. Her face showed elements of hidden strength and integrity that made her overshadow most other clients I had met. Who was she? This woman who's eyes registered every single detail. A woman with white curls along her cheeks and with the body of a ballet dancer. She sat straight outside the sensory room. When she finally entered and sat down in the white recliner she seemed tired and almost uninterested.

'I have been waiting for this for more than a year. My life is so difficult that I no longer want to live. I have lived alone for over twenty years and raised my four children alone. I have lived on almost nothing, and I barely have enough money to get through the day. I just want to die,' she said as she looked intently on me.

As always my strong intuition provided the answer, and it was without hesitation I entered the fight to try saving yet another life.

'I understand that you are thinking about ending your life, but since you're here now let me suggest the following agreement,' I said. 'During the period I am treating you, you will promise not to harm yourself. When the treatment is over you are completely free to do as you wish with your body.'

The suggestion appealed to Isis. She accepted and I started to inform her about my methodology. She had an almost azure gaze. There was something I suspected but did not yet understand. She had waited for over a year to take her seat in the white chair, yet she only wanted to die. We did some small talk as we familiarised ourselves with each other. At her request I adjusted the room's lighting. She disliked the lava lamps. The light was dimmed. The journey could begin.

During a number of sessions Isis visited past lives. One of the most remarkable was when she described herself as the Queen of Spain at the end of the 17ᵗʰ century. In all likelihood this was of course wishful thinking. The world famous Michael Newton told me at his course in "life-between-lives therapy" that it was not uncommon for clients to project their inner wishes on the outside world. And who would not have wanted a past life as a Queen during one of Spain's most famous periods?

The weeks passed with hard work and a constant requirement for one of my flaws, patience. Inconspicuously our souls began to change by the intense sessions. Like a ray of light on its down into the deepest, darkest waters, we started so sense a new world, a world which would irreversibly change us both, but also bring inner joy and gratitude.

During one of her sessions Isis had visited ancient Alexandria in Egypt, where she lived as a Jewish wife to a rich merchant. She was surprised and almost dismayed when she discovered she had been Jewish, something that she had always perceived as a very distant religious faith. As a child in Egypt she had been mystically initiated into secret knowledge by older, serious looking men. They took her to a cave by a remote oasis in the desert. There she was initiated into a force and ability to help people. A force to observe and guide lost souls with. In her higher consciousness Isis showed no signs of hesitation or doubt regarding this force. However, she was certain that she had been induced to disregard it during her current life. With a smile she described her newfound knowledge of her soul's hidden abilities.

At the next session she once again described life in ancient Egypt. She travelled to the great temple in the south where she listened to a priest talking about higher intelligences in the universe. The priest's words affected her strongly. Out of my own curiosity I asked her how the priest died. She replied confidently.

'It might not be as you think. He was killed with spears'.

I was astounded and speechless. How could this woman know something that coincided so precisely with my own past, with what I had experienced during my own session four years earlier? Was it telepathy or just coincidence? How was it possible that she had seen the death of the priest exactly like I had?

The physical world and all my education had cleverly, and sometimes compulsively, imprinted doubt upon my mind. Yet this was not the place for scientific perfection. Even less a forum for irreproachable proof of the endless love of souls and the spiritual world's perfect plan. Yet this was a wonderful, and extremely unusual room to bring about spiritual healing far beyond any expectations. A long list of colleagues had started to bear witness to this. But in a closed and conformist scientific world where people suspiciously watch the progress of others I was probably just another one in the long line of egocentric charlatans no one would pay any notice of. Nothing to waste time upon in a world full of important conquests and physical creations.

But one day something unthinkable happened. Still today I try to remind myself of the improbability of what occurred in this existence that we are all trained to try to control as mundane and predictable. The Queen of Thebes had suddenly returned and sat in front of me in the white chair.

'They want to take us back to the ancient times,' Isis said.

'Does that mean Egypt?' I asked, considering all her earlier sessions with that theme.

'Very high pillars. I am standing by some very tall pillars. Very high.'

'Does it feel like Egypt?'

'I actually think this is Egypt, we have been here before. No, I do not know why I am back here.'

'What are you doing in this temple, or whatever it is?' I asked.

'It is a temple,' Isis replied.

'Why are you there?'

'When I travel to Egypt I am always dressed in the most amazing blue colours,' she replied instead.

'Are you dressed in blue now?'

'Yes… Always blue.'

'What kind of hair do you have?'

'I do believe it is a wig,' Isis answered.

'Why a wig?'

'Black... black.'

'What are you doing in the temple? Do you have a mission?'

'I have no entered it yet. I am standing outside. There is something important that I need to know.'

'I understand. Now you proceed straight ahead. You continue through this building. Is it great or small?' I asked.

'It is enormous... so tall... there is a beautiful marble floor. I think it is shiny marble,' Isis continued.

'Where do you go now?'

'To a statue.'

'A statue of what?'

'I don't know... It is a man. He is sitting down and it is something resembling Amen-Ra. But I don't know what that is... Amen something.'

'Look into his eyes now! He looks at you' I said. 'Through his eyes you can see his soul,' I urged her.

'I think that somehow our souls are related... There is a statue and there is a living man. The man is a related soul, he is a priest,' Isis said.

'Have you seen him before or in this life?'

'Mm, yes, it is strange, I think he could be my father. He looks like my father. He looks like him, but the colour of the eyes is not quite right.'

Isis had often referred to herself as an observer, and I asked her to move closer. 'Now you can see him really close. Is it still your father?' I asked.

'Yes, I think... mm, I was wrong about the eyes because he had something black around his eyes... yes,' she said.

'What is he doing there?'

'He is a healer,' she replied.

'Why have you come to see your father?'

'He's my father from this world. He is not my father in Egypt. He is my father in...'

'Your spiritual father?' I asked.

'Yes,' she answered.

'Who is the woman who visits her father in the temple? Who is she?'

218

'I think I am a Queen… that is silly… I have been a Queen before,' she replied, almost irritated and dismissive towards herself.

'Why have you come to the temple?'

'It is my soul, it is deeply unhappy. I have a very heavy heart.'

'Is it the Karnak temple at Luxor? Why are you there?' I asked.

'Yes, it is it, but there are many priests everywhere. Not just this one,' she replied.

'Have you asked the high priest for help?'

'Yes, but I am so unhappy… so unhappy. It feels so right to say this… but I don't know… it… I know that you know. You know what it is I am going to say. You know that I know, right? I do not know… you understand… it is such an extreme coincidence,' she replied heavily.

'Not to me,' I answered, not immediately recognizing that I had not been completely honest.

'But to me it is. My soul is so miserable and my heart is unhappy… because… we have no children.'

'You don't have any children?' I asked.

'I am really unhappy. I am deeply miserable,' she emphasised.

'Do they offer you someone who can heal you, someone who can help you?'

'There is a chance.'

'I did not ask you to go to this place,' I said, stressing that the direction of the session had not in any way been controlled by me.

'Neither did I.'

'So you knew me even before you came here for your sessions?' I asked.

'Yes,' she answered.

'And perhaps the priest is not pleased to find himself in a situation they know is dangerous. Is that correct?'

'It is risky for them.'

'The priest you see before you, is he young, old, wise, kind, spiritual?'

'He is afraid.'

'Why is he afraid?' I asked.

'He is scared of failing,'

219

'What happens if he fails?'

'The Pharaoh will make sure he is executed,' she replied briskly.

'Because he failed?'

'Yes… because he could not help his wife… I cannot put words on this because it is such an intense feeling… because Pharaoh will become very, very angry.'

'Are you sitting in front of him with your guards, or any other people, present?' I asked.

'There are guards with us and other women… my servants,' Isis said.

'Are you in any circumstance allowed to be alone with the priest?'

'It is like a meeting… this is in order to discuss possibilities…'

In order to try and find clues I instructed Isis to experience herself through the priest, to try and speak the ancient language and observe herself through the priest. It was a chance taken because of her skill as an observer, something I thought would fail. However Isis was able to clearly describe the emotions and experiences of the priest.

'I am him and I look at myself… and I can hear the language, but I cannot speak it. I hear it… I really do understand it but I can't speak it now. I'm listening…' There was a long moment of silence as Isis seemed absorbed in another world. I grew impatient.

'Can you translate it to your own language?'

'He says that it is a great honour and privilege, and that he is humbled to be asked to heal me, and that he can use… he has a gift of using a natural force… that he can connect with.'

'From where has he received this gift?' I asked.

'It is from… it is something out there in the universe…' she said.

'I understand. Does he need to ask your permission to use this?'

'He must ask the Pharaoh for permission to use it.'

'Does he get it?'

'Yes… it is… mm… a supernatural force. It comes from something that does not exist on earth. It is not… it is alien.'

'Is it a tool or a form of energy?' I asked with growing interest.

'It is mmm… from another world.'

'Is it a tool they have in the temple or is it something…?'

'No, it is a force,' she replied decisively.

'So he understands how it should be used?'

'He is the tool...he... the tool... and he can use it... an alien force, I would call it.'

'Why just him? Why not the other priests?'

'I think it is because he has descended from another world. It is... I cannot put it into words... hmm... a very strong force...' Isis said.

'And how is he using the force on you now?' I asked.

'He has not touched me. This is a discussion. This is not the meeting for healing. This is a discussion,' she quickly responded, almost offended.

'Is this an ancient kind of art of healing with light?'

'It is an extraordinarily strong alien force,' she replied with certainty.

'Is this the only place on earth where they can use this?'

'No.'

'Why did the aliens leave this force behind?' I asked.

'I think some of them are in Peru...' Isis responded.

'And what does the priest proceed to tell you?'

'There is a date... this must happen on a specific date. It is like an annual celebration of something. If I am to receive the healing it must happen then.'

I instructed Isis via hypnosis to go to the day of her healing, the day when she would give the Pharaoh the possibility of an heir. I knew from before that in ancient Egypt some days were very holy, and it was believed to bring great misfortune if they were not honoured. One of these days was the festival of Opet who was Osiris' mother and was commonly depictured as a combination of a harmless hippopotamus, crocodile, human and lion, even if the hippo aspect was viewed as the most important. Opet was represented by a female hippo, often standing upright with the feet of a lion. In this position her arms often had a human shape even if they ended in lion paws. Sometimes Opet was depicted as a pregnant woman with large, sagging human breasts. Her back and tail was that of a crocodile, and sometimes this part was accentuated by the whole back being covered by a whole crocodile. It was not without reason that I started to grow amazed at Isis's story.

'Are you in the temple now?' I asked her.

'No, I am not,' she replied.

'Where are you?'

'I am in my home with some servants.'

'And what are you doing?'

'They are dressing me in jewels… they are putting jewels on me…'

'Why?'

'It is because there is a big event.'

'I see. Do you wear a blue dress?' I asked.

'I think it is white… with precious stones,' she said.

'Do you have a wig too?'

'Yes, for special occasions.'

'When you leave the room, where do they take you?'

'I have a meeting with someone.'

'Alone?'

'No, my servants are with me… and my guard.'

'Can you see this person? Who is it?' I asked.

'I think it is one of the priests,' she said.

'Is it the same priest you saw who spoke of using this power?'

'Yes, it is,' she replied.

'And where are you now?'

'I'm in a building, a very beautiful building. I am not sure if it is a temple or not. It is… mm… a very spiritual place that I am in.'

'Are you there because you have not been able to have a child with the Pharaoh? Because you could not get pregnant, and you are there to be healed so you can bring Pharaoh a child?' I asked.

'It is the reason,' she answered.

'To secure the throne?'

'Yes.'

'And now when the priest uses the force, can you describe how he uses it?'

'It is something stimulating… very powerful… it affects my mind in relation to my reproductive system… it affects my consciousness… it has an effect on my mind.'

'Does it affect the Pharaoh's reproductive system in the same way as your own?' I asked.

'Mine. It affects my mental relationship to my reproductive system. It is as if the mind is the key,' she answered.

'Does he unlock the mind?'

'Mm.'

'And when you are with the priests and the others, is it your perception that as Queen you believe in a life after death? That you believe in reincarnation, that we all have souls?'

'I have been in Egypt many times,' she replied without the usual wait.

'But when you're there now as a Queen, do you believe that there is a soul?'

'Yes.'

'Can you make out the name of the Queen?'

'I am not very good at names. I never get any names.' Isis proceeded to describe hieroglyphs which represented her name. She described a swimming bird followed by a cat without being able to see or understand her name. It was as if there was a barrier put in somewhere in this knowledge. I knew from experience that there are things that neither I nor the client was meant to know. No matter how much you tried there was an invisible barricade, impossible to break through.

'You are now ready after the healing. Did you get a son or a daughter?' I asked as the intense session drew to a close.

'I had a beautiful little boy.'

'Is Pharaoh satisfied that you have had a son?'

'He is very pleased… very proud,' Isis said.

'What happened to the priest?'

'He… he has been accused of something.'

'What is it he is accused of?' I asked curiously.

'Mm… one of the servants has spread lies… It made Pharaoh furious… and he believes in these lies…'

'And no one except for the Pharaoh is allowed to touch the Queen, correct?'

'No one is allowed! So I wonder who had permission to touch me?'

223

'And what happened to the priest after the servant had spread his lies which the Pharaoh believed?'

'He had to order him executed.'

'Were you pleased of that as a Queen?'

'No, very, very sad... very sad... he did not want to believe me.... I continued to say... told him the truth yet he did not want to believe me. I wanted to save the priest because he had cured me.'

She proceeded to spontaneously talk about how controlling and dominant her father in her current life had been. Isis described it as if her father did not want to let her go.

'Oh, my father was in Egypt. And then it was this young man in Egypt. He was a priest, but there was also an older, wiser priest. My father made sure he died,' she said, obviously deeply shaken.

'Why is this important?'

'I needed to know this. I need to view my father in a different light.'

'But why did he restrict you so heavily in this life?'

'Because I was strong and had my own will, and he feared my attractiveness.'

A truth had now been revealed that fit together well with my own experiences. I would never have suspected that her father once was that high priest who protected me, and finally had to follow the order to execute me. Was this what the Buddhists call karma? That in the end the equation would add up. There would be the same sum on both sides, and eternal balance would finally be achieved.

I had never told Isis of how I saw myself receive a scarab out of pure gold from the Queen after she had given birth to a son. In my only life changing regression to a life many thousands of years ago, I had been a priest and healer in ancient Egypt. Of course it seemed improbable that a person one day would enter my clinic and give me the other half to this impossible story. Yet the unimaginable had occurred.

When I started to accept this I felt an inner peace, to no longer need to convince or be convinced. To accept the river of life as a part of a whole, to follow its course instead of struggling upstream. It felt so right. At the same time I knew that extremely few would accept this story. Mankind's doubt and requirement for concrete evidence could sometimes take gigantic proportions. Yet a majority of people seem to believe in a God that no one has ever seen, even less been healed by. And here was, in spite of the stubborn doubts, a story weaved together by two people who had never before met in their current lives. Two people from different countries made it seem like God does not play with dice. His plan seemed unimaginably ingenious and managed to find a balance after thousands of years.

'The Queen gave the priest something special before he died. To show her joy and gratitude, she gave him something very unusual. What was it?' I asked.

'I think it was made of gold... I don't know... it might be a scarab. I don't know,' she said unassumingly. I gave a short confirmation that her response fit with my own experience. There was not a hint of surprise in her voice.

'When the priest was buried you ensured the scarab was placed with him, is that right?'

'Yes, I ensured this... I made sure that the high priest... that he knew that it would happen... I have been two people at the same time, haven't I?' she said suddenly before we ended the intense session.

'Why did your master and your guides wish to show us this?' I finally asked.

'It is proof for us both. So you know that what you are doing is real.'

***

During the weeks that followed we began to explore the spiritual world. We were always humbly and kindly guided by Isis's seven guides and masters. She described eons of time of training in the spiritual world in order to become a spiritual master in the mystical school of observation. She described herself being an Observer.

We explored particle physics and the journeys of souls in our parallel dimension. Sometimes the questions became so many that Isis became confused from exhaustion. She had, according to herself, not come here with an especially advanced intellect.

'You had the possibility of choosing between many different lives. Am I permitted to know why specifically this life?' I asked.

'It had to be this life. I must rise above all difficulties and struggles… the human nature… I needed to learn to rise above it all,' Isis answered.

'Are you suspenseful or excited about this?'

'Ah, excited about the challenge and that I can accomplish greater things from the experience.'

'So when you planned your life Isis, was it a small part of your plan that our paths would cross?'

'It is possible… for me to get in touch with my intuition. And I cannot do it alone.'

'And why do they allow us to discuss your soul and your… your accomplishments and progress?' I asked.

'In order for both of us to reach a higher knowledge,' she said.

'But why do they erase your memory as soon as you are born as Isis?'

'We must operate on a human level.'

'But if you remember your past lives and your time as a soul, but lack maturity and an ability to understand, what happens if you by accident remember all of this? What would happen to such a person?' I asked.

'The rest of the society would think they are crazy.'

'Who surrounds you right now?'

'My seven guides and my master. All my guides are men and my master is male. I am the only woman,' Isis said.

Amongst the different advanced souls and masters you encounter during the spiritual journeys with people, there is a structure and an order. Some masters work with souls, others work with creating and changing worlds. But nothing seems to stem from random, unorganised meetings. In the end, there is a meaning to everything. And when all of this starts to take shape from a steady flow of independent clients who bear witness to the same spiritual experiences, a great joy is experienced. People exhibit the same awakening of spiritual liberation and deep insights regardless of wealth, race or personality types. The realisation that we are all souls collecting spiritual experience through one or another human form. When clients discover that we do not exist in the shape of biological, soulless machines, they experience a shock that slowly changes into indescribable joy.

Why has no one spoken about this? Why are people forced to live lives without access to the truth of our real existence? Why are we forced to live under financial, religious and political hypocrisy? These are all questions asked by those individuals who have started the inner journey and the awakening from a spiritual sleep. The awakening gives an aftertaste of surprise and emptiness, almost as if they have felt fooled by political and religious leaders in a world dominated by constructed and manipulated truths. Never the people's own inner truth, but someone else's with completely different material goals. Yet the answers never lie anywhere else but in the unique, inner self. In a place where they constantly and faithfully lie, ready to be discovered. Slumbering and patiently lies the truth in the own super consciousness. Inside of what we always have called our soul.

'Is this life as Isis especially important?'

'Mm, I have special gifts,' she said.

'What kind of gifts?'

'They are gifts of the soul... but these gifts have followed me in all my lives.'

'Can you try to explain what the gifts are if you ask your master?'

'They have a powerful effect on souls.'

'What kind of effect?' I asked.

'A good influence. It regards controlling souls. I need to learn how I can use it. In my spiritual state I know, but in my current life I need to learn. I must be wise in order to be able to use it,' Isis answered.

'When you meet your guides and your master in the spiritual world, do they tell you if you need to return for any more lives before you are finished here?'

'I think I have one more. But it is important in this life before I die, that I... that I really learn to use the intuition and the gift I have been given in this life. And I must use them now. And I must learn how I should use them now.'

'And what is it that you must do?' I asked.

'It doesn't have to do with me. I could not do this before my children had grown up. I must, no I must dedicate myself to this now. My... children don't need me in the same way now,' she answered.

'Are you prepared?'

'If I knew what it was, I would be...'

'I would claim that it is extremely unusual with seven guides in the spiritual world. Ask them through your own soul! Why is it important to protect you Isis?'

'I cannot fall into the hands of evil. I cannot fall into the hands of people who want to do harm,' she said.

'What is it the dark, negative forces? What is it that makes you vulnerable? Look into your soul, take all the time you need. I will show you. This is one of your keys.'

'Mm, I have not really learnt enough to answer this, but it has something to do with my spiritual knowledge.'

'Is it then like I'm thinking, that advanced souls currently on earth are trying to come in contact with each other in order to influence one another? And that they make it more possible to achieve these goals... that we have set, and that this is a goal that we are trying to reach... through development and change? Is it really so that there is a purpose, a higher meaning, a higher power?' I asked after almost rambling on.

'There is a higher purpose and a higher power,' she answered with a calm smile.

'Does that mean that highly advanced souls try to meet?'

'They would.'

'Why would they meet?'

'Because there is like a... collective knowledge and wisdom. And all this benefits the world.'

'Why did you decide to reincarnate again? Would you not do a better job on the other side?' I asked.

'Mm, no, it requires a physical form to touch a person who is not aware of the spiritual side. You need to be a human to do it,' Isis replied.

'And what is an Observer then?'

'Mm, it is coming back to me… I think I must… when you are an Observer… observing souls… you need to try to save as many of them as possible.'

'Is it your job to watch and to save?'

'Save… through guidance… you need to try to direct them away from… everything that is going to affect their lives that is wrong and evil.'

'Do you observe souls for your own sake?' I asked.

'No, it isn't for me, it is for their sake,' Isis said.

'Can you use your skill as an Observer on earth?'

'All the time… I do it all the time.'

'I understand.'

'But I do not always notice it much.'

'Since you are an Observer Isis, do you ever have the right to change the course of events, or are you only able to observe, and not intervene?'

'I can intervene sometimes,' she replied.

'When?'

'I then have to find a window of opportunity. If I miss it, I cannot interfere. It is like when a rocket leaves the atmosphere, you know. It must pass through a special zone in the atmosphere. That is how it is. If I miss the zone I cannot do anything. I need to be aware, and pay attention to this zone. If I pay heed to the zone I have my window of opportunity and my soul… my soul can touch the other person's soul or other souls.'

Isis spoke so quickly that when I later listened to the audio recording I had to play this sequence several times. It was as if she spoke as rapidly as she experienced the other side. It made me undoubtedly believe that the Earth seemed to move in slow-motion in comparison to the spiritual dimension.

'You are like a missing piece of the puzzle in my life and I in yours… because without this piece I cannot start what I am meant to do, and neither can you. It is the reason as to why you and I must work together, because… mm… what is happening in the world is that people… people's spiritual souls will be lost and we need to be there for them.'

'And when you say lost, do you mean that people will die?' I asked.

'Yes… but not everyone will die…' Isis said.

'So what we have witnessed, a tsunami that took more than 300 000 lives, an earthquake took another few hundred thousand… a half million people who just disappeared within…'

'It is going to increase,' she proclaimed suddenly.

'So it is just the beginning of something even more difficult?'

'Yes… I believe… I believe… I am not sure… it has something to do with the downfall of capitalism in the west… and terrorism… and it is the conflicts of bombs and natural catastrophes… and it is going to be terrible.'

'Does that mean there are many souls who feel lost?'

'Yes… because they don't have anything spiritual in their lives', Isis answered, visibly exhausted.

***

For every passing minute, for every session, this spiritual flower started to bloom, a colourful, deeply wise and experienced soul which suddenly discovered that it had fallen into slumber in a sealed physical state. Now she had awakened from a state of loneliness, mental repression and economic poverty. During each session we found a joy in the exchange of knowledge in every imaginable area. In her spiritual condition there was nothing that was not too difficult for Isis, even if she often complained over a lack of words with which to describe and express the knowledge she possessed.

'There is something very similar in our souls,' she finished.

'One step at a time,' she said as we once again met for our weekly session.

'And what does that step concern?'

'Mm, not about… but it regards quantum physics.'

'Which questions are we not entitled to have answered?'

'Mm… it is things… I am not… I cannot be specific… it is like trying to run before you know how to walk… so there are things that you cannot know yet.'

230

'But that does not mean that you are not allowed to ask?'

'No, you may ask, but it means that perhaps you will not get an answer…'

I was taken aback. How could she have known that I had prepared a series of questions regarding quantum physics and humanity's role in the Creation?

'Did they already know that we were going to do this work?'

'Yes.'

'Why did they wait for us?'

The silence seemed to last forever before she replied. 'Mm… I think it has to do with a higher level of our knowledge.'

'When you have all these souls around you today, did they know that we would ask very specific questions?' I wondered with increasing astonishment.

'Absolutely,' she answered with conviction.

'How could they know it?'

'Because they are in touch with your soul.'

'So they knew that I prepared these questions?' I asked.

'Yes,' she said.

'That means they are always one step ahead of us?'

'Yes, of course they are.'

'The pool of souls on earth is enormous today with around 7 billion souls. Does that mean we will exhaust the pool of available souls?'

'No, space is full of black holes, and on the other side of these black holes there is an infinite number of new universes.'

'With other souls?' I asked.

'With other souls,' she replied as confidently as before.

'And the number of souls is finite?'

'Infinite!'

'I would like to ask your guides, yourself and your master one thing. When you travel with your soul, is my belief correct, that the soul travels faster than light?'

'Yes, it can be anywhere in the blink of an eye,' Isis answered.

231

'Yes, then you can travel faster than light, and then that also explains why there is no space-time factor where you are now, since it is absolute now,' I said.

'There is no space-time factor.'

'And is it then like I believe that we don't need spaceships to travel? That we only need to use the most brilliant tool we have, the soul?' I asked.

'It is true.'

'Does that mean you can travel to other planets, other worlds?'

'Only in spirit form. You can't as human. Only if you if you leave the body. You can do this if you leave the body, but then only as a soul,' Isis replied after a long pause.

'But then you can travel to pretty much any world?'

'Yes.'

'When you travel as a soul, is there a difference between the souls' perception of time and the human one?'

'There is a huge difference,' Isis said.

'Yes, because the human thinks that it has only been a short while, but the soul knows it has experienced a wealth of knowledge. The time has in one way been very short, but in another human shape it has been very long. Hundred years on earth can pass in the blink of an eye,' I said, as I lost myself in a short daydream.

'Hmm. It is correct.'

'Do they think it is right by you and me to try to educate people about the importance of this? That we need to use our souls to make it possible to travel through space-time?' I asked.

'It is very important. Your work is very important,' Isis answered.

'So just as Einstein immediately realised something crucial as he watched the clock towers to understand the difference between matter, the speed of light and time, you and many others have made me realise it is almost the same thing when the mind travels with the power of the soul. It suddenly hits you, is it right?' I asked.

'It is right. Einstein had a very powerful soul. Einstein was spiritually aware. But a large number of people in the world are unable to understand. They are not in touch with their own spirituality. They think too logically, too scientifically. They rely too much on their conscious mind,' Isis said.

Just as difficult as Isis found it to express herself with terms from physics and mathematics in a conscious state, as astonishingly easy it was for all of this in her super conscious state.

'I am going to quote something from my colleague Michael Newton from USA. Something important he has written about the soul,' I said as I recited loudly: "*Intelligent waves of energy create subatomic particles of matter, and it is the frequency of the vibrations of these waves which makes matter react in the desired direction.*"

'I have always known this, but never had the ability to express it!' she exclaimed.

'Do you believe all of this is real?'

'Absolutely. I would never have... I have always known this... but never had the ability to express just what I meant, but it is absolutely true!' Isis said.

'Does that mean Isis, that when people create a nuclear explosion, that his enormous amount of energy also affects their dimension as much as our own?'

'It spreads far out into the universe.'

'Do souls notice the force of a nuclear explosion?' I asked.

'No... it is really difficult... mm... I am no scientist... mm. It is as if... mhmm... yes... I think they do. It affects them, but I do not think it has any lasting effect... it doesn't cause them any lasting damage. They can somehow twist the energy and send it back... but I am not sure... I don't really understand. We are living in a very dangerous time,' Isis answered.

'Why do you believe we live in a very dangerous time?'

'It is obvious as to why it is dangerous, is it not?' she asked me.

'Yes, but I am asking you why it is obvious? Is it because people don't believe or because they are trying to destroy each other?'

'Yes... but you don't even need to think about it to see. Constantly, all around you is the potential for... for complete destruction and annihilation in every way. Not only in the physical state of the Earth, but in people's souls, and in people's spirits…'

'Why have we come to a point where we risk complete annihilation?' I asked.

'One of the most important points which has gone wrong is that people turn their backs on their souls,' Isis said.

'Is that something you have observed?'

'Yes, especially in the West… and in the western world the superpowers have nuclear weapons, they have the power to destroy the rest of the earth… and the people in the west have no time in their lives for the soul… and they need to be saved from it. They have to be brought back… to understand that they have a spiritual side.'

'Does that mean, according to your experience as a soul and Observer, that many people in the western world risk dying from their arrogance?' I asked.

'Mm… yes… absolutely, without a doubt they will die because of their arrogance,' she replied calmly and factually.

'Where will they go?'

'They will be lost.'

'Will they continue on another planet or come back here? Reincarnate?' I asked.

'They must… they need… they must be completely retrained,' she answered.

'Do you and I also stand before this dilemma? That we will be killed when we try to save some?'

'No! Because… if I end up in a situation… where my physical body dies, my soul will remain the same, and it will help these souls. I do not need a physical body for this.'

'So what you are saying is that other souls face other problems, because they are not yet mature enough to understand,' I said.

'Yes, and if I can help them with their spiritual life on Earth, and the Earth is destroyed… if people are killed, my soul does not die, their souls do not die, your soul does not die, and you will be able to continue your work in the spiritual world,' she said.

'How great is the risk currently?'

'It is growing… a very dangerous era.'

'Is there any place on Earth which is safe then?'

'Only a pyramid,' she laughed softly. To remain unaffected by… inside the pyramid. They are the safest place. All this destructive, negative energy inside you only creates doubts. You need to free yourself from it. And you know that if people have doubts regarding you, you cannot help them,' Isis concluded her deep thoughts about humanity and the Earth.

'When we make use of altered time or a space dimension in transformation, does that mean that we are protected from the influence of cause and effect-causality?' I asked.

'We are protected, yes,' she said.

'And how is it possible? Why can we not affect something that is going to occur?'

'It is not part of our plan, is it? You cannot change it if it isn't part of your plan. Only if it is,' she stated assertively.

'I understand. And then why are scientists wrong when they claim that time travel is impossible, when we are actually doing it right here and now?'

'They think of physical time travel, when it is spiritual time travel.'

'There is a famous experiment, the so called double-slit experiment. It shows that photons which travel towards photographic film through a barrier with double slits must choose one of these openings. The truth is that the photons do not travel through one of the slits but both. This creates what is called an interference pattern, which according to modern science should be impossible. Practically this means that these photons exist in two places at the same time. We could claim that the photons make a quantum-leap,' I finished, feeling I made a too long exposition.

'Yes, absolutely. Scientists do not have too much left to learn about quantum physics, but they do not understand this fully yet. But absolutely, it is true!'

'How is this possible?' I asked.

'It must have something to do with the power of the soul, since souls can be in two places at once. I can be in two places at the same time,' Isis said.

'But light and light energy has no mass… no charge… it is free…'

'Ah, I think it has something to do with the breakdown and rearrangement of atoms… but light is still particles, isn't it?' she asked.

'Particles of light, yes,' I replied.

'Still particles,' she continued.

'But photons are different. We can assume that the photons can travel through different dimensions. Is that correct?'

'Yes… Because you are a soul and you consist of light. Eternal light. You don't travel with your body, you travel with your soul. It will take the human race a long, long time to understand this, and it isn't needed for my soul,' she answered. 'Mm, I have a special gift. They are spiritual gifts… they have followed me in all of my lives. It is a powerful influence on souls. A good influence,' Isis said.

'And more?' I asked.

'It is about showing souls the way. I must learn how to use it. In the afterlife I know how it is used. In this life I have to learn how to use it. I must be very wise in order to have the possibility to do that. And I am like a step on a staircase which takes you further.'

'Does souls need to meet on earth Isis?'

'They should…'

'Why?'

'Because it is… a collective knowledge and wisdom. And it benefits the entire world.'

'How many lives do you have left on earth?' I asked.

'I think I have one left. But it is important in this life before I die, that I really… must learn to use my intuition and the gift I have received in this life. I must use them now, and I must learn how I can use them now. I cannot fall into the hands of evil… I am not allowed to fall into the hands of the people who want to create evil,' she replied.

'Is there any time where you are now?'

'There is no timeframe.'

'Can you travel to other worlds?'

'Only in spiritual form. You cannot as a human, unless you leave the body,' she answered.

'Can a hundred years be like a blink of an eye in the afterlife?' I asked her.

'That is correct. When you go back after finishing a life, it is just like... to have just spent an hour watching a movie.'

'How can we make our work more understood amongst colleagues?' I asked.

'It is very hard to do... It is extremely difficult. You meet quite a large scepticism. You should not allow your colleagues to discourage you from your work, because what you do is right... But a large number of people in our world do not understand. They are not in touch with any spiritual side within themselves. They think too logically. They think all too scientifically. They use their conscious mind too much. The human consciousness... is like interference during the TV-news. One cannot let the human mind stand in the way of this. The first step is that you accept that this is a part of you.'

'How will you be able to influence people Isis?'

'I am thinking, hmm... by influencing I can also inspire. I think that my actions will inspire people. And then I can affect... you are like a piece which is missing in a large puzzle in my life, and I in yours... because without these pieces, I cannot change to what I am expected to do, and neither can you.'

'Why do some souls feel lost here?' I asked.

'Because we are not a part of... it really explains... we are spiritually aware and they are not... therefore we feel that we are different... therefore we do not fit into the rest of society... because we are not like them...' she answered.

'What is the presence?'

'It feels as some sort of protection... a force of some kind...'

'Do you often meet the Elders on the other side?' I asked.

'You know what, I do not think they look older, you just know that they are through their souls... it is not as if you're looking at older people. They have very old souls. And... yes... quite... I truly see them... I see them more than I see younger souls,' Isis said.

'And why is it that?'

'I think it is due to my own wisdom.'

'You have spoken of older souls, what is then the difference between converting and to heal?' I asked.

'When you are a converter... when you are a converter you allow souls to later reach enlightenment... ah... mmm... because you must heal a soul before you can enlighten it... if the soul needs healing,' Isis said.

'Could we describe their dimension through the use of a hypercube, a cube with more dimensions than those three we are normally surrounded by?' I asked.

'You ask such huge questions! Really enormous questions... multidimensional no... they do not exist in the shape we see them... circles... shapes... they are multidimensional... you understand... we do not see them as they truly are,' Isis answered.

'And how can one describe the afterlife and those who are there?' I asked.

'It is like trying to describe computer programming... but my conscious self always tries to interfere... I am trying to understand this... shapes which overlap... makes everything multi-dimensional. Shapes within shapes which intertwine... which makes everything multi-dimensional in any direction you look. I submit myself because I can see a higher purpose. I can see something far more important than my own needs.'

'And when you submit yourself something happens?'

'Oh yes, by submitting yourself you gain great knowledge and wisdom. It is the reward.'

'And is one of the reasons that humanity gets stuck in its system that it does not wish to submit itself? That humans grow selfish and self-absorbed?' I asked.

'Yes, it is very true. They are also unaware of... unaware of what rewards awaits them. It is like a utopia when you give yourself over,' Isis said.

'How can your knowledge improve mine?'

'By observing what is right and wrong. I am in the hall with the books of life. I am alone'

'Is this what the plan is about?'

'I have to discover it myself.'

'What does the hall look like?' I asked.

'It is enormous. It continues in eternity. I sit at a table. Someone, a master, stands behind me. These are the books with my lives,' Isis said.

'And what do you discover?'

She took a deep breath and I noticed that something important caught her attention. 'Oh, my father was in Egypt. And then there was this young man in Egypt. A priest and an older and wiser priest. My father carried out his death sentence,' she said, visibly and deeply shaken.

'Why is this important?'

'I need to know this. I need to view him in a different light.'

'Why did you father feel a need to control you?' I asked.

'Because I was strong and had my own will, and he feared my physical attractiveness, Isis replied.'

'What are you learning about yourself now?'

'What my purpose is. It is so much. I have a lot to regain. Life subdued me, and I had no possibility to make progress. I think this has to do with the past... and the present... of course the present. I believe that in Egypt there existed such an overwhelming love between us, which continued for several hundred years. It is a force.'

'Did Pharaoh really know that you loved the priest?' I asked.

'He knew. I did not need to tell him. He knew. There are many gatherings and people. It is all about how you think and how you act. We have the knowledge and wisdom to lead them. We have an enormous power,' Isis said.

'How can we use this plan?'

Isis fell silent for several minutes, as she seemed completely overwhelmed by her experience. I heard her breath deeply whilst she dismissed me.

'Oh, this is enormous. I cannot share this with you now, but I will share it with you later. I have just been lavished with so many gifts.'

'Why?' I asked.

'Because I passed the trial,' she said.

'Where is this? Can you describe it?'

'It is pure. I cannot talk about what I am part of. It is nothing ordinary. We share supernatural powers, but it is blocked by humans... so many lost humans.'

'Why do you need so much power?'

'So that I can speak with authorities and be listened to. Our super-consciousness knows and it gets us to awaken.'

'Why cannot young souls be given this knowledge to help them advance?' I asked her.

'We are advanced. Young souls are inexperienced, and they cannot see behind the human form. A soul with so much knowledge would be too much to bear. It is very logical if you know too much. The human mind tries to solve problems, but we need the super-consciousness to solve it.'

'I can see myself and my father, the high priest. The love he showed towards you, he never showed me in this life... he was forced to do it.'

'What was the meaning with the death of the priest? How did it feel for you as Queen?'

'Oh, it is a long story. I was forced to carry my loss and pain a long time. There was mercy and love in the healing of me. You surely know this... do you know that part of... part of the spiritual strength you get, actually comes from pain. Did you know this?' she asked.

'Yes,' I replied.

'So you must perhaps experience some pain...'

'Like I did last year,' I said.

'No, now. It is a type of emotional pain. For some reason when we are on earth, some emotional pain is much more intense, and that brings one to another level... some people who go through emotional pain become very destructive. They become surrounded by negative forces. Therefore, you must use your pain in a wise manner in order to grow.'

Isis then left the library containing the books of life. She had found the truth about herself, but she had also found the truth about her therapist, the priest from Karnak. After thousands of years the circle had closed again. The priest met the Queen he once died for. Now there was no longer any sorrow or wrath, but instead they both smiled at life's and the afterlife's inexplicable mysteries.

***

Isis recovered completely. After having been unemployed for 20 years she got herself a fulltime job as a support worker. I have met her a few times to follow up on her recovery. Her development shows the enormous ability of the soul to not only heal itself but also the body. Regardless of materialistic worries and a legal struggle she has continued her life standing tall. Some of her words still resonate in my mind.

'I was Queen of Egypt and I had unfathomable riches. There was nothing materialistic which I could not get. And now I sit broke in an English town, wondering how to get enough money for food. Why do you live such different lives?' she asked while her azure blue eyes calmly observed me.

Journey into the Afterlife

Marie Fredriksson from Roxette has said that the inner journey is the biggest and most important journey one can make. She is completely right. In truth it is your birth right to be your own authority and to completely be in charge of the shape your own life will take. Sadly most of us humans are caught in conventions, rules and expectations both from ourselves and others. After the relative freedom of our childhood the requirements of the physical life grow so large that we ultimately lose that world which lived so strongly in the new-born child. My anatomy professor at the Faculty of Medicine in Lund used to say: "The soul is like your lungs. The passing years blackens it".

In one way this is true. It is an extremely demanding task having a life where you as a child cannot decide yourself how to dress, choose what to have for breakfast, decide about your early education and which career path should be followed. Freedom of speech and religion, as well as political and economic freedom are other areas where many people lack real freedom. In some cultures not even love is allowed free expression, and the young girl has already received a husband before her first period. Her genitals are mutilated because she is not regarded to have a right to pleasure, and her divine face is covered because it is considered sinful. Real human freedom seems reserved for very few!

In western society a person's right to their own body is actively discussed, as well as if one has a right to suicide or in some cases help a loved one to end their life after many years of painful suffering.

What seems obvious in the hearts and souls of many people is not at all a given in that jungle of laws and regulations which control what people may and may not do. Some people cannot stand it any longer, but commit suicide. In the spiritual world there are many who gratefully decline to be born. To live on planet Earth is according to the guides of some clients, considered to be pure hell.

What happens to people who have far progressed plans of suicide, but who after the journey into the afterlife seem to undergo a complete metamorphosis? What does the journey look like in simple terms, and which areas are common to the souls of everyone?

Many clients have often had a belief in a higher power, a life after death or a faith in God. I have however met individuals from Jehovah's Witnesses and Muslims who consider hypnosis to be created by the devil. On such occasions I wish the individual good luck in life. There are no reasons whatsoever to involve oneself in an individual's faith or life choices. Au contraire, it is a choice that is to be respected.

Other individuals have had no faith whatsoever, and some have emphasized that they believe in neither a life after death nor a divine power. For those people life appears a strictly mechanical affair. We are here to procreate and move civilisation forward technologically. To these people spending energy on the spiritual world seems like a complete waste of time and effort.

When finally concluding the treatment it is not unusual that those who previously had no faith at all have changed the most. A woman from Poland suddenly reunited with her mother, changed profession, wanted to have children and grew an interest in spirituality. To her, God had finally received a face.

The angry carer changed completely and could for the first time in his life shelf his wrath and the physical violence. He changed to such a degree that his old work colleagues would have believed that he had been religiously converted. That was not the case. Instead it was the spiritual journey and his absolute conviction of the existence of an afterlife which created a psychotherapeutic framework for a complete inner personal change. When he left on his motorbike after the last session he was as gentle as a lamb.

We've already met the gentleman Mike, who previously had a high position in the Government and who came for help due to his existential anxiety. He had always had complete intellectual control. During the journey into the afterlife he discovered something he had completely overlooked, that a human's life continues and that the suffering ends. This was a turning point for him. With his sharp intellect he was able to give extremely detailed accounts of the spiritual world. He reunited with the woman he had loved and lost. He received unexpected messages from dead friends, and a previous boss at the Government confirmed, from the afterlife, what an unselfish and considerate person he had been. Finally Mike found the answer to where he came from and where he was going. He found everything he needed to continue living with joy within himself.

Stops Along the Road

Of course, not everyone responds to hypnosis. A rule of thumb is that around 10% cannot handle the method. People with great need for control, inner rigidness and extreme sectarian or religious ideas can either oppose the treatment method itself, or simply just not respond. Others have a fear of the unknown and do simply not dare to begin the search. Some consider the whole field to be drivel. A female English psychotherapist wrote, without a single scientific reference in her opinion, to my English employer: "In the best case this is pure speculation, in the worst case simply pseudoscientific nonsense."

It requires mental and spiritual courage as doctor, therapist and psychiatrist to take the step into a world which is invisible to the physical senses. It is of course encouraging that all psychotherapeutic change occurs in the unseen, whether it is psychological or spiritual.

An excellent way to find the way back to the afterlife is to start at the client's "latest death", i.e. the person he or she was before death occurred. From the moment of death it is natural to most souls to make their way back to the afterlife. Commonly this happens via the famous tunnel of light, back towards an opening with an intense blinding light.

Many clients proceed to report of meetings with loved ones by the gate and the continued journey. Some souls are exhausted by heavy suffering while others carry with them strong, negative energies. Just like a sick body requires care and compassion, the soul needs energy and healing. In most cases this is provided relatively soon after death, through treatment in the centre of healing.

Souls sometimes continue to their respective groups. In other cases they seek the Council of the Elders, the Place of Recognition, the Ring of Destiny, the Library, or sometimes just a place for rest and relaxation. Guides and masters ensure that each soul is given the level of knowledge and the level of challenges that it is mature enough to handle. The number of levels and possibilities seem infinite. This book can only give a brief glimpse of that spiritual world which so many clients speak of during that state of higher consciousness which hypnosis induces.

Before the departure to the physical life, more experienced souls are given the opportunity to select a life in the Room of Life Selection. The youngest souls are allocated lives by the masters of these issues. Briefings are given in the Room of Preparation, just like before a difficult human mission to an unknown environment on Earth. Sometimes a soul might be shown important sequences from the coming life.

Before the departure a more or less global barrier is put on the memory, and when the child is born it has usually few or no memories of the spiritual world. All of this is done to create optimal conditions for learning. If we as souls had all the answers and knew how to handle the issues of life on Earth, the reincarnations would give nothing. Instead there would be great risk of a catastrophic development, because an immature soul with this enormous level of knowledge in a human body would create a world of complete callousness. In the end everything would consist of evil and selfishness. Everything would be "mine" and compassion, mercy and charity would be as devoid of meaning as to the most twisted psychopath.

In the light of this we should be grateful that pain and suffering coexists together with memory erasure. Without these we would have insufficient conditions to allow us to develop into the loving and unselfish people required to become full members in the cosmic federation.

When the individual is born at last, the circle is complete. The birth is in itself a kind of a spiritual death, while the physical death amounts to a spiritual rebirth.

Clients report of experiences in the womb and the process which precedes the birth itself. Many clients have reported that it is more painful to be born than to die. Something we naturally must give some consideration. That giving birth is painful to the mother is seen as obvious.

You will systematically encounter all these spiritual experiences in the following section. The journey has just begun.

THE SPIRIT WORLD

Death

F ew people live without fear of death. At the same time, our deaths are as certain as our births. In modern society death is almost an annoyance when we have been raised in materialistic illusions of a world where we need to stop and delay death at any cost. The nature oriented human lived much closer to death yet was at the same time much more alive than most of us.

The modern world creates addictions to fictional digital realms where avatars achieve those dreams we never made into reality ourselves. An increasing number of people are led into the dependency on machines which control everything from fictional currencies to calculating the latest geomagnetic storms on the sun. More and more time is wasted on insignificant tasks at the cost of decreased closeness, relaxation, meditation, self-awareness and joy. Humanity's astonishing technological revolution has not been followed by the same explosive development on the mental or spiritual plane. The same questions which were asked in the Temple of Karnak by Egyptians, who sought guidance to interpret their dreams, are asked today by people who seek help from everything from mediums to computerised cognisant treatment methods.

"Who am I? Where do I come from? Where do I go? Is death the end of everything or the beginning of something new? Will I ever see my loved ones again?" The anxiety will sooner or later grab even the toughest and most resilient opponent to the concept of a human soul. The atheist, who denies faith, believes in nothing. The religious find comfort and love in their faith in God.

Studies have conclusively shown that those who have some kind of faith meet death with greater peace and assurance than individuals who have never given any time or attention for neither God nor spirituality.

Regardless of race, language or religion we will all meet death. Just like good preparations enrich a long and eventful journey, it is likely that we could meet death with confidence and less worry if only we made death more living. The old Egyptians understood this.

To live not only one, but many lives, gives us a meaningful responsibility for all our actions. This knowledge ought to make the world more loving and forgiving. Because the soldier who dies today in fear of his enemy's bullet, perhaps won't seek rebirth where he once met death. Instead he will perhaps seek the home of the enemy who killed him. Not only due to karmic reasons, but also to paradoxically neutralise the hate, create safety and understand that the enemy is just like himself.

The old Egyptians were of course masters at preparing themselves for what they called the afterlife, or "duat". Perhaps we laugh at all those things the rich, but to some degree also the poor, were given to carry with them in death. It was not only superstitious and magical thinking, but their lifestyle had engrained the belief that the soul never died, and that it continued its journey into eternity. We can recreate this comfort at the same time as we mature spiritually. Billions of people actually believe in a life after death.

Hundreds of clients have told about a long list of different deaths. As painfully as they die, as surprised they all are when they tell of the "awakening" on the other side. No one on the other side seems to reward the religiously fanatic. Instead those whose actions have shown love, compassion, unselfishness and spiritual courage find their rewards waiting for them. Death has always been patient, and never racist. Systematically he reaches every living creature.

At the moment of death it is prominent that many clients experience a journey through a tunnel of light. Retrospectively death has often been liberating, and once the individual starts to experience their existence in the afterlife, I have never met anyone who has eagerly wished to come back to the physical life.

What follows is a selection of clients' descriptions of their death and journey into the afterlife. The first is a roman gladiator's account of his death.

'I and my best friend are in strange clothes, each of us with a sword and shield. There are a number of spectators around the place, but not as many as at Coliseum. Oh... we are farmers... the Romans have forced me to fight another farmer.'

'When you look through the eyes of this man, who can you see?' I asked.

'Oh, it is my best friend from this life... Roger... it is terrible... we fight... and in the end I kill my best friend. I felt so demoralized that I took a dagger and slit my own throat... I died a few minutes later.'

***

In this vivid account the woman takes us into a battle in Germany 1072.

'I live in a village named Fall. As a Saxon we have been instructed to prepare to defend ourselves against the Normans. I am in the middle of the battle now. Oh, my right arm has been chopped off. I ask my best friend to cut my throat because I do not want to slowly bleed to death from my wounds... I am now pulled towards the light together with other people who have died during the battle. There are a number of elders who take care of us. I feel confused because I cannot see my arm... mentally I tell myself that I have no arm. Then I am healed in the light. I stay there for 50 years...'

***

In the following unusual account the female client is disappointed to discover that life continues in afterlife.

'I feel just like a prisoner in this great house. I can look out but not participate in the outside world. My marriage was arranged... something terrible happened to me... I realise now that I hanged myself. My husband was somewhat responsible. He was not happy, but he never missed me. I am very disappointed to discover that I have a consciousness after death.'

***

Not unexpectedly, considering how many people that actually died during WWII, there are numerous accounts of deaths during WWII.

'I came from the Netherlands and my wife and children have been taken from me. I never saw them again. I lived in the concentration camp for two years before I died. I speak with the German soldiers... I do not think that I will die here. Oh... it is terrible... I have lost my dignity... I am a traitor... because I inform the guards about other prisoners... I enter a room, still thinking that I won't die. There are others and they have their clothes on... all together we are gassed... before I die I am gripped by panic. It is over now. I knew that I must go, even if it would be difficult. The experience of being a traitor would give me the possibility to evolve as a soul and reach higher experience and knowledge... I am at the gate now. My father is the first to meet me in a diamond shaped formation of people. I recognize my brother and some children. I cannot... I feel exhausted after being executed at Dachau... I go towards the sea... I like the waves... it is pure.'

In the sea this woman felt refreshed and could wash off the bad energy and negative thoughts that she had carried with her when she died.

'How many lives have you had in total?'

'481... lives on planet Earth. The Earth is usually extremely demanding with its complexity of life. I am a younger teacher in the spiritual world. I try to reach as much knowledge as possible. I teach other souls about life on Earth, and especially communication and the complex relationships between people and souls.'

***

The next death describes an 18 year old soldier arriving at the front 1915.

'I say goodbye to someone I love. It is a train station. It is sad. My name is Jean. I am 18 years old. When we arrive at the frontlines we have to immediately depart for the trenches. I have one of those silly flat French helmets on my head. You really look stupid. I try to get a glimpse of the Germans over the trench. I am dead. It just explodes. It is a bullet that hit me straight in the forehead. I leave my body very quickly. I know precisely what I am doing. I have died before. I don't waste any time staying around my dead body. I just disappear straight up towards the light... I have so many other things to do... I don't miss my body or the trenches.'

***

This man described how he was killed by Japanese forces, probably on an occupied island in the Pacific Ocean during the Second World War. At the end of the session he felt sure that his father also fought in the war somewhere else.

'My name is Tom. It is 1942. We run off the landing craft as an intense battle rages around us. Bullets fly everywhere. Grenades and bombs. It is absolutely insufferable. I run as my friends fall down around me. I am killed... a bullet goes straight through my right eye. I die immediately. I float above my body. I feel freed... there are so many other souls leaving their bodies from all these young men. It is a complete waste of a young person's life...'

***

A male client in England describes how he is ambushed and killed in the jungle 1359.

'I am with some men discussing how we should defend our village. I am outside the village where we hide women and children to protect them from bandits and murderers. We knew that they would come to kill us, to rape our women and then kill our children... The battle has started and I move immediately towards their leader. He is horribly ugly and he laughs and is very strong. We fought with swords and in the end only I was left. I am surrounded by these men, even though we managed

252

to kill a few of them. One of the intruders went up to me and cut of one of my legs. I fell to the ground. I see their leader watching me and how he enjoys seeing my pain and death struggle. The leader knows that they will kill the women and children. The leader killed me with a sword through my chest. My arms limp on my sides. Then I went pale and it felt as if I could breathe normally again. I felt and understood that I had a consciousness outside my dead body. I never returned to the village.'

***

Death has many shapes and forms and Sara describes how she dies due to an accident in Italy 1458.

'I am a young woman named Sara. I am around twenty years old and I live in the village of Serrano in south Italy... the year is 1458... I have trouble walking because there is something wrong with my legs. I carry something on my head as I am on my way to the village well to fetch water. I fall down in the well... The water is so deep.... There is a man who tries to help me. Then I move towards the gate and I can see a light at the end of the tunnel. Out in the light there is a group of people in like a diamond formation who greet me welcome home. Close ones and loved ones I know. The shadow in the background could be my father... I fly amongst the stars... and you fly amongst the stars' this Finnish woman finished.

***

There are naturally some clients who cannot give any account of the transition between the physical life and spiritual life. However, I have never met any client who have told of a markedly different gate into the world of souls than that one which all clients have described in the transition phase, life–death–soul. It is actually surprising that so many people have, independently of each other, been able to leave largely coherent details about the Gate into the afterlife. Some have been short, while others have given extremely detailed descriptions of the meeting

253

with the other side. The arrival itself to the Gate is commonly described as the arrival lounge after a long journey.

After an initial period of confusion, most clients describe what they see as a bright light. Many feel certain that they are travelling faster than the speed of light through a tunnel towards the light or a string of light.

Earthly successes, language, race, sexual orientation, religion, politics or capital have always been completely immaterial in that world where the true self of the soul appears. In truth, it seems more often than not that there is a reverse order in the afterlife.

The most advanced souls often take on the heaviest tasks on Earth. My own perception is that you are more likely to find an old and wise soul amongst people who care for the disabled or sick animals, than naively believe that they would move amongst celebrities, financiers and political leaders. Of course there are exceptions in all areas, but old souls are seldom interested in fame or money!

My teacher Michael Newton has in his excellent books described the different steps into the spiritual world. What follows are a few clients' descriptions of the passing through the Gate into the afterlife. At the Gate itself they are often met by loved ones standing in a half circle or diamond shaped groups. After having died and arrived at the Gate of light through the famous tunnel, some souls continue to their soul groups while others require immediate "spiritual health care".

Asking about small details slowly creates a simple mapping of the structure of this invisible world. When some details are repeatedly described by independent clients you are of course given clearer evidence that all of this can surely not just be coincidence. After having met hundreds of clients my own opinion is that the afterlife has a very clear structure in an infinite number of dimensions.

***

A fifty-five year old Englishman has just died 1802 in Australia.

'I passed through a tunnel of light at high speed. At the end of the tunnel I saw a bright light. When I came to the end of the light I was met by people standing in a half circle. They all greeted me. I was one of hundreds of thousands of people who passed through the gate, but only two came up to meet me. One came from the centre of the half-circle, and looked like a very old monk I perceived as my guide. His name was Albert. The other person was a woman I felt very scared of. She had some sort of negative energy that went many lives back.'

***

A fifty-six year old English woman dies in Italy and describes her return back to afterlife.

'I am an Italian woman... I think it is in the southern parts of Italy where I live, but I don't know which year. I see a man without a face. He stabs me, and I die slowly in pain. I continue through a tunnel of light. It doesn't feel hard in any way.'

Katie lit up as if she had met some very old friend or acquaintance.

'There are a lot of people here at the Gate to greet me after death. They form like a half-circle. The first one who comes up to me is my old aunt.'

'If you imagine a clock, where on the clock do you see someone you know well?' I asked.

'At 1 o'clock I can see my husband,' she exclaimed with joy. 'There are others here as well, and the last one to come up to me is actually my grandfather. He apologises and regrets that he was so mean to me.'

***

Some clients have actually reported that their group of souls have arranged the most wonderful welcome parties. A female college teacher reported the following:

'Oh, my friends have arranged a welcome party! And to be really sure that I remember, they have arranged everything precisely as it was during one of the wonderful moments I had in my life when my daughter got married during the early part of the 17th century. We dance and enjoy everything one more time!'

255

Soul Healing

As everyone knows, living on Earth can be very challenging, and often life is full of suffering, sorrow and pain, but also joy and success. People who die suddenly in great anxiety such as in accidents, war, torture or serious crimes will naturally carry an exhausted soul filled with strong negative energies. Sometimes these energies also carry traces of wrath, greed, revenge, selfishness and many other forms of negative behaviour.

With the experience of hundreds of clients it seems as if the place for spiritual healing can also be used by clients under hypnosis. Many clients who have arrived worn down, full of anxiety, depression and physical pains, have been freed from the symptoms after returning from 1½ hour of hypnosis.

Some clients describe the experience of healing as either a focus effect or an experience of being enveloped by energy. Of course critics could claim that this is placebo or suggested by the therapist. My own experience differs. Those clients who have had serious spiritual or physical issues have often recovered for a few days only to relapse. This reflects itself in a type of energy influence.

Sometimes it seems as if the soul itself is so strongly tied to an event, people, desire or material possessions, that the individual's soul gets stuck in an empty space in between the physical and spiritual world. Sometimes the mental energies that an individual carries can ensure a series of events repeats again and again in an apparently unbreakable circle. The individual sometimes does not perceive him- or herself as dead, or simply refuses to accept the change. The story of the woman who was buried alive is a good example of a soul who, due to a terrible crime, gets stuck in a dimension outside of time. Unsurprisingly such a soul needs extraordinary help, something which is always available if only the soul accepts change in its own situation. Sometimes help only comes after hundreds or, in extreme cases, thousands of earthly years. Not due to a lack of love and compassion from the entities of the afterlife, but due to human hate, wrath, desire or fear of the unknown. However, I have never heard of a soul being lost. Nevertheless, there seems to be methods in the afterlife for handling extremely violent prone and evil souls, something which is described under the heading 'Reconstruction.'

How does the spiritual world handle broken and tormented souls? What methods are used to correct these disorders?

***

Roxanne suffered chronic depression and chronic fatigue. She had consciously brought too low an energy level with her into life. We will later see examples of different souls' energy levels and how these reflect the afterlife and on the physical body itself.

'I enter the Garden of Souls, and there is a blue woman waiting for me. She is wonderfully beautiful with large blue eyes. She takes my hand and leads me to the centre of healing. There is a cloud above my head... and suddenly a beam of light comes down from the sky. Just like a shower... I feel vitalised... the Master of Healing tells me that I must return.'

When Roxanne left my clinic she smiled, and acted almost as a freshly recharged battery, full of vitality and energy. Regardless, she had a chronic problem. The energy of her soul could never exceed 40% of her total energy reserves.

'Why do you only have 40% energy in your soul?' I asked.

'I selfishly thought that I'd do just fine with 40% but that was a mistake...' Roxanne said.

'But you have 60% more, right?' I asked, certain that she had misunderstood something essential.

'Of course I do, but not here on Earth. That part is in the afterlife. You always leave part of it there when you are born. I left too much.'

***

Carol was a retired and experienced social worker fighting with all sorts of physical symptoms. Her hypnotherapy helped her to come to terms with these symptoms.

Carol had undergone a long line of blood tests, including gastroscopy and ERCP (Endoscopic Retrograde Cholangio Pancreatography) of her gallbladder because she felt physically ill. Her surgeon thought that she had a problem in the tube between the liver and the gallbladder. Carol agreed to explore her problems on a spiritual level. What really surprised me was that she described the same Master of Healing as Roxanne. The two women had never met, and I had not mentioned anything about healing on the other side to Carol.

'I am walking through a wonderful garden with lovely trees and a lake. I have walked around the lake and meet a gorgeous woman on the other side. The woman looks like she is in her twenties. She has a white shroud, intense blue eyes, and long light curly hair down to her ankles. Her eyes are intensely blue. She acts mildly and with great compassion. She takes me into a pagoda. I get the impression that she almost floats around me. She says that I have deserted myself... but I have nothing physically wrong. She gets me to understand myself from a higher plane...' Carol said.

***

Other clients have on a few occasions spoken about more advanced healing in afterlife. In a few uncommon cases souls have described how they are brought to the Centre of Healing after a very demanding life. This client describes how she is healed by a Master.

'There is a sphere around me which circles me from head to toe. It reminds me of a CAT scan at the hospital. The apparatus seems to measure my soul's energy level and where I have holes in the energy. As soon as the sphere has finished the measurement the Master grabs it. I then understand that the machine has taken some form of energy from my soul, as I can see a carbon copy of my soul stretched through the room in front of the Master. He then proceeds to repair those energy fields which have been damaged by my traumatising experiences. The copy is then sent back into the sphere which puts the energy back into my soul. I feel completely reinvigorated, like a recharged battery!'

***

The girl from Bergstein was severely traumatized with severe anxiety after her encounter with the Nazis that killed her outside her home in Austria.

'I am with a Master of Healing. I receive a blue healing light around my body. He tells me to trust my doctor. I feel so calm with this old man who uses the blue light as a healing force.'

***

Light seems to be the most important ingredient in the healing process after death. This young woman suffered from depressions and chronic fatigue. In one of her past lives she had been brutally murdered by her parents and buried in the garden. Sharon's experiences seems to constantly haunt her current life on a subconscious level.

'She has blue... it is so nice... she has green-blue eyes... she has taken me to this place... it is like a dome... she gives me a bowl of light and I am asked to pour the light over my chest. The light flows over my entire soul and purifies it. I feel so happy!' Sharon said.

***

And Meg from England who had also lived in Nigeria in 1883, reported from a life in Spain in 1873. A man kept her prisoner in a castle. He violated her and seemed to have murdered her in the end. After her death Meg describes her spiritual healing. Independently of previous clients she once again describes a female Master of Healing in blue.

'This lady has long hair and blue eyes. She smiles and is very kind. She is dressed in blue. She takes me to a cylinder and we move slowly downwards...' Meg said.

'We?' I asked.

'Yes, me, you and her. We move to the bottom and then we move upwards in circles. Up and down in the cylinder with circles of light through my body. I need to do this to reboot myself. I heal my shoulder... my emotional injuries... it doesn't take long at all... Along the sides of the cylinder I can see the symbol of a cone which the chairman of the Council of the Elders had around his neck. All of this heals me! She has done it! This is a place I have been to many times.'

The Nursery of Souls

Sheila was one of the very few clients who spoke of the origin and birth of souls. A natural reason for the visit to the nursery of souls was of course her thoughts regarding her sick son and his congenital muscular disease.

'I am enveloped by energy.' Sheila said.

'Does it feel like a cocoon?' I asked.

'Mm... yes... I feel that there are carers around here but I can't see them. There are other new born souls just like me, and they all wait in this special condition.'

'Where does the soul come from?'

'I don't know,' she replied.

'Do you stay in this condition for a year, a hundred, or thousands of years?'

'Several hundred years,' Sheila said.

'Why?' I asked.

'It is necessary to receive and stabilise the energy,' she replied resolutely.

'But how do you know when you are ready to leave this stage?'

'I just know.'

'Where do you go then?' I asked.

'Into the womb,' she replied.

'And when the soul is done with all its lives, what happens then?'

'Advanced souls return to the source when they finally finish their journey. There are three beings in front of me. They have been selected as my guides. Two are women and one is male. Their colour is mainly white. They tell me that I must go to Earth to live a life.'

'How do you know when you should depart for Earth Sheila?'

'I just went because I knew that I had to,' she said.

The Colours and Groups of Souls

E ven my first clients mentioned different colours of souls, Masters and not the least the Council of the Elders. It became readily apparent that the colours played some essential role in the spirit world. Michael Newton in California, has in his amazing books described these colours of souls.

In the spiritual world there is a very clear structure and order, even though you sometimes get confused by multi-dimensional worlds with events completely independent of time. Souls are divided into groups, and some have what is commonly spoken of as "soul mates".

In reality it seems that we all travel in groups with those near and dear to us. We are our children's parents in one life, only to in the next life become siblings or children to our previous children. Everything creates optimal conditions for spiritual learning and development.

Souls also have some type of specialisation from an early stage. It can concern mastering energies or perhaps teach or heal damaged souls who are returning from life on Earth. Just as we humans are individually unique with different interests and knowledge, all souls are each and every one unique in their creation. Some souls are adventurous, while others might be more strong and rebellious. On Earth this might express itself in a person constantly hunting for new challenges or experiences, live a quiet and spiritual life or perhaps throw themselves into dangers like wars and catastrophes to try their own limits.

The "new born" souls have an explicitly white colour, probably because they have not yet attained the knowledge and development level which stands in direct proportion to the colour scale. Below is a very simple scale which could be used to describe the souls in relation to their colours.

The Colours of Souls	
Colour	**Spiritual Level**
White	New-born
Red	Beginner
Orange	Early Intermediary
Yellow	Intermediary
Green	Late Intermediary
Light blue	Early Advanced
Dark blue	Intermediary Advanced
Violet	Advanced

If we put this in relation to those colour scales used by colour therapists we can notice striking similarities. According to their point of view the colours stand for the following attributes to the individual.

WHITE:	Purity, clarity, restlessness
SILVER:	Ethereal, trust, flexibility
RED:	Passion, intensity, emotion
ORANGE:	Sprouting, impulsive, open
YELLOW:	Protecting, strength, courage
GREEN:	Healing, nurturing, compassionate
BROWN:	Down-to-earth, tolerant, industrious
BLUE:	Knowledge, forgiveness, revelation
PURPLE:	Wisdom, truth, divinity

A large number of people have independently given coherent details regarding the significance of the colours both regarding the individual and to which group they belong.

Just like in our normal schools the souls have an individual developmental speed. There are examples of a few extremely uncommon souls/people who have reached very high knowledge from just a few lives. The girl from Bergstein is such an example. Other souls require many lives and many failures before the knowledge is acquired.

It seems to be a shared common goal to finally avoid rebirth and the experience of pain and suffering, something we recognize from some religions, for example Buddhism and Hinduism. When that level is reached the souls seem to continue towards new heights and challenges. To finally achieve the Master grade in healing or creation is no stranger than being a master of jewellery or athletics. The barrier is our inability to accept or reconcile this world in our conscious way of thinking.

Due to the extreme difficulty of living on earth some souls chose to stay in the afterlife and guide those "departing" for new lives. There are likely an infinite number of soul specializations and levels which I and my colleagues around the world have yet to discover.

The colour of souls and their group affinity is a fascinating world and that is why I am giving a large number of examples of these experiences.

The probability of encountering a truly advanced soul is naturally small, not the least because their numbers are significantly less. This seems to be balanced by the fact that advanced souls, to a much higher degree than the young and inexperienced, seem to control who they meet and under what circumstances. Such a fact naturally poses questions whether they are just random encounters or planned meetings. My own experience of the spiritual world is that we never seem to need to roll a die. Everything follows a higher and inscrutably wise plan.

Souls are Energy

When asked directly many clients respond with unity regarding their energy. The rule seems to be that when a soul is reborn he or she brings a certain percentage of their total energy. Often the answers lie between forty to sixty percent. Sometimes the individual soul brings too little energy. Roxanne was an example of this. When I have asked clients why they do not bring 100% the answer is straight and simple.

'Then the central nervous system would simply collapse due to the high vibration frequency in combination with maximal effect.'

That part of the soul which is left behind also helps when a tired soul returns to the afterlife. It acts as something like a spiritual insurance policy. It is possible that those Masters who are responsible for this are those who Jo calls The Prophets of Souls.

My own opinion is that we remain in touch with this part in our dreams. Carl Gustav Jung used terms like the "collective unconscious" and "anima and animus" to describe the subconsciously male and female in humanity. Jung was far more interested in humanity's spiritual dimensions than Freud, and created terms like "sensation/intuition", "thought/emotion" and not least the "archetypes". The last is according to Jung the inherent prototype of ideas.

Sigmund Freud encountered hypnosis in his youth through his teacher Jean Marie Charcot in Paris, but the unpredictable and unfathomable power of it scared Freud who instead proceeded to create the psychoanalytic school.

In the section "Masters" there is a more comprehensive description of how Jo has a dialogue with her Master regarding the energy of the soul.

The following nine clients give examples of soul colours and soul groups.

***

'My guide Running Water is here. He has feathers in his hair. My dear friend Linda who died during pregnancy is also here. She is a young, white soul.'

'Describe your soul group! They are standing right in front of you now?' I encouraged her.

'I recognize my friend Linda, my grandfather, my ex-husband and my son… mm… my ex tells me that we had an agreement that one of my trials would be to be abandoned through our divorce.'

***

Tony was a fifty-three year old English gentleman. In the conscious state he was a quiet and reserved individual. Through his higher self he told of a long line of astonishing lives. One of them was the earlier account of Queen Elizabeth I tax collector in Wesby, England.

'How many lives have you lived, Tony?'

'1268,' Tony replied with certainty.

'Which was your best and your worst life?'

'My best life was as a farmer somewhere in Europe. My worst was as a roman soldier when I was paid to kill. I hated this and as Romans we battled all over Europe. I was finally killed in Britannia when people threw spears, and one of them finally killed me.'

'Tony, you are now holding a mirror in your hand. When you look into it you can clearly see the colours of your soul. Tell me what you see!'

'My main colour is light blue with a halo of pink.'

***

Sandy had died after a life in the now lost city of Pi Ramesses in north Egypt. Sandy was illiterate and worked with the production of bricks which were taken to a building site near the pyramids. According to Sandy, the clay was mixed with hay before being poured into wooden frames. She carefully emphasised that the needs of the Pharaoh always came first.

'I see a priest wandering around, bowing and mumbling. I think he is praying.'

I asked her to enter the temple and she continued: 'It is a wonderful building of blue, gold and precious gems. The floor is marble, and it is extremely clean. All the people are very busy. They are preparing the burial site for Pharaoh and his wife,' she finished.

When Sandy later described her soul group she described the following: 'I can only see two individuals, Gwen and Judith. Gwen has a mainly pink colour around her soul while Judith has a mix of blue and yellow. My own colour is green with a halo of yellow around it.'

***

A young English woman had lost her husband Peter, and she sought understanding for this and the fact that her son suffered from an autism spectrum disorder.

'Peter's soul colours are yellow and red. My own is mainly green with a halo of yellow. I have lived 16 previous lives on Earth. I can see five other members from my soul group… they are dancing around as lights… I truly miss them.'

***

Sheila was in her early thirties. She had been referred by her GP due to anxiety and depression. Her eight year old son suffered from an incurable muscular disease, and would probably die before his tenth birthday. All of this severely tormented Sheila.

'I did not choose this life. It was given to me and I accepted it without hesitation. There were other lives available... My soul's main colour is red with a halo of blue. Mm... I find out that my son's muscular disease is a gift and that there is nothing wrong with all of this.'

After six sessions she was so strong and self-aware that she concluded the treatment. She no longer took any medication. When I called her one year later, she told me that her life had markedly improved even though her son was dying in his disease. She had accepted his illness, and this made her able to take joy in each day that they were able to spend together. She found herself more close and living in the daily contact with her son. This naturally contributed to her son feeling calmer and more secure in his illness.

***

This sixty-five year old English woman told of her meeting with other souls in what she described as the Place of Recognition.

'I arrive at the Place of Recognition together with a class of around 20 other souls. There is a teacher here and everyone is friendly and welcoming.'

She felt somewhat confused but corrected me when I asked her: 'Perhaps it is because you are leaving this group in order to continue to a higher level?'

'No, that is not right. I arrive because I have just advanced to this level.'

'What colour is your soul and what are you meant to learn?'

'I have a pink colour. I got this life to learn disappointment. It has been a real struggle for me. I can see my dad, my grandfather... oh dear me... I can see my old babysitter! What is he doing here?' she said.

***

Meg arrived at the Gate after having been murdered as a fifteen year old girl in England. A half circle of relatives awaited her. She was first welcomed by her grandfather, mother, aunt and guide.

'It almost feels as if he's sitting on my shoulder. He has very kind eyes. My mother and grandmother are also here. My guide has long brown hair. His name is Edward.'

I asked Meg to imagine seeing herself in a mirror in her left hand. 'What colours does your soul have Meg?'

'It is white, red and with a black line...'

'Does it feel as if this has something to do with the girl who died in the castle?'

'Yes.'

***

Sean had been suspended from his job as a healthcare assistant in an English hospital. This was highly due to his blunt and aggressive manner of handling both colleagues and patients. To his own surprise, Sean had completely changed. He mournfully looked back on his wrath, but he also had the great ability of forgiving others as well as himself in order to be able to move on. Even though he had developed diabetes and had had to struggle physically as well as spiritually, he was developing into a wonderful human being. To me as a doctor, Sean appeared as a radically changed person. Here he describes his meeting with his soul group.

'Me and my wife belong to the same soul group. She has a mainly blue colour around her soul. My two daughters and two close friends are also there.'

Sean recovered completely and was able to slowly wind down and ultimately end his antidepressant medication.

***

Isis is in her current life a poor but strong woman. Every day is a struggle to survive economically. Against all odds she has recovered and found full time work. Her outstanding spiritual qualities are described in "The Return of the Queen".

'I am a very old soul. I am part of a group of souls where 6-7 of them are on the Earth today while others are spread on different worlds. I will soon leave my soul group to move on. That priest I once met in Egypt is one of the souls in my group. His colour was also purple... it was very important that we met,' Isis said.

'How many souls are there?' I asked.

'The number of souls is infinite and if you travel through a black hole you will reach other universes in an infinitely growing number.'

'How many members are you in your special group of souls?'

'Do you mean my guides or others?'

'No, not your guides or your Master. You belong to a special group of souls, is that right?' I asked.

'Yes, I think... but there are many others with me... in this group,' Isis said.

'Do you know how many?'

'Not a large number... maybe 20.'

'How many different colours do you recognize as an advanced soul among them?'

'There are quite many whites...'

'Are they beginners?' I asked with growing curiosity.

'I think so. There are many white... a few in gold... who... quite clearly yellow... and not that many with blue... hmm,' she said.

'What colour are you?'

'I am a mix.'

'Of what?'

'Blue and violet.'

'I understand. Are you perhaps also a guide?' I asked randomly.

'Of white souls,' she responded instantly.

'So one of your responsibilities is taking care of this group?'

'I am like... like a teacher.'

'Do you teach these white souls while you are living on Earth? Are you actually doing two things at once... like women actually...?'

'Yes, I can do it.'

'How is it possible?'

'Because my intellect and my soul work independently of each other. My soul is more powerful than my intellect,' she replied without exaggeration.

'Why? Why did they not give you a more powerful intelligence?' I asked.

'I don't think I need to be especially intellectual because… because… mmm… because I would become too concerned,' she answered.

'By intellectual matters?'

'No, not so much intellectual things. I think it is… materialistic capitalism…'

'How can we as souls affect our environment?' I asked.

'Everything has different levels… okay… so the higher up you are… the higher the level you have reached… the more you are able to accomplish. The greater is your influence. It is hard to explain, because it is not… you tend to think in terms of human consciousness, and it isn't a human sense,' Isis concluded.

Guides

Getting assistance from a knowledgeable guide can enhance the trip to a country with a long, rich cultural history. Guides can help you interpret a language or find that special place you would otherwise have missed. Most of us have probably used guides at some point in our physical life. In life many have also encountered terms such as "guardian angels" or "protective spirit". Is there any kind of basis for this, and what signifies a spiritual guide or guardian angel?

Most clients, once again independently of each other, talk about their guides in the afterlife, but also sometimes about those creatures they would give the name "angels". In many studies regarding people's faith it has been shown again and again that a majority of people believe in a force or a life after death. This acts as an enigmatic deep contrast to that world where established science more or less casually dismisses the possibility of an existence following death.

To maintain and extend life to enormous costs has become the answer in the materialistic society. Politicians, financiers and some religious leaders have in their own ways put controls on people, natural resources, states and capital. Millions of civilians are killed, and soldiers have constantly been regarded a natural force in order to defend a system of ownership and power. Those who guide political leaders and financial titans do of course not have any spiritual motives, but strictly selfish and financial motivations in order to achieve power and status. The system has to be preserved at any cost.

The biggest question is why so many people share the same values regarding death and the afterlife, when so many political and financial leaders have a diametrically opposite view? Why is it so threatening with a world where we all are equal and the lies cannot root?

Hundreds of clients have time and time again showed the same surprise when they are firmly, yet lovingly, reminded of their origin by their guides. Invisibly and constantly these guides follow and direct a two-faced humanity on the great scene of Earth. Faces which expresses both limitless evil, yet also the richest and most wonderful love.

My experience is that all people have one or sometimes several guides. Some guides have earlier lived incarnated on Earth, but for different reasons they chose to become guides. Some have lived so many lives and reached such a level that the earth lives are no longer necessary. Other guides seem to believe that life on Earth is so painful that they have chosen to refrain. What is common is their importance, and that they from a treatment perspective can be an excellent help for that therapist who, freed of prejudice, uses the guides as "colleagues on the other side". Such a relationship was formed between Ron and his guide Omar and me, but also with several other clients.

Some people, who have neither had a spiritual interest or a religion, are at first shocked at this change, but no client of mine has dismissed the experience and considered it as fantasy or madness. Contrarily, many have undergone such major and radical inner changes that their lives have been given a new meaning. The story of "The Crying Policeman" is such an example. These changes have much in common with what has been reported by people who have had near death experiences or out of body experiences. In the following case studies some clients talk about the spiritual guides.

***

Laura who was murdered by Nazis in Austria by the age of twelve, relays what her guides are saying.

'Azaria is soft. Broken Arrow is a strong Indian, while Li Tan is a wise Chinese man. Broken Arrow is disappointed with me because I have got stuck in old emotions. It makes me unable to move on. They remind me that my task on Earth is to work with and heal animals.'

***

Often guides are incorporated in the welcoming home to afterlife. This young Englishman described how he died as a young woman in Scotland.

'I am a young woman who dies suddenly somewhere out in the fields in Scotland. I am completely sure about this. After my death I arrive at the Gate. There I am welcomed by a dozen people in a half circle before me. I don't recognize the one who comes up to me first... he is an old man with a beard... ah... now I see it is my guide Gerald...'

***

Tony, the tax collector from Wesby, England, continues to give us insight.

'Albert is an old monk. He is my guide. He takes me to the library. It is an enormous building with books stacked up to a nearly invisible ceiling. The books continue as far as the eye can see,' Tony said.

***

And the Queen from Thebes has given several accounts of guides.

'Do you discuss questions regarding your soul with your guides and perhaps also with a Master?' I asked Isis.

'Yes,' she said.

'How does he or she look?'

'They are all incredibly beautiful these people... all of them.'

'And why is there more than one Master?'

'No, it is my guides and my Master who is male. It is a man, so mainly he wishes to be male, even if there is likely a female part too I think... I am the only woman. They... are all... the guides are men and my Master is male. And I am the only woman.'

***

And Jake who had premonitions had lost both his parents. His story is found in the chapter "The Premium Bonds". Jake was now keen to explore his own spirituality and to find a solution in his life.

'How many guides do you have Jake?'

'Three or five... one of them is a tall man... Omar. He has a beard and is dressed in a shroud. He says that he has waited for me for a long time. I have been a disobedient boy... again...' Jake said. Omar then proceeded to speak through Jake.

'Human stupidity. Just small pleasures. Jake must learn how to stop drinking alcohol. He can have a glass and 1-2 cigarettes, but no more. I helped him for many years. I was one of the first guides. He has had enough of bad thoughts... there is fear of awakening... a dark side. He can't handle his bad thoughts.'

After the session Jake confessed that everything was true. He had drunk too much alcohol for many years, and had trouble putting up with his dark thoughts.

The Garden of Souls

Many referred clients have great worry, physical illness, economic issues and social problems. When the money was rolling in from the stock market, the new house was ready to be moved into and the wedding planned, there was likely not a single thought spared to existential questions, life after death or other people's pain and suffering. When the personal economy has been ruined, the marriage dissolved and a close relative has suddenly died, there is naturally a psychological, spiritual and physical reaction.

Not all people have invested time and energy in precautionary measures. This obviously has a price. The soul ends up in crisis, while happy pills are prescribed by the doctors.

A few lucky ones get free counselling or sometimes also cognitive therapy, yet the suffering continues, often because the treatment methods focus on the symptoms and not the source. In an increasingly stressed and performance focused world time becomes a scarce resource. There is simply not enough money to give the client 1½ hours to talk about their issues. Prescriptions can be necessary, but with spiritually suffering people they just become an illusionary shortcut away from frustration, desensitization, anger and more pain. That is when the individual also start to search for alternative methods.

The engagement of the individual creates conditions for a more constructive, long term healing. In my own opinion the higher consciousness under hypnosis gives the possibility of closing in on the ultimate source of suffering. The symptoms then become secondary to the treatment method's real goal.

Just like a surgeon removes blast shards from an injured body, the therapist must mentally/spiritually/psychologically remove the charged trauma from the individual soul. The dreadful traumas created by fathers raping their daughters, women's fear after being murdered in a past life, the loss of children from illness, the soldiers experience of violence from war, or violence against a wife in life upon life. All of this needs to be handled carefully, respectfully and without judgement. Such work requires courage, patience, imagination and energy. Sometimes the road to recovery begins in the Garden of Souls. This garden is unique to each individual. Again and again I have seen how people during their first contact in the Garden of Souls experience reunion, love and joy. It cannot really be described, only experienced.

***

One such exceptional experience was when Roxanne lost her father during her therapy. Roxanne suffered from difficult recurring depressions. She had told me at the beginning of our contact that she was distressed by a conflict with her siblings. One of her sisters had alcohol issues and she was insistent that Roxanne would not have the energy to attend her father's funeral.

'Oh, I am by a fountain and I can see my father sitting there with my mother and Roger and his side,' Roxanne said.

'Who is Roger?' I asked.

'He was my brother who died twenty years ago in connection with a seizure... he was twenty-three years old. My father looks happy and healthy. He is smiling, and no longer in a wheelchair. He looks young. He tells me that we should make his funeral a celebration of life... he wants us to stop fighting and to be together... he already knew before he died that I would come to the Garden...'

Roxanne did not only attend her father's funeral, she also wrote a long, and very beautiful, speech. The funeral came together as her father had wished and the family members managed to avoid any conflict with each other.

***

A fifty-five year old woman, who had lost her husband in the past year, describes her first experience from the Garden of Souls. She was thoroughly detailed in her descriptions of both the souls and guides she met as well as the environment.

'I am walking through a wonderful garden with jasmine and honeysuckle. It feels so pleasant. Hmm... I meet an old woman with black hair... dark blue clothes and big blue eyes... her name is Helen.'

***

An eighteen year old woman had been sexually abused by her uncle as a nine year old. Her father also abused her for a year until she finally told her best friend everything. Kate's treatment was successful and she was able to completely free herself from all the anxiety caused by years of abuse.

'I walk through a garden. There are red, yellow and lilac flowers. Trees, green grass, crystal clear water, and it is a wonderful, calm and relaxed environment. Mm... I meet my mother's grandfather Jim. He has been dead for a long time. He tells me a bit about my mother's childhood, especially the trip they took by carriage down to Walton-on-the-Naze.'

***

Keith had been referred by his GP due to panic anxiety. During the treatment a recurring theme was Keith's conflict with his father. When Keith concluded the treatment after five sessions he had completely recovered from his troubles.

'I am in a garden. My father stands in front of me. He tells me that he did not want to come here, but that he came because I wished it. He tells me that he left the family because my mother knew a secret. Dad was not my real dad, and his wife knew this. He tells me that he is proud of me and that I should never leave my children like he did. Before he leaves he tells me that he is busy meeting friends and that he was surprised to discover he had a consciousness after his death.'

During a later session Keith met his father in the garden again. This time the meeting was more light and joyful.

'My father tells me that he was asked by his guides to go to the garden again. That is why he knew of the meeting in advance.'

Keith and his dad managed to mend their relationship, and Keith was relieved to be able to forgive his father's disappearance. A disappearance which had played a major role in his young life.

***

A recently retired English woman suddenly started to breathe violently. She seemed shaken by something which occurred during the session.

'Oh... I have walked through the garden and I suddenly meet dad. He embraces me. We do not even need to speak to each other. He knew that I would come here and that it would happen through this session.'

Before she left she almost started crying due to the experience, yet she radiated genuine happiness.

The Council of the Elders

The pioneer Michael Newton has left a large number of descriptions of the Council of the Elders in his books. This place has also been described by a long list of my own clients, and even though their lives have all been so different I am continuously astonished by the unity that is shown in their descriptions.

The Council of the Elders is a place for counselling before departure to an upcoming life. It is also a core spiritual institution for reflection, support and contemplation regarding a past life. There is never a trace of wrath or condemnation in this place. Instead each soul is given an opportunity to demonstrate their insight and self-knowledge before the oldest and wisest souls. Some clients are accompanied by their guides, either because they need support or because they have difficulty expressing their experiences or questions. Others simply need a little push in order to dare take the next step.

The members of the council naturally do not share everything they know. Just like we know that a child has to learn to walk before they can run, the Council knows that everything has its time and place. When souls communicate it happens instantaneously by a transfer of information and knowledge in a way that differs from speech and hearing. Everything happens immediately here and now for the individual soul. It is precisely during this process that it becomes very clear how much time it takes for the client to transfer information in both directions. Speech, hearing and vision are simply very slow methods of communication in comparison to the invisible language of souls. Sometimes the client gets a little irritated of having to relay the information, and sometimes it simply takes too long. Many of the individual sessions described in this book have taken one to two hours to complete. The process is physically very time-consuming. Some clients have observed that if two souls don't want to share their information with anyone else, they are able to touch each other. There are never any negative intentions with such behaviour.

There are many different experiences from the hundreds of clients I have met throughout the years. Younger souls with few life experiences on Earth, more commonly bring their guides with them before the Council. In addition, the number of members on the Council is often greater the older and more experienced the soul get.

Each Council has a chairman who not uncommonly refers the souls to a specific area that needs to be explored or understood. Usually there is a mix of male and female Council members, even if the soul can choose to manifest any gender. A number of clients have conveyed that the chairman sometimes has a medallion with one or more symbols. The medallion itself seems to stand for an archetype or a symbol which signifies the individual's specific gift, specialisation or ability. Several cases have produced pictures or drawings of the medallion that they have seen. During the session the individual is given a post-hypnotic suggestion to photograph the medallion in their memory and if possible draw it after returning home. Several clients have made excellent drawings of these medallions.

Some clients' guides have occasionally been responsible for the transmission of questions and answers between the Council and the visiting soul. A few clients with few life experiences sometimes have difficulty assimilating the experience. Sometimes I have suspected that the experience itself has not occurred at the right moment. Of course, sometimes the Councils themselves have imparted this by asking why the individual has been taken there.

My consistent experience is still that the Council of the Elders is a deeply fascinating spiritual institution. The chain of events itself obviously challenges our human need for control, but also our learned compulsion to dismiss the unexplainable as irrational and imagined. How is it possible for a relatively non-intellectual person to divulge such incredible knowledge, understanding and insight during a session of hypnosis?

I have chosen to give many accounts from clients' meetings with the Council of the Elders. The reason is mainly because these meetings seem to have played a crucial part in the clients' recovery.

***

Sean is the only client who has had two meetings with the Council of the Elders where something important happened between the meetings. Here we meet Sean during his first meeting with the Council.

'I see seven members in the Council. They seem to be almost dressed in suits. A man is the chairman. There are also two female members. They seem... disappointed that I did not perform well enough in school.'

'Is there enough time for you to change according to the Council?'

'I am starting to get old... they don't judge me. They do not accuse me either, but rather comment on how I have lived my life. I need to become kinder and...'

A few weeks later Sean had been to an additional three sessions. During a motorbike trip with his friends they suddenly left him. Something happened with Sean and he started to pay attention to his inner self. When I discovered Sean's sudden change and how he had grown milder and more humble, I took the chance to see if anything would happen if he was given the possibility of revisiting the Council of the Elders.

'I am in a room with five creatures behind a desk. Two are female and three are male. The chairman is still a man. They are dressed in quite dark blue suits. They are very kind and they say that they are surprised by my change.'

'How do they know that you have changed?'

'They knew it at the same moment as when I felt sorrow in my soul last week when my friends left me. They are saying that my soul and personality can be described as a spiked tower. They say that the spikes have disappeared and that this might also symbolise my personal strength. They say that they are doing this through you...'

Sean's life changed forever. Of all my clients he was the one who changed the most within the shortest timeframe.

***

During another session an extremely talented Indian doctor participated. He has since returned to New Delhi and works on a high level within the nation's health care. Before the session Carol told my Indian colleague that she had never really had any faith and that she had never really cared about God.

'I stand before a Council of eight members. They are dressed in cloaks and the chairman sits in the middle. I perceive them as very wise, yet I feel calm and comfortable. They tell me that they are pleased with my development since I have failed before.'

I asked the Council through Carol if they believed it was appropriate with this type of therapy.

'They confirm that this initially created big issues... it has to be carried out with a pure heart, and not everyone seem to have that. The process is inevitable and they knew that it would happen, but it still has created a lot of issues. No problems regarding you specifically, but worries on a general level.'

'But can they not discover those with negative intentions?' I asked.

'No, that's not it. It is a part of life and they cannot protect people from it... mm... I feel humbled by being able to transmit this discussion regarding this method in general. The gentleman who is sitting here and tries to introduce the method in India will encounter resistance... it isn't as easy as you might think. In that country there are some basic tenants of faith which can create big issues... the chairman of the Council nods... they were all well aware of all the facts around our session... in truth they were aware of all these questions before I visited the Council,' Carol said.

After the session Carol was shocked to find that she had been in a state of higher consciousness for a whole two hours. My Indian colleague told me that he would never forget his surprise when my clients so easily had read his thoughts.

***

Another client gives a good description of her encounter with the elders.

'I am standing before the Council of the Elders with twelve beings sitting behind a desk. Most of them wear white cloaks, and the male chairman, who is sitting in the middle, directs the meeting. They all look kind and look at me with interest.'

'Does the chairman have anything around his neck?' I asked.

'He has a chain connected to something that looks like a locket. It looks like there is a lid on the top. There are no symbols on it,' she replied.

'They say that I will feel well.'

'Is anyone in the Council asking you anything?'

'A few are asking me why I messed up my life with all these relationships... now I can see that I have wasted my time... I feel disappointed.'

During the session she continued to keep an inaudible inner dialogue with the Council. Just like many times before the client only physically conveyed a fraction of her experiences to me. Sometimes this could be frustrating to say the least.

***

Meg from Southend-on-Sea describes her Council.

'I walk through a door under an arch. There are steps which go round and round. The building is round. There are three higher beings behind a table. The middle one is a female chairman. She has a chain around her neck with a necklace of flowers. It seems as if the Council know of my anxiety... it seems as if the Council's members speak to each other. Apparently they think that I have come a little too early. The tell me to come back', said the young woman.

'Ask the Council what the best way of helping you is?' I asked.

'They say that I need continuous support, emotional support. Something within the church can help me… meditations calm me down…'

***

My client from Finland had been carrying a heavy heart for many years. Some would describe it as having had bad luck in love. Through life-after-life therapy she wished to find the answer as to why she lived alone. It turned out to be very easy for Marja to meet the Council, perhaps because she meditated daily.

'There are many beings here… they are very old… the chairman is a woman. Around her neck she has leaves formed as into a necklace. They are joyful and when I ask them about my future they just sing the word LOVE… they sing LOVE over and over.'

After a few months Marja sent me a drawing. She said that the experience had affected her so strongly that it had taken a long time for her to process and integrate the whole event to her inner self. She was completely convinced that the experience was real.

***

An English gentleman described his Council with emphasis on the medallion.

'I am standing before six older beings behind a semi-circular table. The chairman has a medallion in a chain around its neck. In the chain there is a sapphire or ruby,' said Liam.

'Go closer! What can you see now?'

'A small "gremlin"… a part of myself and all the bad things I have done in the past.'

***

The always tired and downtrodden Roxanne smiled in recognition. She seemed so excited and full of energy during the session.

'The chairman has a golden disc around his neck... I cannot see what it represents,' she said.

'Go closer and take a mental photograph when you receive my instruction,' I encouraged her.

'It is a golden disc with a tree in the middle... the Tree symbolises me and the importance of taking care of myself. The Council encourages me to explore myself. There is also another disc on a red ribbon. It has strange letters in a circle around the border. There is a picture of a temple in the middle... I won't forget this.'

***

Laura had great issues with both herself and her foster daughter. There was a long line of conflicts between them, and Laura had a history of violence and emotional issues. Here Laura reports from her meeting with the Council of the Elders.

'They are not pleased with me... I can see a knife... yes, I killed her... and then I took my own life.'

'Look into her eyes! Who is it?'

'It's my foster daughter.'

I encouraged Laura to extend herself to reconcile with her foster daughter and, if possible, to forgive herself.

In her current life Laura's foster daughter suffers from a heart condition from birth. This "hole" causes a special case of palpitations. Her congenital defect affect around 8 out of 1000 new-borns and, together with Laura's story, it has remarkable similarities to those outer birthmarks which Professor Ian Stevenson describes in several of his well-known books. The knife actually did hit the heart!

***

Tony had always been tremendously scared of dying. Perhaps this had its roots in the difficult compulsive disorder which was the reason for his referral by his GP. He suffered from, amongst others, cleaning

286

mania. One of those lives Tony had lived showed to some degree how this fear could have developed.

The session started with Tony regressing back to the age of two. He spastically moved his head towards his right even during hypnosis. Tony told how his mother grew increasingly alarmed by his compulsive actions. After I had told Tony to use his guide Albert to find the cause of his OCD, he proceeded to speak: 'Oh, I am a weak little boy... my name is Harold... he is three years old and he lives in a poorhouse. It is extremely dirty. I don't think he has any parents. He just lives there and survives by eating earwigs, flies, mice and some sort of dirty soup that they give him... there is only a little sunshine which comes through a window with iron bars. Harold never left the building during his short life. He just sits there and has nothing to do...'

I invited Tony to go to the end of Harold's life to see how he died.

'Harold actually lives there until he is 9 years old. He dies from hunger and disease. He used to scrub the floor where the workers were and sometimes they gave him a bit of dirty water so that he could survive.'

'What were you supposed to learn in this harsh life?'

'To find inner strength and to survive against all odds.'

Of course Harold's life stood out as a deep contrast against Tony's obsession of constantly cleaning the house both after his marriage and his later divorce when his wife left him for his best friend. To Tony, the meeting with the Council of the Elders was important.

'My guide follows me to the Council of the Elders. Three men are waiting for me. The middle one has a chain attached to a medallion around his neck. I can see an old man with a beard in the middle of the medallion...' He started to laugh. 'Ha ha, I realise now that the old man is actually myself.' He told me that the Council itself asked him if he had any questions. 'I have a question regarding my whole existence... the chairman tells me that I must let go... They say that I am a good person...'

The Akasha Library

Religious leaders have sometimes spoken of how all peoples' actions are registered in Heaven. Humans have scarcely put any weight to such statements. During their constant hunt for new experiences in an increasingly compromised bubble of time, there usually exists neither interest nor time for contemplating the cause and effects of actions. Naturally, many are completely preoccupied with simply trying to live their lives and to survive in an increasingly pressured existence.

Even the most stubborn opponent to spirituality or religion, is forced to concede that an evil action on Earth obviously has immediate or long term effects. Everyone wants to see justice done, but not everyone is prepared to reveal the truth so that justice can be served.

Sanskrit describes everything which creates cause and effect as karma. An unending cycle which is in strong contrast to the idea of everything being controlled by fate. In some Hindu schools humanity's free choice between good and evil is viewed as a natural part of God's plan. In Bhagavagita Krishna himself stands before the difficult choice of having to wage war against his own family. His divine squires explain that it is of course his duty, dharma, to carry out these deeds.

Every person must through her own choice accept that good and evil are experiences and a consequence of life choices and actions. In eastern religions, such as Buddhism, God is not deemed responsible for this, but rather the present, past and the future is constantly created by people's thoughts and actions. In this way each person receives, as a result of the sum of their actions, neither more nor less good or evil than they deserve. To followers of Hinduism and Buddhists the main goal is to unfetter yourself from Karma.

To my surprise it has been shown that many clients report details which to some degree support the eastern schools of thought. My experience is that a murderer who escapes punishment in the physical life will still be confronted by his actions in the afterlife. Actions have consequences, and sooner or later the murderer himself must experience the suffering of the victim, regardless if it is on a mental, spiritual or physical level. Yet there is still no punishment. All souls are part of a hierarchy of infinite learning, and as hard as it is to accept a life where you enter a German gas chamber, it is equally difficult to choose the role of executioner. Everyone needs to realise the cause and effect of actions.

Many people naturally have trouble of both understanding and accepting such a way of thought. In such cases it often proves fruitful to visit the library of the Akasha books.

In Sanskrit Akasha means "the existence of all things", a knowledge of all infinite events and existences. Time upon time my clients have not only gained knowledge for themselves, but also given me knowledge which in an extraordinary way helps to explain the existence of everything.

Like other spiritual levels, not all souls are able to or want to visit the Akasha Library. The golden rule seems to be that each soul is given the precise level of knowledge that he or she can handle or is ready for. How this is determined is still unclear.

***

In the following examples we will follow some remarkable accounts from some of my clients. Tony starts by telling about the library.

'I walk to the Library together with my guide Albert. It is an enormous building with books up to a nearly invisible ceiling. The books continue as far as the eye can see. I see other people reading books, and there is a white lady here who offers me my first book.'

'Describe the appearance of the book?' I asked.

'The book has a cover of brown leather. As I open it I can read that it is about... all my lost friends... oh... now I understand why they all left me... it was about me... I was too open and gave away too much and they used it and deserted me...' Tony then received another book of red leather. He continued: 'The title says... "The Book of Actions"... each action becomes completely different as I experience them through the book. I do not only read about an action, but I also perceive all the emotions tied to it. It is so unexpected and enlightening.'

Tony now also discovered that he had earlier been quite violent, just like his father, but that this was not a practicable way through life. He saw himself as a quite old soul, and even if he did not wish to appear selfish or self-involved, he often knew more than most.

***

In January 2005, a fascinating session took place. Enzo was actually visiting the Akasha Library to understand herself better. What actually happened was something completely different.

'I see someone reading a book in another room. An older man gives me a book. When I turn the first page I see like a golden leaf around a very distinct picture. I see a human, or a man, inside a circle and his arms and legs are extended towards the circle. Both his feet and arms seem to touch a square but at the same time the circle... I see some strange lines go through the picture at the bottom and I can see the name "da Vinci" under the picture itself.'

When the session had finished I asked Enzo for the first time to come with me to my office. There I showed her the book I was currently reading. The book was called "Holy Geometry" and was written by Melchizedek. On one of the first pages in the book was a copy of Leonardo da Vinci's famous drawing "The Vitruvian Man", or as it is also sometimes know, "The Cannon of Proportions".

The experience showed us both that even though no one knew what I was reading, Enzo was in her enhanced state of consciousness or super consciousness, able to to easily see what I was studying privately. Perhaps the precise intention was to demonstrate the connection between therapist and client, but also art and science, and humanity's relation to nature. Every detail in this drawing stands in exact proportion to the whole, just like her triskele. Perhaps this was also the message we were given from the Akasha Librarian.

***

We have met Sean before in several different chapters. Here he is again, in the Akasha Library.

'It is an enormous library with shelves of books as far as I can see. A guardian gives me three different books.'

'When you open the first book, what can you see?'

'It is about my previous and current life... I have been a scary man... I have been bad at many things, but right now at this point in time, I have found a way to change through my soul.' He grew almost impatient and wanted to move on.

'The second book is about my two sons. They often fight... I realise now that my other son is almost a carbon copy of myself!'

'Do you think you can get them to fight less?' I asked.

'I normally don't get involved in their fights,' Sean said.

'And what is the third book about?' I asked, almost a bit impatiently too.

'It is about my friends and my life in general.'

All of this released a chain reaction within Sean. He took himself into the future, perhaps to find more answers about himself. First he told me a bit more about who he was before he continued to talk about the future.

'I walk by the sea with my two daughters. They are four and six years old. It is in Cornwall, and it is actually quite long ago. When I look at the girls I feel so much love, but I also understand that I made a mistake when I left them... I have not seen them in many years now... one day one of the girls will stand outside my door. She will then be in her twenties. We will have a really nice relationship. They will discover that I have changed a great deal... it seems as if it was more difficult for the girls to live apart than it was for me.'

Before Sean one day forever disappeared on his motorbike, he turned to me and said: 'I didn't believe in anything when I started, but I now realise the full potential of this therapy... it has been like walking on clouds. I was not sure if it had been worth waiting 2 years for this... but I can now honestly say it was worth every second!'

When he left me that day in March 2008, I knew that he would never again turn into wrath. Sean had finally found his way home!

***

Tom, a twenty-six year old English man had compulsive thoughts and actions. It was later revealed that they had their origin in a life he had lived during the 18th century as a farmhand to a rich landlord.

'I sit and stare straight ahead in the kitchen. I feel completely empty. My wife lies in the bedroom and she is dead. We had a fight and I finally strangled her.'

He managed to convince his neighbours and friends that the wife had left him. They believed him because the couple was known for often fighting. He buried the wife in secret. During the therapy Tom discovered that this murder had led him to try to commit suicide repeatedly in his current life. The reason was that he was subconsciously scared of murdering the woman he was currently living with, and deeply in love with. On a subconscious level he was terrified of committing the same crime again.

'It is an enormous room with windows and shelves of books as far as the eye can see. There is a female guardian of the books, and at first she was not happy with the prospect of giving me a book.'

After requesting it again, the guardian gave him a book about himself.

'When I open it I can see that it's about me as a twelve year old boy. I suddenly realise that I am not happy with all the expectations both from myself but also from my family and life in large. I see a list of expectations comprised of being successful, being a proper person, to be of use to others and to have a purpose…'

To Tom this proved meaningful. He could put everything in context about himself. He recognised that he failed even though he had things to help him, and that he actually had access to things he needed. He apprehended that he had the possibility of choice to do or get what he wanted.

***

Shenmo walked through the massive Akasha Library. She was hunting for knowledge to understand her father's violent rage and his physical violence towards her mother. He had, amongst other things, attacked and kicked Shenmo's mother in the stomach when she was pregnant, expecting her daughter. It seemed as if this violence had also been the reason for Shenmo's congenital scoliosis and back pain, an injury which forced Shenmo to use crutches to walk.

'It is an enormous building with lots of books. I am standing in front of a desk where there is some sort of guardian or Master of all books. He gives me a special book.'

'What do you see when you open it?' I asked.

'The book is about my life and I look into the book and see everything that has happened from a multi-dimensional perspective. I can now see my father's horrible actions in the past… it seems as if this haunts him and has made him emotionally disturbed,' she said.

Without the need for instruction she said that she understood that this was the main reason which had contributed to his aggression and violence towards his own family. Shenmo said that it had been incredibly insightful to see her father's background, and to see this as a foundation towards her own life.

'The next book I am given by the guardian has a bull on the front. It is called "The Book of Wrath". In this book I see a lot of angry people. Yes, all sorts of greedy and selfish people who only seek to satisfy themselves, no matter the consequences. In the end of the book I see that this path leads nowhere, and that they all need to turn back. I see a bull, completely controlled by greed and selfishness, running right through these people as he throws them to the sides.'

A bull running through a china shop is an expression for breaking someone's spiritual ability.

Preparatory and Reorientation Classes

After a completed life, a process of reorientation ensues for the soul which might have suffered physical pain as well as mental and spiritual misery. Everything is regarded in a greater context and the souls are given assistance by guides, teachers and Masters to reorient themselves and to return to their natural existence. You could view this as a type of crisis management therapy with the intention to instigate learning and insights which hopefully for ever gives rise to development and change in the individual soul. If the soul fails and for instance repeatedly commits suicide in the physical life, the conflict needs to be resolved so that the soul can move on. Brian in "The Crying Policeman" and Mike in "The Last Straw" are good examples of how this process can get a push forward even in the physical life.

Some clients report of a preparatory room about the life that is planned, most often by the Masters. As a rule a soul is given a specific life, but more advanced souls have the possibility to choose. Language, religion, politics and country almost never seem to matter. A life is something very valuable, and it is honoured in the best possible and imaginable way. When people report about the journey back to life, you often get the impression of a busy train station. People come and go. Some are very anxious to depart for their new life. Others feel tense and worried by the knowledge that their life will be very demanding.

Souls discuss and organize everyday things which create conditions for learning. Family members, parents, lovers and users of violence discuss their roles together. The plan is formed of what they all have agreed to accomplish. On a conscious human level, our ideologies and ways of thought are naturally extremely tested, and no one should be criticized for dismissing a world which so radically changes our way of thought and action.

Thankfully we have been equipped with some tools to use during the course of the physical journey, some of which are named intuition, premonitions, déjà vu and prophetic dreams. Some might have experienced that when the signs are heeded, in the end all problems seem to work out alright.

It occasionally occurs that two very close souls get a comfortable and relaxing life after some tough trials. Physically they seem to live without a single serious problem. There is always money, entertainment and relaxation at hand, and life runs on a simple track. It is not hard to imagine other people's jealousy. Perhaps everything would be easier if we understood what really lies behind it all. When we look back at things in the end perhaps we do not wish to miss that day of falling in love. Let us listen to the planning between a few souls!

***

'When it is the right moment, I travel from London to Brazil. It will seem like a coincidence, but you board the same plane in Madrid because we have a stopover there due to an ill passenger. When you get the seat next to me, you have to trust your intuition and your feelings! If not then we have to wait perhaps another 15 years before we are given a second chance…'

All souls who are going to act on the scene of the great theatre of Earth must agree to have their memories blocked at the moment of incarnation. Otherwise conditions necessary for change and growth would not be available.

***

Some clients have independently spoken of preparatory classes. In those a number of souls and their teacher meet to discuss an especially demanding life, and those general goals which souls strive towards. One client reported the following: 'There is a very advanced teacher here today. He talks about the risk of growing too attracted by the dense body and other physical things. These physical attractions are short lived and serve the lower ego. Memory blocks will always be present, because otherwise no learning could occur. Only advanced souls know in advance… but now we discuss how this group of people will die together. All will die in a big terrorist attack… we all feel elated if we can accomplish this without growing too distracted by the tight gravity compromised of life itself… I can see my wife from my last life, and my grandfather and my two daughters. We will all be a part of this…'

**

Of course, many souls are pleased to be able to return to Earth. The reason is that they wish to change, develop and learn. Souls sometimes chose the opposite gender in order to really learn more about the gender they have had difficulty understanding and integrating. Other souls have a preference for a specific gender, but sometimes they must shift gender in order to create optimal learning conditions. Sometimes I have had clients who have reported that a life as homosexual has been created under just such circumstances. When this knowledge was transferred to me, I instantly realised that sexuality might be controlled on a higher plane, and that the individual sometimes experience lots of pain in order to heed their "true" love. In fact, it seems as if the soul is far more powerful than the body's primitive way of expressing sexuality. Perhaps this can help religious people to more easily accept homosexuality.

Sometimes the rapist is forced to reincarnate as a woman to experience for himself what sexual violence and duress means to the woman. I would guess that such a lesson will hopefully create fewer relapses than prison.

Through other clients it has come to light that those who die very young in connection with accidents, violence or disease, often reincarnate very quickly. In his books about reincarnation Professor Ian Stevenson has given plenty of proof of this process.

When I ask clients how they know when it is time to depart for a new life, they reply: 'I just know that it is time, and I just go. It just happens...'

If we allow ourselves for a short moment to consider the possibility of a higher plan, perhaps we would be more reluctant to blame our own misfortune on others. The answer might instead be that the misfortune is a part of our own learning, something we have accepted in the afterlife as a necessary part of the learning process.

Most clients' souls repeat that the difficulty does not lie in preparing for a life, but rather in the fact that the human does not follow the created plan. The temptations grow too large on the material plane, not least due to humanity possessing free will. Soon those intuitions and dreams which showed what really needed to be done wilt away, relegated to a corner of human forgetfulness.

***

This fifty-five year old English woman described her experience of education in the afterlife.

'I am sitting in a room which you could describe as made out of clouds. I listen to a teacher who speaks of the struggle to understand that not all good actions are good. Sometimes they can cause harm. I can see other souls, but I can't really describe them. I participate in this class because I am soon leaving the afterlife for my current life in England. It almost feels as an honour...'

Life Choices

After a time of healing, recovery and reunion after a painful life, new challenges await. The souls seem to constantly seek higher and tougher challenges. Preparations and planning seem as natural in the afterlife as in our physical everyday life.

The Council of the Elders give possibility to evaluation and insights. In the Ring of Destiny the possibility is given of understanding on a higher level, but also a possibility to study the life that is being planned in greater detail. The guides are a basic requirement for most souls to be able to even handle life on Earth. Before a new life takes shape, more experienced souls are given the chance to choose a life.

Many clients have independently reported about a fascinating part of the afterlife. In the room of life selection one or several Masters give the soul the possibility to choose among several lives. How these choices are made is described in the following stories by my clients.

***

Sheila, who kept caring for her dying son, visited the place of life selection.

'There is an advanced higher being here who helps me. I do not choose a life, but I get one and I accept it without hesitation. There are other lives available in this place. I get to sit down in a chair and I can see almost like snapshots of myself as a child and when I get older. I feel secure with this.'

***

Another young woman visited the room for life selections. She described that as a rule she chose to live as a woman. She also said that she had chosen to live in an Asperger family. Asperger's is a autism spectrum disorder which is signified by lacking social competence, emotional disconnection but also compulsive obsession by specific areas of interest in anything from bus time tables to advanced mathematics. Sometimes this young woman wished that she could exchange her anxiety filled life for another.

'There is a person in a cloak here who helps me. He looks almost medieval. I am offered a life and I accept it. It was about emotional suffering... painful... to teach us... different aspects of life,' she finished.

***

A fellow colleague and woman told of how she came to the room of life selection. In her latest life she died hungry and malnourished in Auschwitz. It was a dreadful experience which remained in her soul.

'I am in a room where I can choose a life. It is almost like a clothes shop... I can see up to five different lives. I can choose to be a rich Chinese woman, but then my liberty is rather compromised. I can also choose a life in New York, in luxury and extravagance. Now I can see a life I really fall for. It is in north Norway. I have warm, comfortable clothes. I get to be healthy and never need to go hungry. We aren't rich, but my family loves me, and that is where I want to live.'

Hybrids

On some rare occasion it has happened that a client refers to a life in other, distant civilisations, and sometimes even other life forms. It is obviously naïve to believe that humanity is the crown of creation, or the only existing life form in the universe. Such a mindset would constitute human narcissism on a cosmic level.

Of course, we are trained to not believe, or even to want to believe, in stories like S'rlian's. That was also her own sentiment. She had never dared to tell any of this to her relatives, and even less to her psychiatrists. Her experience was fascinating, and naturally raised questions in my mind. I understood that those questions could create hysteria, wrath and persecution. A few years earlier I spoke to the now late and wonderful Professor John Mack, Harvard University. He was a well-respected Professor of Psychiatry until the day when he published the book "Abduction".

The only problem was that he had been asked to investigate the issue of abduction by aliens and that his conclusion was that there was no evidence that any of the independent individuals either lied or fabricated evidence. Professor Mack taught me that science, religions and even governments are not yet ready to meet uncomfortable truths in public. The truth is that we are not alone in the universe. Today Professor Mack is dead, hit by a car in London as he crossed the street from his hotel.

Clients, who claim that they have had previous lives in other civilisations, sometimes find it incredibly difficult as souls to stand the destructivity and animosity which the Earth's environment offers. Some claim that they have been born on Earth as an extraordinary challenge. A planet like Earth with its extreme challenges is cosmically regarded as more demanding than most other civilisation in the universe.

You are obviously free to dismiss these claims or perhaps other life forms, but are you absolutely sure that they are not already studying you? The souls in the afterlife truly seem to study every step we take, and their worry about our capability for self-destruction does not seem to have decreased during the last few years. It is naturally doubtful if any civilisation would currently like to contact a race which is not only capable of repeated genocides, but also of dropping atom bombs on civilians.

S'rlian's strange story was imparted by an English woman in her late middle age. She claimed to be intellectually slow, but nothing was revealed pointing towards any type of developmental disorders. As a semi-hybrid–she was abducted by aliens–she always tried to hide from attention. Her childhood was marred by sexual abuse from a relative, and through large portions of her life she was controlled by self-involved and aggressive men. She had always been used to people never noticing her existence. She was happy with that, largely depending on the immense fear which had once been created in a previous life.

I have compiled the following story from a large number of sessions, mainly to bring order to all the details and to enable a greater overview. This stands in distinction to other cases in this book, which are mainly direct transcripts from the sessions. S'rlian's story consists of memories from an earlier life that she has always carried with her. During the conversations with me she was able, for the first time, to share her memories in a continuous flow. She is the only client who did not undergo classic hypnosis.

It was a great personal shock when another young English male patient who I had never treated informed me in May 2011 that S'rlian had suddenly passed away with heart problems. In the light of her story it is easy to understand that she finally found peace. S'rlian's strength and courage was astonishing. T'Caana is her story.

T'Caana

Everything has come forth through my body and my hands. Before you read this I ask you not to judge or condemn me. I am a quiet woman, and I think that I am without purpose on this planet.

In reality I would rather go back to T'Caana because the Earth is in itself too difficult for me. I have never before even dared to entertain the thought of telling anyone, because they would obviously believe that I am insane.

I have given you my story with honesty and integrity. My doctor got me to share this, and he is the only person I can trust in this world. You have the right to not believe me, but when you have finished reading, remember this: Every reasonable person or government would deny it. It is nothing but nonsense and madness. For me this was a terrible nightmare which became real. I survived and I received a new life on another planet far away in a distant galaxy. I have decided to allow my doctor to publish this to honour the 19 people who died on the alien spaceship. This is my story.

There were 20 of us in total. We had all been abducted by aliens on Earth, and we knew there would be no chance for us to get back. There aliens used us for experiments. It was completely terrifying. I cannot say how long ago this was, but it was in one of my previous lives. I was sixteen or seventeen years old when I was abducted. I was on a field together with other people from the village. We harvested vegetables or something that we all collected to save and collect. I wore a heavy brown dress made of some cotton material. It was partly hitched up to not drag in the mud. Since I was barefoot I needed to wash my feet in the stream. In the spaceship we got some type of disgusting porridge as food and we all knew we were lost. Everyone especially felt for the five year old girl. In the end I killed her. I wanted to save her from all the terrible experiments and these evil grey aliens. They were very short, and just used us as experimental animals.

I managed to hide from them. There was a loud bang and I managed to escape. My abductors searched for me. I heard screams, but not from them. I hid in the tall grass and amongst the bushes.

It was very dark and I could hear shouting. They were killed. Suddenly I heard footsteps close to me. I did not dare to breathe or move, and I did not know where the others were. My memory seemed to disappear. Everything was silent and I decided to make a move. It was a mistake. They threw themselves onto me and dragged me away.

I then remember a creature in a room which I could not see out of. They observed me. I was questioned but did not reply. Finally, I was taken back to the dark room.

One day I was marched away to another part of the building. A hooded cape was thrown over me from head to toe. I remember looking at the floor as they escorted me away. The floor was so black it seemed as if you could fall right through it. The massive doors opened and I was marched through and then pushed down to the floor.

When I finally dared to look up I saw three steps leading up to a great chair. There he sat, slouching. Just like me he wore a cape, so I could not see his face.

He then spoke, and everyone left the room. He stepped down and pulled back my hood. He stared at me and then started to speak. He asked if I knew who he was. I did not, but he seemed familiar. I felt safe with him.

I was then taken to another room, bright and spotless. Another man awaited me. He was a doctor. I was left alone with him as he examined me. All he did was, as I remember it, press a button and the bed I lay on scanned me and a diagnosis came up. I kept looking on his face. He had brown eyes, and like a raised ridge over the nose. I felt my own nose to see if I had a similar ridge, but I felt nothing.

The doctor took me back to the great room where he waited for us. He had his hood down and I could see his face. He was tall with dark shoulder length hair, and with the most sparkling blue eyes I have ever seen. He also had a ridge over his nose.

All who I could see had dark skin, but not black. They talked and looked over me. I later learned that they saw each other as brothers, even though they were not.

When I was out walking with F'rell everyone looked at me with kindness and curiosity. They all knew I was from a different planet. They later told me that they had visited our planet once or twice.

Somehow I started to eat with them. Not the first ones I met, but there were three others. An older lady, and old man and a young boy. We were in a small room compared to the big building I had first come to, but it was cosy. We all eat some sort of vegetable stew.

'We are not from your galaxy. We are from much further away, but we travel far and wide. Our planet is about the same size as yours, perhaps slightly larger. There is an ocean of islands, of which one belongs only to Sh Ch Ki. We used that island when we wanted to be alone. The planet is protected by an invisible force field which protects us from another species who wishes to eradicate us. We are stronger and more intelligent than them. There are rivers, fish in the sea, trees and diverse plants and animals, even if nothing is similar to yours. Some trees have almost blue leaves. We also have a sun and a moon,' F'rell told me as we washed ourselves. We bathed in a pool of something strange, as I felt a light tingle over my whole body. It was very refreshing.

We do not use cars. We have small vehicles which fly to where we wish to go. They have a humming sound. We also have cities where we trade. Our planet is not unlike yours, but we are more advanced. No one smokes, and we do not consume meat. We drink, but never in excess. I cannot remember what fuel source we use, but we have no pollution. One day there was a storm on the planet. It lasted several days. No one dared to go outside during the storm-it was much too dangerous.

As I lay on the medical examining table the doctor must have done something, because I could understand their language. Ch'Ki asked me many questions, but I could not answer all of them because the others had messed about with my memory.

It was not until much later I started to remember things. F'rell grew annoyed with me because he thought that I tried to avoid him. I was annoyed at him because he did not believe me. He got so angry because I dared to raise my voice to him, so that I ended up back in that small room. It was not long until I was escorted to a small room where they all sat waiting for me. They gave me some sort of vegetable stew again. They were all kind to me, but I could not see on his face if he was still unhappy with me. It was not until I started eating that his expression changed into a smile. I gawked as he smiled. The stew was so hot from spices that all I wanted was something to drink. Everyone laughed at me, so I could not help but to laugh at myself. It was the beginning of our friendship. I suppose I should tell you their names, but I cannot place the tongue right, so I will translate them as well as I can into our language.

Sh Ch Ki means "My lord", which is his title.

F'rell is his name.

L'ell is the lady

Sh'tare is the young boy.

L'kia is the old man.

I cannot quite remember the doctor's name because he was like a brother to Sh Ch Ki. I am not sure where to start the story of my life with F'rell and the others, because I am not sure if you want to know.

We live in some kind of fortification, with guards not far away. The building is very dark, and it is made out of some sort of stone. It does not look very inviting, but it was not meant to. Apparently it was built a hundred years ago when F'rell's ancestors ruled the planet as tyrants, until the death of his father.

F'rell was around twelve years old when he inherited the title. He was raised by L'ell and L'kia who trained him to be hard but fair. He still has a bad temper, but L'kia spoke with him now and then to sort things out. I did not see much of him during the day. Especially during the mornings as he was always in meetings with the High Council, trying to understand what was happening around the planet and making certain decisions. That was the only room I was not allowed to visit. No woman was, unless she had special permission by the court, and then she had to wear a cloak from head to foot.

If nothing special was happening, F'rell would often leave the meetings and we went to sit under the old tree by the river. Sometimes he showed me the inside of the building. Most rooms were very large, and seemed devoid of comfort and love. He was uninterested by them, and used to walk off.

You remind me of him slightly, with the way you walk with steps of authority. I tried to keep up to him in vain. Sometimes he took my hand and pulled me along with a smile on his face.

It was decided by L'kia that I would be taught to write their language as F'rell sat in his meetings. It wouldn't have been so bad except that I had to sit next to Sh'tare, who could be a mischievous little monkey. To read their language was not like words, but more like symbols or letters. It is very difficult to learn their language because so many letters look so similar.

I do not know how much more you would like to hear. I could tell you a lot more. About when F'rell and I united–we married. F'rell drank enough to shake the earth. I don't know what you would like to know.

Sometimes I sat under a tree with F'rell as the river passed us by. I kept splashing F'rell, which did not amuse him. He picked me up and threw me into the river. Then he jumped in after me.

Sh'tare was educated to follow in L'kia's footsteps. He was only eight years old, but already possessed an aura of wisdom. He was an orphan, and L'kia looked after him. L'kia knew that the boy would be the one to take over when the time came.

L'kia and L'ell were old, but I cannot say how old as I never asked them. But we had a gardener who was a wonderful man. He was 113 years old when he passed away. He had fallen down and broken his neck. I cried, but L'kia asked me why I cried for him.

'He has passed through time, and his journey continues,' she said.

I had to learn things over and over again, but in a different way. It was really difficult sometimes not to cry over people who died.

F'rell took me out on a flight over the ocean once. We just hovered around there. He asked me if I could see anything, which I could not.

He then landed the craft and we went over to some doors built into the cliff. It was massive inside. We sat in a capsule which seemed to float in the air. It took us deeper into the building. When it finally stopped my breath was taken away. It was like the inside of a building without walls, and you could see fishes swimming around the building itself.

I think this was the heart of their energy system, but I don't know what it was. There were enormous tubes everywhere and the lights from some kind of computers blinked on and off continuously. I think F'rell mentioned that there were several hundred people who worked there. I only saw around half a dozen during my visit.

L'ell was always so maternal towards me, if you can put it that way. She always took care of me, and made sure everything was well. She never allowed me to help with anything. She took care of everything in the household, even if she didn't do everything. There were others who worked there, but L'ell always cooked the food. She never allowed anyone else, although she had started to teach me. She used to make me laugh, even though I knew I shouldn't, by the way she reprimanded F'rell after doing something stupid or for shovelling down his food. It was like he was still a little boy. He didn't care. I think there are always such moments, no matter which world they live on.

Since I could not remember my name, F'rell received the pleasure of giving me one. He took his time, even if he later told me that he had kept the name in mind the whole time… He just wanted us to wait. It was his way of teasing or annoying us. I understand that I should try to write it down if I can. My name is S'rlian or something similar. F'rell and I loved each other so much that L'kia said it was time for us to be united. When two people were united, they could never be parted again. Not that they would want to. If one of them died, the other could never again become united.

As the time grew closer the preparations started. I started to feel nervous, because L'kia had explained what would happen. I did not look forward to that part of the ceremony. In a way I did, but not in front of the High Council. It was their custom and they never saw anything wrong with it. Normally a pair would have their whole family and friends there. Like a wedding here, but since it was Ch'Ki it had to be more official, and since F'rell did not feel comfortable with that, he decided that the ceremony would occur only in front of the Council. We would have a reception for all the others later.

The day came and L'kia had dressed himself in an ornamental cloak and then he went together with us into the temple. I thought the building would be like the inside of one of our churches, but it was not. It was a very old building, and it was very simple on the inside with only a stone altar in the centre of the great hall. As we entered I felt a great presence there. It was as if a warm and loving feeling enveloped me. I no longer felt nervous. I came to feel that presence later.

L'kia began the ceremony. He spoke for so long that I never thought he'd finish. F'rell and I stood with our faces to each other as in a trance. Then L'kia removed our cloaks and we felt the presence enclose us as we united. We made love before the Council and I did not care. It was the most wonderful feeling in the world, and I wish it had never ended.

The council did not stay, they had just ensured that we united. L'kia later grabbed us to prepare us for the reception. It was wonderful to meet all of F'rell's friends, even if I knew a few of them already.

F'rell was not allowed to drink more than two cups of alcohol due to reasons I will get to later. In any case I thought drinking was despicable. After he had drunk one cup L'kia told him to just drink fruit juice. He did. We had two wonderful weeks on the island, just the two of us. There are lots of bits I have left out, like all the silly and lovely moments we shared, but they would be too trivial for you.

F'rell and the captain of the guards were good friends. They had trained together. One day F'rell discovered that D'rin had an affair with another woman. It was not allowed, especially since he was already united and had children. During this special day they were out hunting. They only hunted wounded animals, because they could be dangerous to people in that condition. The animal they were hunting was one of the most dangerous. They loved the thrill of the hunt, but they did not use guns. Instead they used their knives. It was like a game to them. He who first got close to the animal would kill it. The animal was like a rhino, but it had more horns or tusks or both. I only saw one at a distance. F'rell said they were almost blind, their hearing was bad, but their sense of smell was brilliant. I do not remember who killed it in the end, but they returned to the guard quarters to celebrate. I don't know how F'rell got drunk, because he knew that he shouldn't drink more than a certain amount. D'rin was also drunk, and it was then that F'rell discovered it. He became so angry that they started to fight. D'rin pulled out his knife and attacked F'rell, and he grabbed his arm. At that moment F'rell had also pulled out his knife, and he stabbed D'rin in the chest. He fell to the floor. F'rell just left the rooms and left him where he lay. I only got to know all of this much later, when F'rell knew that he could tell me, but it was not the end of the matter. F'rell was still angry when he got home. I was in bed when I heard him shouting. I went out to see what the noise was.

F'rell was arguing with L'kia, and he asked him to move out of the way. When I saw him he did not at all look like the F'rell I knew and loved. Stupidly I went to him because I saw blood running down his body. He looked down at me and grabbed my arm. L'kia tried to go in between but F'rell just pushed him to the side. He dragged me into the bedroom, I did not stand a chance. He was much too strong—he was like an animal. I can't remember how long it lasted—I fell unconscious.

When I woke up Sh'ban was looking down at me. I was in the medical room. Sh'ban had repaired me physically, but my psyche was something else. I couldn't speak to anyone as I was in too much shock. Then L'kia carried me to the temple. I was put towards the altar. L'kia sat on my side and looked straight into my eyes, as if his gaze could pierce deep into me. Then I felt the presence again. It enveloped me, warm and pleasant. Then it went into my head and my whole body. It was a wonderful feeling. L'kia still looked into my eyes. I could see him speaking, but couldn't hear him. My soul was starting to clear up again. When it was over L'kia looked exhausted. We remained for a while as L'kia recovered, then he took me home. I knew that I had to speak with F'rell, but he wasn't there.

Apparently he had put himself before the Council to answer for his actions. Even if he was Ch'Ki he was not immune to punishment. The High Council ruled that D'rin's death was in self-defence, but what he had done to me would now be ruled on by the Council. They could punish him if I wanted it, but I didn't. I just wanted to find F'rell, which I did.

I should have understood that he would go to the island. I nagged L'kia to let me go to him. Finally he relented, but said that he would come with me. When we arrived we found F'rell sitting by the edge of the lake. He stared out into the thin air. He seemed lost. I sat down and put my hand over his. He grabbed it, and pulled me to him. I knew then that everything would be alright, and it was. Or I should say that it was for two years after that horrible night.

I told F'rell the good news that I was pregnant. We never thought we would conceive.

F'rell was busy as usual when the news came of an earthquake in the west quadrant. There had been an unusually difficult storm this year with extensive flooding. As usual F'rell took no time to rest. He and Sh'ban went there to help. I wanted to come along, but of course I was not allowed. I was in the sixth month then, and women there normally give birth after seven.

Sh'ban said he didn't know when I would deliver since I wasn't from T'Caana. But from all the scans it looked like I was getting there. We knew that it would be a boy, and F'rell was ecstatic since he found out he would have a son to secure the bloodline. He already had a name ready, but he did not tell me it. I nagged him to tell it to me. Finally he said he would tell me when he got back. I stared at him, and he just laughed in his teasing manner. He said he would not be gone for long. I loved him so much.

It was three weeks later that I got the news that F'rell had been seriously wounded. He was on his way home. I didn't care that I was getting close to the birth, I had to go to him. Apparently he had told Sh'ban that he'd take the ship with the other workers while Sh'ban stayed to keep working things out, because he wanted to get back to me as soon as possible.

They later told me that the ship had somehow lost its power. I never got a chance to say farewell or tell him how much I loved him. He would never get to hold his son, and neither would I. Then I went to see his dead body.

Now I just need to tell you how I died… One week later I gave birth to our child. I had a dreadful time. I kept thinking about how much I missed F'rell. I could not stop crying, and I did not care about what L'kia had once said. Sh'ban held the child before me, but I was too weak to hold him. He was a copy of F'rell with wonderful eyes, but he missed one thing. He did not have the ridge across the nose. In that way he looked like me. I started to shake. I grew cold. Then everything went dark. I have told you everything now. There is nothing left to be said.

The Ring of Destiny

Burdens from trials in past and current lives can make the journey through the afterlife occasionally unintelligible and difficult. With the help of Michael Newton's earlier discoveries from over 7000 cases, it has sometimes helped to use Newton's structured methodology and great knowledge.

An important station in the search for answers to existential questions is the Ring of Destiny. This place is the afterlife's multi-dimensional super machine, which makes today's appreciated 3D cinemas seem as black and white silent movies.

The clients are once again unanimously united in their descriptions of both how the place works and how they experience the life which is played back. Of course, there are individuals who are unable to visit the Ring of Destiny. As a rule it depends on the individual's spiritual developmental level and ability to benefit from the experience. There is always a Master who controls the flow of information. Sometimes the Master also contributes with technical assistance.

I have yet to discover a client who has experienced the Ring of Destiny as a negative. On the contrary they have all described how clearly they have found deeper insights and decisions about themselves. Many clients describe the Ring as looking through water. Suddenly he or she looks into a specific life. Everything feels absolutely real, except that space-time has been manipulated by the Master. Some clients have said that the gate in the TV show "Stargate" is a good image of the phenomenon.

When the client arrives at the Ring of Destiny she is told to either stand or sit. Some clients have reported that they were given something similar to headphones which they were able to use to roll through a chain of events. Except from the visit to the Council of the Elders, this place

313

is, according to many clients, the strongest and most useful experience from the whole life between lives therapy. Often the individual's whole approach to life changes radically as life receives new meaning, which is not to be wasted.

***

After having contemplating suicide, a young woman was given the opportunity in the Ring of Destiny to view an earlier life from the conservative Victorian England. During her life as a young woman in England she had given birth to a child out of wedlock. Her parents sent her away and told her to never come back. The Ring of Destiny chose the fact that even though she was depressed and committed suicide, there was still place for joy and a happy ending. Suddenly she could see herself as an old lady surrounded by young children in a day care centre. When she now again thought about suicide in her current life, she realised that it was a bad solution that she had tried too many times before.

Roxanne had previously worked as a garden designer. She loved her work, but after suffering depression and chronic exhaustion she had no energy left for her passion. The Ring of Destiny became like a call for help as she had gotten stuck on her spiritual journey.

'It is a ring which looks to have almost like water on the inside. Now I can see Chelsea Flower Show. I am arranging a garden there. It seems like an English garden, but with mainly red flowers. I see a man there who smiles… it seems as if he will become my love,' said Roxanne. I asked her to continue exploring her own future. 'I see a quite nice detached house. There is a front and back garden. I walk through the house but can't see anyone… I don't understand how I would get such a wonderful house in the future.'

***

Meg who was murdered after having suffered sexual abuse in Spain 1873, and who later died in a military battle in Africa, tells of her meeting in the room of life selection.

'She is around 40 years old. Very cute, with red lip gloss. She is wise… She has a choice of windows. There is one with the castle in Spain, another with a ship, and one just like a house, and one is a farm… the one with the boat… she says that life was special. She suggests that I go there…'

***

Keith, who freed himself from his anxiety after meeting his father in the Garden of Souls, here tells of his experiences from the Ring of Destiny.

'They show me something almost like a bubble. Inside the bubble I see myself holding a small child. It is my son's baby… and I can also see my son's wife.'

This short and simple experience made Keith very happy. He said that he realised that he had managed to break a negative cycle, and that he had managed to continue forward with his own family.

***

A woman describes briskly how she can see another part of her current or a coming life.

'I see myself standing by the side of a road looking down towards some simple sheds. There are a large number of black children with their mothers. Now I am inside one of the houses, and they seem to be of much better quality than the ones I could see from the road. I don't know what I do… it feels like I am much respected by these black people.'

***

This middle aged woman experienced hope through her visit to the Ring of Destiny.

'It feels as if there is someone in the background, preparing me for the experience. I see a large ball before my eyes as I sit down. I see myself in a multi-dimensional perspective… Now I am a young woman out for a walk. Then I see myself in my current age. Finally I see myself as older, thinner and happier. I am involved in some kind of printing work,' she finished.

***

Tom, who discovered that his compulsive symptoms were connected to the murder of his wife in the 18th century, here visits the Ring of Destiny.

'Someone gives me a type of headphones. I then watch an enormous ring which looks like plasma or water. Suddenly I can see myself. I am extremely happy… I am holding a small child in my arms… I am in my thirties… I know we have something in common… there is a blonde woman in the background, I can't see her clearly.'

After the session he told me that the images of the future had given him a deeper understanding of his own life and especially the experience of the suicides and the consequences these would have had if he succeeded. He viewed this as deeply therapeutic.

***

In our final meeting with Sean, he is visiting the Ring of Destiny. The place played a major part in Sean's recovery.

'I have been given the possibility to look back on my past in this life, and to also have a glimpse of the future. I can see myself living as an old man together with Lisa in a bungalow. I look thin and fragile compared to when I was young. I am happy and I have two grandchildren… I must leave now…' Sean asked me to take him back to reality due to the intensity of the experience he had just had.

'I only have one wish left. I want you to take me to my mother's funeral where I previously was so bitter and angry.'

Finally Sean was back with his mother and the circle was closed. Wrath and anger had been neutralised and disappeared like fog in the sun. Sean had found his way home.

'Mom, I forgive you everything and I am sincerely sorry over all I have done.'

Departing for Life

The departure of the souls to life requires preparations. The youngest and most inexperienced souls seem less aware of the process itself regarding incarnation on Earth. Just like knowledge grows as a child matures and develops, the knowledge and awareness grows among the souls regarding the spiritual process' diversity and brilliance. Step by step every piece is integrated into the soul. And for each level that is reached in the afterlife, a colour is achieved which signifies advancement.

Sometimes I imagine this as being like the Shoto-Kan karate I once trained. For each kata and knowledge I had gained after about 6 months of hard physical training, I would receive a belt. All my peers knew exactly at which level I was from seeing my belt. In the same way we can see the progress of the soul.

Sometimes I imagine departure like a gigantic station with departing travellers to all corners of the Earth. Here and there you can see groups bidding each other farewell. Millions of travellers leave this station of the afterlife each second. After just a short while many are back again in the hall for arrivals. And so the process continues through eons of time. In the afterlife there is no time aspect. Everything is now.

The Womb

The parents are tense and nervous during their wait for their first child. How will the delivery go? How will he or she look? Some parents already know the gender from the appearance from today's 3d ultrasound pictures. It is really only the step out into life itself that awaits the child.

Not everyone might have asked themselves when the existence of the child begins. When is it a human? As doctors we know today that children can be saved earlier than the moment at which it is legal to abort the foetus. Does the small child really have its own consciousness? If so, when did it come to exist?

For me some of these answers created a completely different outlook at life. My journey into this invisible, and wonderful world began when I visited the previous president of The South-African Society of Clinical Hypnoanalysis, Dr J Leeb's, lecture at the Royal Society of Medicine in London

Dr Leeb, who had worked as a maternity doctor for many years, told us that if anyone had told him 25 years earlier that the unborn child very early has a consciousness, he would have laughed out loud.

'Now I know better,' he concluded his hour long lecture.

A majority of my clients talks briefly or sometimes at length about how he or she as a soul entered the unborn body. As always the stories have been very coherent from both men and women, even though each time their accounts have been given independently of each another.

A simple rule of thumb seems to be that the older the soul is, the later it takes its place in the new body. Experience seems to be of great importance, and the older souls seem to go in and out of the unborn child's body all the way to the birth. The birth itself does not necessarily mean a stop to the child's soul making journeys out of the body, but it is undoubtedly true that after a few years in the physical form there are extremely few souls that are able or want to alternate between these distinct life forms.

Scientific research has in later years confirmed that the unborn child reacts to sounds, music and activity that the mother encounters. You do not need a medical degree to realise that what the mother absorbs in terms of food and drink constantly affects the child. The whole thing gets a bit more complicated when the mother's experiences and thoughts also affect the child.

Reports from Unborn Children

'It is quiet and safe. Mommy is happy. I went into the child early. I can see small pitiful legs. I feel panic... I feel my mother's panic', said the young English woman.

***

Shenmo speaks about how her father not only abused his pregnant wife, but how the violence affected herself as an unborn child. It is quite astonishing that we have not yet integrated the idea and possibility that the unborn child can be hurt not only physically, but also mentally, whilst in the womb.

'It is very noisy...'

'What do you mean?'

'He is very aggressive and he kicks mom in the stomach... it hurts.'

'When did you take your place in the child?'

'In the middle of my mother's pregnancy. This girl is strong, but difficult to unite with.'

***

This client enters late due to the age of the soul.

'I feel that my mother is quite tense... I went into the child late... because I am an old soul.'

***

This client is unhappy with the choice.

'It feels pleasant inside the womb. But I can clearly feel that my parents don't want me... I go into the child's body in the middle of my mother's pregnancy. I don't feel satisfied with the body I've received... I already know that I will become physically aggressive and strong.'

***

A woman reports: 'I feel safe inside the womb... I also feel that my mother and father do not want me... I decide that as soon as I've been born I have to be silent. I somehow know that my body is weak and that later in life I will have to suffer physical health issues.'

***

Roxanne's soul gives a vivid picture of her choice.
'I know that my body will be weak... I did not bring enough energy with me... it is too late now... I explore the central nervous system in the child... she is mentally weak... her body will not listen to her soul... it will be difficult.'

***

This gentleman reports: 'This is a strong body... a very strong body... it will serve my soul well... I need a strong body... I have a mission... I must make my body aware of my higher purpose... I will not fail...'

***

'It feels warm and protected in here. I can feel my mom's worry. She is worried because there is war out there...' said this retired English woman.

***

Jo, who you met in "Buried Alive", here tells us about an experience as a baby. The story shows that all human beings, even the unborn, seem to have a consciousness, and that we must naturally show them all the same love and respect regardless of whether or not they have a language.

'Oh, it feels like I'm falling… I start crying. The doctor looks at me and grumbles something about it being just another one of these children. He is not emotionally involved. Oh… I now discover there is a nurse with a funny hat. She looks stern and puts me on a scale… that is why I'm falling. … I would like to tell them that I can hear them… I wish I could tell the truth… mm, later… I know that I will die… I will die in a traffic accident when I am fifty-seven years old… no, it doesn't frighten me… it helps me to appreciate each moment…' said Jo.

A Higher Order

From hundreds of clients appears sometimes an individual with extraordinary knowledge. It is not uncommon for the individual to be relatively unaware of the soul's high level. When the person suddenly finds themselves on a higher plane with access to an unfathomable amount of knowledge, by natural reasons a large curiosity and desire is awakened in both the client and the therapist.

The work which I have pursued is just a scratch on the surface of the spiritual world. Just as certainly as we still find unexplored places and new species on Earth, it is that this work on the afterlife has just glimpsed through the door to a new world.

In the concluding sections of this book the experiences of Masters and a few very specific places in the afterlife will be described. They get to represent the higher dimensional order which rules the afterlife.

The Hall of Divine Knowledge

It was Isis who, during one of her very last sessions, was showed to the Place of Divine Knowledge. Other authors might have called this the place "The World of Omniscience". Isis is the only one of my clients to describe this place.

'Where are you now?'

'Mm, I am with my Master in an enormous... it looks like a huge archive...'

'What kind of archive?' I asked.

'There are very high columns. Very high ceiling. It is like, it is strange... it is as if... you saw Earth through a window...yeah... so that it's like you can look... like you can look down and see what happens on Earth at a certain moment in time,' Isis said.

'I understand. Then you can look down on Earth now... and what do you see?'

'I can see the whole world.'

'And has the Master taken you there to show you something? What is it?'

'Some type of things... it is hard to find the words... because... I have difficulty expressing it... but it is like the planet has problems...'

'Is it dangerous physically or spiritually?' I asked.

'It is because... eh... the people are not perfect, and they commit truly stupid mistakes, and they do not care about physical problems in the way it should be done, to save the Earth,' Isis replied.

'Does the Master show us if there will be more earthquakes, tsunamis, nuclear war... what is it?'

'Oh, it is a combination of all those things... it could make the whole planet uninhabitable. To the spiritual world, Earth is so valuable.

It is a beautiful thing, something we all love. We have many previous experiences of lives there, and we... in the spiritual world, we do not want it destroyed. We want to preserve it.'

'Okay, so that is why this Master has brought you and me to this loft to look down from. Let him tell you what it is they want us to know,' I asked.

'I do not get a lot of information, but we are like saviours, and I think it is because you... we are such... beings which are used as saving instruments. Not used in the sense of being taken advantage of or anything, but... the spiritual world uses us as tools... because it is so important to save our precious Earth. It is difficult, because it is so completely different from being a human being. I don't have... I do not have the restrictions of the human mind... I do not have... I am not... I have no sense of time here. I have no influence on the surrounding world here. Everything is real,' Isis said.

'Is there a name for this place?'

'This is the Hall of Divine Knowledge.'

'Why did he take you there?'

'Because I am a very advanced soul, and maybe I will return here one more time with my Master. Then I will have permission to come here on my own. I am with my Master. You have to possess knowledge, wisdom and experience before you can come here. It is really nice... I have just been... it feels so good... I have been enveloped in light... it is so nice... it is set as truth... the light is the truth... it feels so good.'

'What do the colours look like in the Hall of Divine Knowledge?' I asked.

'I cannot see any colours. The light... the light which surrounds me.... It is white... it is not white... not like I paint white. It is almost as if it came from God... it is so... indescribably beautiful...' Isis said.

Evil

As a human you might sometimes wonder what happens to a soul which in life after life continues to manifest evil in increasingly growing ways, and who refuses to listen to their guides. From the simple reports I have received from clients it seems that even here there is a higher order. Just like the creation of new souls is handled by Masters, a soul with too much negative energy can finally reach a turning point.

Masters can in extreme cases take the decision that the energy in an extremely negative soul should be adjusted and transformed. A part of the original soul's energy always remains, but the larger part of the negative energy returns to its source. The small remaining part of soul's energy is then mixed with new energy. It is natural that there is very scarce information surrounding this, since this process is unique and extreme in the afterlife.

The All-seeing Eye

Isis reported during one of her sessions that she as an Observer came close to the All-seeing Eye.

'It sees everything, it knows everything, but it doesn't interfere. No secret is hidden from this eye. It looks into all dimensions and through all people,' she said.

The place could be described as the place of all knowledge, or the world without ego. Throughout human history we can observe that the human ego has been the biggest hindrance to development and change. A place where the ego does not exist, does hardly create any conflicts.

Play and Leisure

O f course there are moments when souls just rest and revel. It would be strange not to after a trip to our planet! Several clients have told of how after returning from a painful life, they have just let themselves follow the movements in the crystal clear water, or sat down to relax and enjoy some place in nature.

It does occur that clients refer to alternative existential life forms. During a session Isis spoke of a life as a more psychic form. Perhaps this is more the question of an energy form, rather than a physical and solid life form. Here a woman tells of herself playing as a soul.

'I am together with seven other souls in my group. We really amuse ourselves. We kind of float up towards a rainbow. We all have colours around our souls which consist of white circles, yellow, orange, red and purple.'

***

A psychiatrist in England tried life-between–lives hypnosis during one occasion. According to him, it took him several days to process and to understand the fascinating experience he had. As a soul on the other side he discovered that he was training to become a Master of Energy in the future. On the current level he learned together with his soul mates to manufacture and control small amounts of energy. These amounts of energy could then be used in the construction of simple life within the animal and plant world. The colleague said that it was extremely difficult just to create a small insect. The doctor reported amongst other things, the following.

'I am together with other souls and we create balls of energy which we throw up into the air between us. We enjoy ourselves and it is wonderful.'

329

Masters

Out of all the meetings with clients, soul groups and different places in the afterlife, I have without doubt found meetings with the Masters the most exciting and fascinating experience in the spiritual world. The Masters have irresistibly taken command over the session. Suddenly I have found myself addressed and questioned. The answers from the Masters have often completely overwhelmed me. Their knowledge appears enormous regardless of whether the subject is humanity's role on Earth or quantum physics.

Michael Newton and Brian Weiss have described the phenomenon in their books, and here I a few very detailed accounts of meetings with the Masters have already been given. All dialogues were direct extracts from those conversations which I have had. Only a few words or sentences have been changed to make the text more readable. Elisabeth, Jo and Isis have already introduced you into the world of Masters.

The Masters appear as souls who have completed their work on Earth, and who have ascended to Masters within different areas. We have previously encountered the Masters within areas like the Council of the Elders, the guardians of the books of life, in the place as nurses of new born souls, the Ring of Destiny, the place of life selection, observers, the philosophers and the place for healing of exhausted and broken souls. My impression is that in the dimension of the afterlife the Masters are distinguished as the spiritual elite. A foundation to perhaps even higher dimensions of angels and what we call God but which the spiritual world could describe as the great "presence".

The masters themselves have both younger and older souls which are trained and educated in the afterlife to one day reach the level of Master. My impression is that this is a process which might take many thousand earthly years. The areas I have encountered where Masters have a clear role are:

The Redeemer of Lost Souls
The Wise (The Sage)
The Philosophers
The Masters of Healing
Masters in the choice of life
Masters in change of space-time and room-time
Masters in the healing of animals
Masters of energies (Rainbow Spring)
The Observers
The Prophet of Souls
The Guardians of the Books of Life
The Carer of new born souls (Nurses)

The Future

F ew remember even what happened just a couple of weeks ago. The details fade and only events of great significance or large emotional attachment etch themselves into memory. Many know exactly what they did that specific day of some major global event, but they also remember their first love, their wedding or their divorce.

Of course consciousness and its ability to filter plays an important role. For a lot of people everyday life and the present would become insufferable if they constantly had all the details of the past in their conscious mind. Those who naturally have the greatest ability to live in the present are our children. Young children live absolutely here and now, and they often struggle to understand when the adults plan for a trip which they themselves already have started packing for.

Regardless of all this, every detail and every moment of our lives are stored in what I like to call our super-consciousness. In a state of raised awareness under correct hypnosis, the consciousness is displaced to that sea of experiences we have of both past lives and our current existence.

Most people would naturally like to know if they will get that house they placed a bid on. They would like to know when shares go up or down, if that man is the right one or if that woman is a future wife. Humanity's history is lined with oracles, medicine men, dream seers, mediums, astrologists, fortune tellers and a long line with other experts and charlatans. To know the future is both frightening yet appealing. Everyone from ministers of state to the poor have sought comfort in predictions of the future. Religions have unsuccessfully tried to act as a bitter barrier in order to stop this search. Violence, torture, executions and thousands of years of persecution has still not managed to stop this force. Hand in hand with the belief in God, people have still sought an answer to their own future.

Many millennia ago in Egypt, it was fully acceptable for people to venture to the temple and have their dreams interpreted by the priests. To sleep and dream in the temples was not unusual for those leaders going into war. The wise leader took no risks but rather every piece of knowledge which could finally decide the outcome in the approaching battle was important. A small proof for the power of dreams is the stele which todays stand at the site of the Great Sphinx of Giza. On this stele Tuthmosis IV, son of Amenhotep II, tells of how he had been promised in a dream to become pharaoh, if he in return dug the sphinx out of the sand. Tuthmosis kept his promise and became pharaoh for nine years.

Freud himself became famous for his dream interpretations. Therefore it is natural to ask oneself why hypnosis with REM-activity shows physical response which barely differs from dreaming when we sleep. The main difference is that the person is awake and to some degree in control of his or her experiences. There is a state of higher consciousness which plenty of studies evidently has noted both with electric brain curves (EEG), breathing, skin responses, muscle activity and brain activity by the use of functional computed tomography scans or magnet camera examinations.

In modern times some countries intelligence services have been involved with what is referred to as "remote viewing"–to gather information from the enemy via a state of raised consciousness. This is obviously a very dangerous way to attempt to manipulate humanity's existence. There are a few books published in the subject. This is of course not my area of work.

Just as natural as it is to go back to life's all past events–the moment of birth, the latest moment of death, past lives and finally the afterlife, it is to try to explore the future. Is it possible? Is it dangerous? Who needs to know their future?

The following cases are the most fascinating I have encountered during those years when I have worked with hypnosis. There are naturally a lot of opinions regarding the value of this. What is absolutely clear is that few clients can really go into the future. Just as there are memory blocks in place regarding what will happen in a life, as surely some information is actually not accessible. It would be naïve to think that we as physical humans could control this world.

Sometimes a brief look into a limited part of the future can release and help a suffering person. "The Wedding" is such a case. In other cases the information conveyed can be used to verify the accuracy of the recollections in the future. "The Olympic Games in London 2012" is such an example.

There was a time when I as a young man wanted to know my future. My experience of that made me prefer to seize the day and live in the present. To know another person's exact death is something that most should be protected from. Professional mediums know this well, and mediums such as Sally Morgan and Gordon Smith in England have through the years shown what enormous responsibility rests on their shoulders. In my opinion they are masters at what they do, and the amount of people who seek their help is in itself a good measure of their great importance.

In a super-conscious state those clients who respond to the method can become their own mediums. In that state each and every one get precisely what they need. The difference in regards to a skilled medium is that a medium can turn their super-conscious state on and off without requiring to be induced in trance or hypnosis.

One also has to remember the most important principle which affects both mediums as well as clients under hypnosis. It is almost never possible to say precisely when an event will or won't occur. In the super-conscious state there is no space-time axis, and sometimes the past, the present and the future get mixed up together.

She will Die due to Medicine

I was 18 years old and had just sat down opposite one of Scandinavia's most famous mediums. It was autumn 1977 in Malmö. In truth I was only there to youthfully and light-heartedly test her ability. Nevertheless my chest grew tense with worry, because even before I had opened my mouth she had started telling me who I was.

'You don't actually come from Sweden. You would have been named Jukka or Heikki. You come from Finland. You will have three sons. You have four guides and you will become a psychologist or psychiatrist. You will write something important in the future…' said Charlotte von Arenstorp. When she continued I became critical and annoyed. 'You have a Danish girlfriend. Her mother will not get so old. She will die from medication,' she said.

'No, I cannot accept that. Surely I can stop it,' I replied.

'You cannot affect this in any way. It is already decided,' the old lady said pleasantly yet with certainty.

The years passed but as it would be revealed her predictions would be fulfilled on every point. I always carried an inner worry that what Arenstorp had said would truly come to pass. I constantly carried this dark secret of existential anxiety without being able to tell anyone.

As time progressed the romantic interest of my youth studied to become a dentist and married in Germany. At the beginning of summer in 1999 my adoptive parents told me one day that her mother had passed away suddenly and unexpectedly. After having been diagnosed with breast cancer, treated and largely been declared healthy, she went in for one last check up at the Rigs-Hospital in Copenhagen. Once there she underwent a computed tomography (CT) scan of her brain. In order to do this contrast dye was injected into her veins. Abruptly thin blood vessels around undiscovered metastasis in her brain burst. She died within a few hours from a massive inner cerebral haemorrhage caused by medicine.

From that day on I knew that I would not want so much information about the deaths of those near and dear to me. I wanted to live life and do as well as I could.

The Wedding

A very talented and prominent academic contacted me regarding his wife Vicky. He wanted me to meet her due to her depression. She told me that something that had occurred in their relationship bothered her a great deal. She was dejected and very worried that her husband would leave her. We decided to try a session with hypnosis. This turned out to be the only session she would need.

'Oh, it is so beautiful… we are waiting outside of church… here comes the bridal couple… my god how beautiful she is.'

'What wedding is it?' I asked.

'Oh, it is my son who is getting married today, he is so handsome!' Vicky said.

'Who else is there together with you?'

'My husband is right behind me, and the rest of the extended family.'

'How old is your son when he marries?'

'He is twenty-one years old I think.'

When Vicky had finished the session she told me that her son was only a few years old. Staggeringly we noted that she had immediately taken a step twenty years into the future. Her face was radiant. I asked her to write down all the details and put the letter in a safe-deposit box, so that she could compare the details in the future.

A few months later I called Vicky. She sounded happy and I asked her if she was pregnant.

'How did you know that?' she asked.

'I heard it in your voice.' I replied for some strange reason.

I recommended her to stop taking her anti-depressant medication. Everything went well and Vicky did not need to contact me again. She continues to live happily with her husband and children.

The Olympic Games in London 2012

This middle aged woman asked me to get to enter the future out of straight curiosity. She had no symptoms of any psychiatrically serious illness and always stood with both feet firmly planted on the ground. With her permission I publish her glimpses of 2012. Whether or not they are accurate or not is another question. Her predictions were made in November 2006. No one knew then who the main candidates would be for the presidential elections of 2008, and neither had the financial crisis begun. It is possible that some details come far later than 2012, but that was the year that her journey departed from.

'I'm sitting in my house in Southend-on-Sea. Mom and dad have left me now. My father asked me to forgive him before he died. I live alone but have plenty of friends. The garden at the back of the house has been cleared up and I have some trees and bushes there now. I sit in my favourite swing. I look back at my therapy and how much it helped me. I do not use medication any longer. I still have physical issues, but I make do.

The Olympic Games went off in London. Parking prices skyrocketed. There were plenty of police, but no serious incidents. In the USA the police have received help from special "Marshals" and things have improved. They did not elect a female president.

Fuel is available and has not run out like some believed. It was connected to some people's greed to make money out of the crisis. More cars are now built running mainly on electricity. The weather has gotten warmer and China suffered a major earthquake. People died in thousands.

A journey to Mars failed as the spacecraft exploded once they had left the atmosphere and reached space. Six astronauts died. The troops came back from Iraq in 2009… one more thing… the religions have slowly begun to meld together into one faith.'

2113

Elisabeth approves my suggestion. My main idea is that since she easily goes back, perhaps she can also go forward in time. Something I perhaps grab straight out of the air. In which Swedish psychiatric clinic would they understand this? The only consolation and joy is that the patient would never report me to the Healthcare Board of Responsibility. She wanted all this from the start.

'What a paradox,' I think while Elisabeth gets comfortable with some soft pillows under her thin arms.

Around all the hypnotically regressed patients I have experienced, there seems to be one main universal rule. In the state outside of current physical lives, the space-time perspective disappears. Instead the latest models of modern physics seem to become real.

Non-space-time enters and humanity's fourth dimension, time, cease. To understand this you need models with 10 or 26 dimensions. Of these two are always width and length, i.e. just what you see now. A page with text before you. Only in the fifth dimension are Einstein's, Maxwell's, Bohr's, Kaluza-Klein's and the other physicists' calculations unified. Only there the mirage in the deserts desists evading the thirsty man. There suddenly an oasis springs forth in a chaos of sand. Every particle, from atom, electron and down to the smallest meson and fermion, resonate in super symmetry which moves into super gravity. In contrast to quantum physics all particles can mix in the super symmetry. Finally string theory emerges which says that everything in existence consist of, at its lowest level, vibrations.

Within string theory an absolute magnification of an elementary particle means that we would observe a vibrating string. String theory can thereby not only explain the particles themselves, but also space-time. A string moves in space-time, and passes through a series of complex motions. A string can according to the hyperspace physicists only vibrate in 10 dimensions. The strings can break down, collide and create longer strings. These quantum changes or loops can be calculated. Sometime in the future perhaps we will be able to make calculations before we move in the space-time dimension. Maybe we will be able to make dimensional quantum leaps on shortcuts made of antimatter and multidimensional wormholes. Our ships will no longer be powered by rockets weighed down by gravity, but by light-quanta which give the possibility of intergalactic quant-movements. The spaceship and the human shall then be viewed as vibrating strings. The strings move faster than the speed of light to new coordinates. When "braking" the matter reverts to its original vibrational frequency. The thoughts swirl through my mind while Elisabeth rapidly moves into complete relaxation.

I never divert from the technique, so regardless of their ability to relax the patients always go through the same programme. Her eyes move under the eyelids. She seems to experience something. Consciously I move her into the future.

'You have now entered the future. Far beyond in another century. I am by your side. I never leave you. You do not need to be afraid. What are you doing?' I asked.

'I am sitting in the sand on the beach. There are palm trees further away. I see a small boy at a distance,' Elisabeth said.

'Look into his eyes! Do you recognize him?'

'No.'

'How old are you?'

'5-6 years...' she replies hesitantly.

I let her walk towards her home.

'What does your house look like?'

'It is a green house with a flat roof. It lies close to the beach,' Elisabeth said.

With help from the visualised globe and the chronometer I find out that it is somewhere in South America and the year is 2138 or 2188. She sees cars outside the family's house, and they have rounded shapes and move completely silently. I move her further ahead in the life to when she is eighteen years old. She is with the family in the kitchen. She has three siblings. She only recognizes her mother from her current life in one of her siblings' eyes.

'My parents are upset. Something is going to happen. It comes from the outside... not from earth,' she says disjointedly. Elisabeth seems strained, as if she used a lot of energy to talk.

'Does humanity have contact with alien civilizations?' I asked.

'Yes, they made contact after the great war,' she says suddenly.

'The great war?' I instruct her to use whatever computer systems that the family reasonably might own. Elisabeth reports that they have an extensive database. I urge her to use an encyclopaedia to get details of the past war.

'It breaks out 2113 as a nuclear war. I see China involved. Large parts are destroyed. The destruction is vast. Many humans and animals perished,' she reports neutrally.

'What other countries are affected?'

'I see large parts of the USA devastated. Parts of Russia are also affected.'

'How about Europe and Scandinavia?'

'Parts of Europe, but not Scandinavia. The war leads up to contact with the others.'

Even though the experiences seem so short and quick, a great amount of time is used during the session. It is as if the time is never enough. Every time the clock is the opposition, a reminder that human life is dense, heavy, slow and always on limited time.

At the end of the session Elisabeth is an adult. She says that she works as a researcher with some kind of advanced technology. She fails in conveying what kind of technology she works with.

'I wear a white overall. It is very advanced. I do not understand.'

When I later on tell her that the light envelops her and allows her to relax she spontaneously burst out: 'Now I know, I work with light energy. We develop technology for space travel to reach the speed of light.'

'Does humanity travel far away in space?' I asked.
'Yes, but no one comes back,' Elisabeth said.
'Why?' I ask with curiosity.
'It takes too long.'
'Do humans still get as old as before?'
'Yes.'

***

When we during the following week's session find ourselves back in the same life more specific details emerge regarding her work. Before Elisabeth enters the relaxed state she tells me that she never before has experienced such exhaustion as she did after the journey into the future.

'I work together with other engineers. We are developing a machine which is of importance to the earth's energy system and space travel. We have... some kind of black sticks... we put them into a cylinder. It is complicated.'

The following week we decide to visit the future one last time. The excursions are too demanding, and neither of us have any interest in knowing whether all of this will really happen. I take her back to the life as an engineer in the 22nd century.

'I have a white overall with text across one side of my chest. You also work there. There are many who work with the machine. The work is complex.'

'How do we solve the problem?' I asked.

'Hmm, it has something to do with alien civilizations...' Elisabeth said.

I considered how gleefully critics might claim that I had projected my own thoughts and interests onto the patient.

'Could I have imparted this?' I say surprised.

'Hmm, yes, you have received some sort of knowledge. There are three alien civilizations known on earth,' she says, just as in the previous session.

'We use small, short black sticks which we put inside a cylinder.'

'You are now in your apartment. Does anyone else live there too?' I asked.

'Yes. He does not like being disturbed when he's reading. He is so focused,' she says serenely with a smile upon her lips.

'Do you have any children?'

'Yes, two sons.'

I asked myself if I really understood any of this. 'How do we communicate with each other? Are there telephones or something similar?'

Following a long silence she replied: 'We have small boxes in our pockets. You can hear someone talking very clearly.'

I convince her that she is now using her computer of some kind. I ask her to describe how the information is visualized.

'The computers are very small. The images are not on screens, they come out straight on the wall.'

Influenced by science's constant requirement for proof, and the undebated truths of the double-blind controlled studies of 2002, I get an urge to check Elisabeth's details. I instruct her to see historic events. The 2000s. The attack against New York in September 2001 is a suitable point of reference, and all that which happens then. I ask her if she sees any new attacks later on.

'Mm, I see August 2021, it is some kind of gas disaster. The country is flat and dry, but no, I cannot see what country it is, it is so vague.'

I move her further along her life as an engineer to her old age.

'Did you succeed in constructing the light machine?'

'Yes, it went well. It is used to improve space travel and it has given earth a new, safer source of energy,' she replies happily.

'Has the environment changed?'

'Yes, it has improved,' she answers.

'Was the work appreciated?'

'Yes, we received many prizes.'

'What do we proceed to do?'

'I see how you teach others.'

My Dog will Die

Elisabeth had received visions which became reality even before the hypnosis sessions. She had seen the deaths of her father and mother before they occurred. She considered these experiences a burden rather than a gift.

She was quiet for a longer time than previous sessions. Her eyes moved intensely under her eyelids. Occasionally she twisted her head, and sometimes she seemed to gasp for air. Then she began to speak. 'I have always know it. Why has no one told me this?' It was obvious she was experiencing something far beyond what she was conveying to me as her doctor.

'What is happening?' I asked quite impatiently.

'They tell me that I am an observer. It was meant for me to meet you so that you could take the step. I had to meet you. That is what they tell me.'

'You mean that there always was a plan,' I said astonished.

'Yes, it was agreed in that way,' said Elisabeth. 'Oh, it is so difficult. My dog will die soon... and soon a very good friend will die...'

Elisabeth told me that she never intended to ask for such information. She was only informed, and felt stressed and uncomfortable from her experience.

Our friendship always remained, and a few years ago I once again had contact with Elisabeth. During the summer of 2003 after her contact with the masters, a very good friend of hers had done some work on her house. A few months later he fell unexpectedly ill, and died within a month from liver cancer.

Elisabeth never complained, because she had been given a possibility to do things she would not have done without her predictions. Some more months passed, and then her beloved dog died.

344

My impression of Elisabeth was that her predictions helped her focus on things she knew to be important. I know that she appreciated the time she had with her dog before he died. She was able to prepare herself. Many know that the loss of a loved pet can sometimes be as painful as the loss of a close relative.

My own experience is that this kind of information is only available for a very select few. To know that you will win the lottery is great, but to know when someone will die is another thing entirely. It seems as if many people have premonitions and suspect when something major will occur in life. The invisible, and for many unacceptable plan, seems to roll on regardless of what we think. Luckily we have been equipped with memory blocks of our own future. Otherwise, it is doubtful if anyone would like to continue the journey. Similarly the conditions for learning would decrease if we knew everything in advance. From a spiritual perspective we are all ultimately here to gather spiritual experience in our physical shape.

The Terrorist Attack

If we cannot influence a future event, what use is there to know that it will occur? In everyday life many know how modern it is with risk evaluations. The more variables and complex relationships, the more difficult it is to accurately assess the risk of something occurring. Unsurprisingly people and leaders wish for a world under human control, and more than anything a predictable one. Reality is not so simple. Sometimes simple things happen which helps or interferes. This middle aged gentleman referred to a future terrorist attack in London. Now we have suffered one attack in London, but this one is of an entirely different level. Let us hope that he is completely wrong.

'It is very strange but I see Big Ben's clock tower and there are vultures on the roofs... there should not be vultures on the roofs of London. There are no people left. Most have departed. I now see that there are some people who stayed and many of them built their own bomb safe shelters since they had so much money, and they knew times were bad and something could happen. Many have stayed in these shelters, but if they leave them they will die from the radiation.'

'What has happened to the city?' I asked him after this unpleasant beginning.

'A neutron bomb exploded. The bomb destroyed all advanced technology and especially the economic heart of London which seemed to be its purpose. Buildings were not affected but a neutron bomb does not damage buildings. The radioactive fallout was serious and many people were killed both due to the bomb and the later radiation. The Thames is very low and there is not much water left. Strange... they have also closed London's barrier.'

'Perhaps it is closed so that no one can get in,' I suggested.

'No, they don't want water which has been contaminated with radiation to leave the area.'

'How do people manage this?'

'They live in camp sites throughout England.'

I asked him to get a newspaper in order to read about this terrible catastrophe. He proceeded to speak. 'I can see the word "talisman"... it had something to do with them... not an object... they issued a warning regarding the attack... the government knew something would happened, and in secret they arranged a move of the capital... it later became Edinburgh.' When I questioned it all he continued. 'There was not much people could do and times were bad. Other parts of Europe has also been affected but not Scandinavia... it is strange... just like the first and second world war the Scandinavian countries are somehow spared. People cannot move back and live in the area for hundreds of years.'

Having regained his regular consciousness Tony said: 'If I had told someone this they would have viewed me as insane and committed me to some ward.'

'And you're telling me as a psychiatrist,' I said with a smile.

MENTAL PHYSICS

In the World of Cut-outs

A cut-out shape of a priest, for instance, is a two dimensional toy. It has no depth, just two flat dimensions. Trapped in this world, the priest experiences his congregation from a truly flat perspective. One day God in his infinite wisdom drops an apple straight down into the priest's cathedral. The apple does not fall down simple and whole, but shows up as spots and circles. First a dot, and then increasingly wider rings which finally culminate to a dot of the twig. Astounded the flat congregation witness this divine revelation.

This divine apple's visit is perhaps interpreted as a heavenly revelation in the priest's flat diocese. Perhaps he travels far and wide to tell others of his vision. Many years after the death of the priest the flat church leaders decide to sanctify the priest. He who only saw an apple fall down from our world into a box of flat cut-outs.

Reasonably there are exceptions even in our priest's flat world. In 2002 Lawrence Schulman at Clarkson University, New York, introduced the possibility of regions in the universe where time runs backward. Our priest would in this dimension literally see the apple leave the congregation the same way it arrived!

The world of cut-outs is important for us to be able to progress and understand our own limited three-dimensional world which has been equipped with the fourth dimension of time.

In our youth we learned Pythagoras theorem, that the square of the short sides of a right angled triangle is equal to the square of the long side, the hypotenuse. We write:

$a^2+b^2 = c^2$

In a three-dimensional cube there is the same simple relationship. The sum of the squares of the three sides is equal to the squared diagonal line. We can thus write:

$$a^2+b^2+c^2=d^2$$

Generally the same equation holds for an infinite number of dimensions, i.e. n-dimensional cubes. We could give an expression for this in the form of:

$$a^2+b^2+c^2+d^2+\ldots\ldots = z^2$$

On an ordinary sheet of paper we are thereby curiously enough able to imagine n-dimensional cubes, even though our fantastic brains still have a hard time imagining what these cubes or states would look like. In other words, we are beginning to understand that states outside our sensory abilities can both be hopeless to try to measure, and even more hopeless to try to understand. Sometimes it is just easier to accept the state we live in and experience, and leave everything else to the physicists or the priests–the metaphysicians.

The N-dimensional Theory

The German mathematician Georg Bernhard Riemann introduced the 4th or n-dimensional geometry in the middle of the 19th century. He was likely far ahead of his time.

In fact Riemann's theories provided the foundations for Einstein's theory of relativity. Riemann introduced three mathematical points for every point in the flat priest's 2-dimensional world. In 3D-space Riemann discovered that you needed 10 numbers to describe every point in space. Without having really understood the consequences, Riemann had taken the first steps towards describing wormholes in space. Holes which physicists theoretically assume can provide points of contact between parallel dimensions or universes.

Riemann discovered that in order to manipulate something in 3d-space, you needed to use shortcuts in what came to be called the fifth dimension. Why?

In the fifth dimension there is more space to manipulate matter and the states bound by the pure laws of physics. By moving our flat priest straight up into the air from an imagined circle he cannot escape, we liberate him in one move from hopeless imprisonment. Through a movement made from the third dimension our priest is moved from the circle to a free unlimited state.

In the same way a ship in a bottle could be moved into the fifth dimension. There the expanded space would give the possibility to literally lift out the ship without damaging the bottle. Probably we would experience this as just as great a miracle as our flat priest. The priests would argue for a divine revelation, while laboratory enclosed scientists would prefer manipulation or fraud as the cause. Who would be able to prove anything?

Our flat priest begins to experience doubt. Is there perhaps a world beyond his own? Is it then divine, or just different? He is assaulted by more and more questions and is tormented by his worry that his faith is lacking.

When contact finally is established between the 2D and 3D worlds, the 3D-world's scientists try to prove their existence to the priest. They use a cube which they fold out into the shape of a cross with six squares. They are frustrated when the priest still does not believe them. The cube is still flat. When someone finally comes up with the idea of shining a torch through a transparent cube, the shocked priest discovers for the first time the shadow of a cube inside a square cube. This shadow changes shape as the 3D-scientists twists it.

A small step has been taken towards a higher consciousness for our flat priests. Constantly attacked by anxiety and doubt, he tries to explain his model. Ridiculed and regarded as mad he is left alone. Many years after his death, he is sanctified.

The Fifth Dimension

In the fifth dimension other principles apply than in our three dimensional world (The 4th is the illusory time). In order for the normal human brain to handle the external world's constant bombardment of stimuli, it has been equipped with a sophisticated filtering function. The filter does not only provide an effective barrier to the external world, but also to the great ocean of subconscious and possibly collective archaic knowledge. Without the filter most of us would go crazy from stimuli. How many can today in the modern society find a place of peace and silence where the mind can rest? Naturally few manage this in the buzz of the cities, yet we all long for tranquillity.

Manic patients are afflicted by an inner bombardment of signals and their brain can be likened to a runaway engine, constantly increasing in speed.

It is then naturally more difficult to go to a hospital where people shout, music is playing, doors are slammed, telephones call, mobiles send texts and computer screens flicker. The modern/unmodern life simply risks overloading the brains like a server can be overloaded with email-requests on the internet.

In an awake state only around 10 billion neurons are active in the brain. Slumbering and in a REM-phase the neuron activity increases drastically as several billion more neurons are activated. The real supercomputer appears in the consciously relaxed state which then reigns. This supercomputer or quantum brain requires peace and quiet. Like an advanced computer processor it needs to be cooled down. Everything to give maximum return.

Theoretically an interaction could begin to appear through hyper fast movements between the brain's neurons and the fifth dimension of a hyperspace state. In order to understand this we can use Einstein's theory of relativity.

A person travelling at the speed of light will, according to the theory of relativity, always see the light a bit ahead of himself, even if the person finally is close to the absolute speed of light. Einstein pondered upon this and realised that the solution was astonishing. When the person approaches the speed of light (c), time slows down. For someone standing on the ground observing a traveller at the speed of light, enormous disruptions and anomalies naturally arise. The same phenomenon could theoretically explain the unique loss of the patients' sense of time. Everyone report in unity that the sessions last 10-20 minutes, when they in reality often last for longer than an hour. During visits in other "imagined" dimensional states, i.e. pasts or future lives, patients, not unsurprisingly, lose their sense of time. I have experienced the same disruption many times. It is like shouting at someone far away. Sometimes you get an answer. Sometimes the questions I ask become annoyances. The patient/traveller experiences unimaginable amounts of information in just a few minutes. Sometimes their tales are reminiscent of out of body experiences. The time expands in the experiences themselves (horizontally), but accelerates away from me as an observer (vertically). When the patient/traveller returns the opposite occurs. Time contracts in the present for the disappointed patient who wanted to stay in their quantum state. For me a noticeable expansion follows. All too much time has passed… only 60-90 minutes.

The currently imagined neuron activity could be described in terms of light or above light speed. It almost seems as if the individual's complete existence becomes a multidimensional map, where the individual made short stops here and there. All these movements between the time zones sometimes create a condition of jetlag in hyperspace. Perhaps it is here that the real quantum brain reveals itself.

'Has it been 60 minutes? You're joking?'

The Swedish physicist Gunnar Nordstram was first to publish thoughts regarding the 5th dimension. 1919 Theodor Kaluza at Königsberg University came up with a brilliant mathematical way to show that it was not just imagination. It was an absolute, real possibility. In Kaluza's important breakthrough he described how to unite Einstein's field equations for gravity and Maxwell's for light. 1938 Oscar Klein independently of the others carried out research which showed the same thing. Kaluza-Klein's model was born.

Even though this was just the beginning of our intellectual understanding of other dimensions, these theories were left gathering dust when quantum mechanics entered the picture. In 1971 however, hyperspace got its comeback when a theory began closing in on a complete picture of the cosmos.

Yang-Mills field described more components than the light, and that they can carry electric charges. The light itself carries no charge.

Since earlier it was known that the elementary particles were made up of quarks. The weak forces which hold quarks together in the quantum world are called gluons. This is described by Yang-Mills field by that which the physicists call a W-particle. It can carry the charge $+1$, 0 and -1. These charges bind together mesons (a quark and an anti-quark) and protons/neutrons (three quarks). Their common denominator is an exchange of quantum energy. Something that could possibly occur in our quantum brain.

Now it starts getting really exciting. Something that reasonably has a theoretical implication as an explanatory model to the patients' experiences in a dimension without time. According to the physicists an exchange of information can occur on a sub-nuclear level without the movement of particles. We begin to imagine a quantum brain.

The only particle known today which can carry information to an imagined "mirror-world" and back to our own is unsurprisingly the photon. It has no matter, and therefore it can travel immeasurable or infinite distances. The question is if the photon at one point enters above light speed, or if it uses wormholes in space to convey information between different dimensions. Hocus pocus or magic no longer applies here. Instead we look to Niels Bohr's words when Wolfgang Pauli had taught Heisenberg-Paul's unified field theory: 'We all agree that your theory is crazy. The question which divides us is if it is crazy enough.'

Synchronous Coincidences

Even if it might seem uninteresting and irrelevant, I think it is important to tie together the patients' experiences with modern, and for many perhaps difficult, quantum physics. The 5D-world is too small to be measured and the amount of energy we need to penetrate into it from our physical world is unimaginable. Just like the priest in the 2D-world we can only see secondary effects of this world. In the shape of blips, blobs and unexplainable events, these manifestations show up uninterrupted in our world. Some wish to call them random occurrences. Others, like Carl Jung, preferred to describe them as synchronous events.

Normally we wish to act according to cause and effect. He who truly wishes to live a life in proximity to other dimensions has to start living according to synchronous events. Meaningful coincidences without causality will therefore rule instead of cause and effect. When these experiences are mentally accepted and truly confirmed, an immediate change occurs. The human goes through a change of consciousness. Instead of an unceasing practice of cosmological isms, the first steps are taken towards a life through harmony with cosmos. One becomes a part of the harmony.

If we imagine that the human brain already at the moment of birth contains a matrix of the creation, its purpose and meaning, there is always on a deeper level a possibility to understand our origin and our goal. Through the inertia and slow movement we face at birth, we quite soon risk to lose contact with the true quantum brain of ourselves. Do we not envy the child's complete untethered relationship to time and matter? They live in the complete present until the adult world require their presence. And what was it that Jesus said? 'Let the little children come to me and do not hinder them, for to such belongs the kingdom of heaven.'

The children's state of mind is still full of a creative ability which is absolutely now and unbound by time. Nothing is impossible. When the consciousness is allowed to delve down into the subconscious, and what I would like to call, the Jungian sea of total collective knowledge–then the soul is filled with an astounding understanding of the past, the present and the future. All faiths, isms and paradigms which have previously restricted out creative consciousness, dissolve and disappear.

Einstein himself was not a stranger to these thoughts, and he would likely have spoken of scientific intuition to suspect but not fully understand the existence of other worlds.

Yet one problem remains with the study of all subatomic elementary particles and quarks. Something called Heisenberg's principle of uncertainty. Our priest must decide if he should go public and talk about his experience. If he only mentally imagines doing it, whilst not carrying it through, his energy will mentally play pinball between his own reality and the dream of telling the truth. Just the fact that we concentrate on a scientific idea or method, affects the outcome of our results. This realistically ought to apply to all types of studies, and of course also a psychiatrist's observations of his patient. A simple attempt where we try to study our thoughts, will immediately change our experiences. Therefore, thoughts become strange things in the quantum physical world. They cannot systematically be broken down into ordered structures.

This implies that an observer attempting to study a particle, discovers that it is changed at the very moment of observation when we attempt to measure it. Perhaps you are experiencing the same phenomenon at this very moment. A physicist has to decide to either measure a particle's velocity or position. He cannot measure both at once.

If we transpose this onto humans, it means that we can never know everything about an individual. Just those parts we have decided to explore. Certainly we know just as little about ourselves.

According to Einstein-Podolsky-Rosen's (ERP) paradox a system always consist of an absolute balance. We can describe this in terms of non-locality, i.e. that something can be affected without cause. A particle can (why not souls?) be split in two parts, and when these move in opposite directions from each other, they are affected by each other's movement. The whole naturally has to remain constant.

The patients' delivery of information according to my quantum-psychological hypothesis, therefore occurs without the doctor or therapist knowing its actual origin. If one half of a "particle's" information of an earlier life is affected by a quantum-psychological intrusion (the therapy), naturally the other half will also be affected. Like ripples on the water the information is carried above the boundaries and creates the basic conditions for healing. Buddhist teacher might perhaps talk about breaking karmic patterns.

The information transmitted across quantum processes is almost impossible to measure as a chain of events. Researchers like Freedman, Clauser, Aspect and Grangier have shown this by measuring rotational changes in polarised light.

In actuality it is nothing extraordinary that the patients collectively pass on a clear picture of primarily past lives, but sometimes also of the future. On a quantum level it is completely reasonably that singular neurons are stimulated to activity. Individually the threshold level for activity for each neuron is not easier to predict than a subatomic particle's collision with another. Of the brain's 100 billion neurons, it is statistically estimated that 10 billion neurons are constantly stimulated or are close to the threshold for quantum sensitivity.

When the brain is asleep, in a meditative state or according to my view REM-phase, the number of sensitive neurons increases explosively. Psychic or quantum-psychological phenomenon are therefore not coincidence but an absolute possibility. Within quantum theory the world does not consist of separate and divided parts, but everything is connected in an invisible network. A network as invisible as today's internet, which extremely few doubt the existence of.

The quantum-psychological hypothesis is a small step for physics, but a giant leap for psychology. Gone forever are the behaviourists. Those who mechanically assumed that the human was just an object giving response to a stimuli. Pavlov's dog is a famous example. Neither can anyone deny Darwin's importance when it comes to his thoughts in "The Origin of Species". But this was strictly biological/genetic and had absolutely nothing to do with the question of whether humans happen to have a soul.

Freud contributed to the knowledge about dreams. Something that ultimately is more essential than hysterical neurosis amongst well-off upper class women in the late 19th century Vienna.

Despite Freud's thoughts of the preconscious/subconscious/unconscious mind, and Jung's hypotheses of the collective unconscious mind, questions remained. The intimidating and challenging question of whether humanity truly has a higher consciousness and if there is a life after death.

According to my hypothesis the quantum psychology allows, through its meld of physics and psychology, physicists to calculate the brain's possibility to quantum operations. Suddenly the possibility arises for a biological quantum computer far more sophisticated than those quantum computers which today lie in their cradles. When the physicists have assisted psychiatrists and psychologist to develop supersensitive instruments which can measure the brain's quantum operations, the possibility for a new world emerges. A world which consists of the on a quantum level immortal humans mental operations.

When you unite Kaluza-Klein's theory of the 5th dimension with Yang-Mills field theory, hyperspace theory ascends. This is only possible through calculations in an infinite number of dimensions (N). The first to carry out these calculations was the physicist Bryce DeWitt from Texas.

Super Symmetry and String Theory

In hyperspace there is symmetry, i.e. super-symmetry. The super-symmetry has given rise to mathematics which in ordinary schools would be viewed as pure madness.

a x b is no longer = b x a. Instead a x b = - b x a

This super-symmetry has later paved way for super-gravity. This is the gravitational force which occurs between subatomic elementary particles. In order to calculate events in this world they have used the Indian mathematician Srinivasa Ramanujan's mathematical term which is raised to a power of 24. By adding the two dimensions physicists calculate, 26 dimensions emerge which make up the world of the so called string theory. These have then been generalised to 8 + 2 dimensions. Just like the strings on a violin vibrate and create tones, the subatomic elements tremble and create unimaginably small vibrations. When these strings meet or break down, stretch or pull together, vibrations arise. Information is transferred, and a possibility for communication appears. This is called adjusted symmetry in two dimensions.

Modern physics has now reached a stadium which for most people seems to have nothing to do with reality. At the same time we must remind ourselves of the established culture in our society which largely builds its assumptions on a conformist material world view, shaped by Newton and Darwin. Today's modern physics has as little in common with the old world view, as we have with Aristotle's view that the earth was the centre of the universe. Modern physics has actually given way to a philosophy which has more in common with ancient Indian wisdom and spiritualism. Something many religious and political leaders fear will deprive them of power and control over humanity's minds.

Is this the beginning of our understanding of how information can be transmitted across different dimensions without physically moving? And do we need to fear finally seeing our true selves?

My answer is that many fear the truth more than lies, and that courage is required to truly meet yourself. If we choose untruths and lies to maintain the illusion of control, only more anxiety, suffering and hopelessness awaits. The true meaning of life will remain hidden.

If we choose the truth we will sooner or later understand that the biological brain also contains a knowledge and a depth which surpasses our wildest dreams. The quantum brain can make its entrance.

The Quantum Brain

The future is always a statistical possibility. No matter if we want it or not, a synchronisation occurs with the present. What we do today affects tomorrow. The consciousness seems to control chance by reaching synchronicity. It happens daily in people's lives, and we usually just end up saying "what's the chance?"

The ruling scientific view is that the cosmos is ruled by the second law of thermodynamics, i.e. that everything moves towards disorder and chaos. The question is if we in reality do not move towards a more developed, super conscious and beautiful world. A sign of this is our possibility to understand that we can go from using 10% of the brain to 100%. Such a brain could be described as a quantum brain.

The physical body would require an absurd amount of energy to move at light or above light speeds. Paradoxically enough the mind or hyperconsciousness would not require the same amount of energy. Through a, for me still mysterious, inter-dimensional interaction, knowledge is transferred between the 3D-brain and hyperspace. Psychologists would talk about events in the subconscious or collective unconscious, without further contemplating how this occurs. Physicists would talk of quantum processes without daring to draw any premature conclusions regarding eventual effects on the brain's neurons. The question one should ask is if the brain on a subatomic level reflects a hologram of the whole.

A hologram is a picture of for instance a person, created by two laser beams. When the beams meet interference is created, and a picture of the light pattern appears. This image can only be seen when the picture is affected by light. If we decide to split the image in smaller pieces, they will all show the same person but with fewer details. Micro cosmos begins to reflect macro cosmos.

In my view the human brain reflects the same thing. It recalls, independent of time, events from past, current and sometimes frighteningly enough also future lives. The case of Leif showed according to the same model, reflections of this hologram from a past life, and Elisabeth might possibly show something similar of a future we yet do not know. Many would naturally talk of pure speculation, but we must remember that within modern physics this is far more than just speculation. We speak of multidimensional states and the possibility of a quantum brain. A state which arises from the subconscious' possible connections to a super consciousness, or according to Jung a collective unconscious state.

It may sound like a naïve thought, but it is still a regularly recurring experience. When the patients feel a state of absolute white light after carefully completed relaxation, a boundless state of experiences rises. Often patients return to memories of early childhood, and recall in great detail long forgotten events. This is naturally nothing unique. It has occurred in many regressive and hypnotic states in the past. Anton Mesmer, Sigmund Freud, Carl Jung and many others have all worked with this world.

Yet it is important to demonstrate the differences between hypnosis and regressive relaxation. During hypnosis it is not uncommon that the patient completely lacks memory of the session. The therapist therefore presents a tape or tells them. Personally I believe it is incredibly important that the patient always is conscious and thereby has full control, or can help to control. A recurring experience is that no one is exposed to more than he or she seems able to handle. Why this is so is naturally again speculation, but I believe that the quantum brain once again is the answer. In this subatomic synchronous non-casual state, there is the possibility of absolute knowledge. But just like with computers not all events (files) are accessible. Some are simply protected. It is not possible to access this knowledge. It seems as if it is here that the individual state of consciousness is decisive in regards to whether access is given or not. And why would consciousness be given access to something it would not understand anyway?

In total each individual is still given such a formidable experience that it is more than enough. Sandy described this well as she said with simple words: 'I have gotten to where I wanted. I neither want nor need any more sessions. Life has been given a completely new meaning.'

On a deeper plane there is a purpose. This purpose is not to become rich or famous. Instead we probably choose between different states and lives in order to through these experiences create a foundation for true spiritual development and evolution in consciousness. Often we lose the holographic matrix we created before we were born. The physical life is condensed by matter, and soon we are trapped in circles of other people's joy, hate, suffering, greed and love. Sometimes something extreme is required to awake a slumbering soul in the stiff and sluggish body. Gone is the absolute spiritual awareness.

Everything is created so that we through our bodies can reach a maximum of experiences. As many know, a life is all too short to experience or do just a fraction of everything we want. Probably we decide already in the matrix-state, what will be our main theme. And the years pass. When death approaches we would like to turn everything right. We feel anxiety and regret. Some of us even become religious. The main part of humanity is also convinced that life is more than a body which breathes and dies. What differs among us is the view on life after death and not the least karma, cause and effect.

In the end all our lives are given a meaning. A meaning which for the individual themselves often seems no less reasonable that the current life's different stages from childhood to old age and death. Life and death is for many given a whole new meaning. The experience could be described as religious, but involves a complete turnaround in the view on both the ego and the surrounding world. The body lives and dies, but the soul seems to eternally and inextinguishably continue its work towards perfections. All isms and dogmas ultimately become meaningless. The respect for life expands explosively.

Finally Michael Newton's explanation of how our physical life operates in unity with the afterlife appears not only understandable, but also fully possible: '*Intelligent waves of energy create subatomic particles of matter, and it is the vibrational frequencies of these waves which make matter react in the desired direction.'*

Cause and effect over time and space becomes apparent, and none can better than Isis describe the experience of understanding exactly this: 'I have always known it, but I did not have the ability to express it!'

References

Anderson George and Barone Andrew, Walking In The Garden Of Souls: Berkley Books New York (2002). ISBN 0-399-14790-X

Capra Fritjof, The Tao of Physics: Flamingo (1982). ISBN 0-00-6544-894

Esdaile J. The introduction of mesmerism as an anaesthetic and curative agent into the hospitals of India. 1852.

Chown, Marcus, The Universe Next Door: Review, (2002) ISBN 0-7472-35287

Clark H. Hull, Carmarthen., Wales, Hypnosis and Suggestibility: An Experimental Approach. Crown House Publishing. 2002. (Originally published 1933).

Freud, Sigmund, *Origins of Religion* "Totem and Taboo" and "Moses and Monotheism", The Penguin Freud Library, ISBN-10: 014013803X, 1990.

James, William, *The Principles of Psychology*, (1890), Dover Publications, paperback, vol. one, 696 p. ISBN 0-486-20381-6, vol. two, 708 p. ISBN 0-486-20382-4, 1950.

Kaku Michio, Hyperspace: A Scientific Odyssey Through Parallel Universes, Time Warps, and the Tenth Dimension. Oxford: Oxford University Press (1994). ISBN 0192861891.

Grant Joan, Speaking from the Heart; Ethics, Reincarnation & What It Means to Be Human: Overlook Press/Duckworth Press (2007). ISBN 9780715636510

Grant Joan and Kelsey Denys, Many Lifetimes: Ariel Press (1997). ISBN 0-89804-161-9

Hartland J, *Medical and Dental Hypnosis and Its Clinical Applications.* 2nd ed. Baltimore: Williams and Wilkins, 1971.

REFERENCES

Hilgard, Ernest R., A neodissociation interpretation of pain reduction in hypnosis, <u>Psychological Review</u>, <u>Volume 80, Issue 5</u>, September 1973, Pages 396-411

Kastenbaum Robert & Aisenberg Ruth, Dödens Psykologi: Forum (1979). ISBN 91-37-07001-0

Kampman Reima, du är inte ensam: Askild / Kärnekull (1975). ISBN 91-7008-568-4

Kübler-Ross Elisabeth, The Wheel of Life: Bantam Books, (1997). ISBN 0-553-5054-40

Kübler-Ross Elisabeth, Samtal Inför Döden: Bonniers, (1978). ISBN 91-0-027429-1

Kübler-Ross Elisabeth, Döden är livsviktig: Natur och Kultur, (1991). ISBN 91-27-02751-1

Magueijo Joã, Faster Than The Speed Of Light: William Heinemann: London (2003). ISBN 0-434-00948-2

Leskowitz, Eric, MD, Transpersonal hypnosis, gateway to Body, Mind and Spirit, CRC Press (2000), ISBN 0-8493-2237-5

Newton Michael, Journey of Souls (1994). **ISBN**-10: 1567184855

Newton, Michael, Destiny of Souls (2000). **ISBN**- 1567184995

Newton Michael, Life Between Lives: Hypnotherapy for Spiritual Regression (2004). ISBN 0738704652

Rossi, E., The Psychobiology of Mind Body Healing, Revised Edition. New York: Norton. 1987.

Segal Alan F, Life after Death: Doubleday (2004). ISBN 0-385-42299-7

Schroeder Tom, Old Souls: A Fireside Book (2001). ISBN 0-684-85192-X

Schwartz Gary E, The Afterlife Experiments: ATRIA Books, (2003), ISBN 0-7434-3658-X

Weiss Brian, Many Lives, Many Masters. ISBN 0671657860

Weiss Brian, Messages From the Masters. ISBN 0749921676

Weiss Brian, Same Soul, Many Bodies. ISBN 0749925418

Zukav Gary, The Dancing Wu Li Masters: Rider Books (1991). ISBN 0-7126-4872-0

Zukav Gary, The Seat Of The Soul, An Inspiring Vision Of Humanity's Spiritual Destiny, Rider Books (1990). ISBN 0-7126-4674-4

Made in the USA
Las Vegas, NV
14 October 2021